CW01642998

Opening up Ezekiel

ANDY OLIVER

DayOne

Ezekiel is a prophet for our times, and Andy Oliver guides us on a fresh and compelling journey through this ancient word that challenges the contemporary world. He has done a thorough job of distilling the key findings of scholarship but he doesn't leave it there. The prophet's authority speaks still and all who study him in Andy's company will not fail to be changed by the experience.

Mark Meynell, Associate Director (Europe & Caribbean) of Langham Preaching. He was previously on the ministry team of All Souls Church, Langham Place, London. Mark is also the author of several books including *Cross Examined*, and *Colossians: Confident Christianity*

Ezekiel is possibly the most neglected prophetic book in the Bible. The prophet does some very bizarre things, preached some pretty scorching messages, and introduces us to his wife only to watch her die in the next verse! Yet he brought God's word to God's people at the lowest point in their history, and helped them eventually to look up and look forward to a future filled with hope - a hope that we can now see fulfilled in Christ. We need to hear his message afresh today. Andy Oliver's commentary will be very helpful to anyone trying to get their head around the book. It is simply and clearly written, explains difficult passages without getting bogged down, and regularly comes back from Ezekiel's day to our own, to suggest ways in which the text can challenge or comfort us in the church today.

Chris Wright, Langham Partnership, Author of *The Message of Ezekiel* in *The Bible Speaks Today* series

I have been a pastor for 30 years but have shied away from dealing with the book of Ezekiel apart from a few individual sermons. When I finished reading Andy Oliver's commentary on Ezekiel, I immediately said to my wife, 'I think I want to preach through Ezekiel!' I found the commentary to be immensely helpful and the applications made were especially relevant and timely. I was informed, challenged and encouraged in equal measure.

Pastor Harry Dowds, Stonepark Baptist Church, Northern Ireland

Ezekiel is an unfamiliar part of the Bible to many people today. Here Andy Oliver provides a helpful guide to the context and content of the book. It is also a book that is unafraid to challenge readers to consider the often hard-hitting implications of Ezekiel's message for today.

Dr. David Luke, Director of Postgraduate Studies, Irish Baptist College

© Day One Publications 2019

First printed 2019

All Scripture quotations, unless stated otherwise, are from the anglicized edition of the ESV Bible copyright © 2002 Collins, part of HarperCollins Publishers.

All rights reserved.

ISBN 978-1-84625-632-5

British Library Cataloguing in Publication Data available

Published by Day One Publications

Ryelands Road, Leominster, England, HR6 8NZ

Telephone 01568 613 740 FAX 01568 611 473

email—sales@dayone.co.uk

web site—www.dayone.co.uk

All rights reserved

No part of this publication may be reproduced, or stored in a retrieval system, or transmitted, in any form or by any means, mechanical, electronic, photocopying, recording or otherwise, without the prior permission of Day One Publications.

Printed by 4edge Limited

Dedication

To George Baskin, Kenneth Martin, and
Stanley Trouton.
Just three names from among the many that
have been hugely influential in my
Christian walk.

Acknowledgements

This book began as a series of messages in the Rruga e Paqes (Way of Peace) church in Tirana, Albania some time ago. I am thankful to my friends and spiritual family there who so readily received those lessons. You remain very special to me.

It is with much gratitude that I express my thanks to friends who have taken the time to read my manuscript and have offered much encouragement and practical advice for its improvement: Pastor William Wade, Pastor Harry Dowds and Dr. David Luke of the Irish Baptist College. Lastly I am indebted to Ela, Rakela, Emma and Jack, who patiently bore with me as I disappeared during a number of leave periods to work on the book. I hope that I have made up for my disappearing act in other ways.

Contents

Preface 12

Introduction 15

Table 1 19

Table 2 24

Overview 25

Background and summary—Ezek. 1:1–3 and 2 Kings 23:4–27 27

1 Ezekiel's master and ministry—Ezek. 1–3 32

Judgement against Israel 45

2 Mimes and models—Ezek. 4–5 46

3 High places and hearts—Ezek. 6–7 57

4 The glory of God departs—Ezek. 8–11 80

5 Pay attention—Ezek. 12 95

6 False teachers and fortune tellers—Ezek. 13 107

7 Idols of the heart—Ezek. 14 116

8 Shocking images—Ezek. 15–17 127

9 Personal responsibility—Ezek. 18 143

10 A funeral song with a difference—Ezek. 19 156

11 Old habits die hard—Ezek. 20 165

12 The painful side of leadership—Ezek. 21–23 179

13 The dangers of presumption—Ezek. chapter 24 191

Judgement against the nations 202

14 Schadenfreude—Ezek. chapters 25–32 203

	Hope and restoration	219
15	The watchman—Ezek. chapter 33	220
16	The King of love my Shepherd is—Ezek. chapter 34	232
17	God heals the broken–hearted—Ezek. chapter 35:1–36:15	245
18	A change of heart—Ezek. chapter 36:16–38	263
19	Can these bones live?—Ezek. chapter 37	282
20	The enemies of God will not succeed—Ezek. chapters 38–39	300
21	The final temple—Ezek. chapters 40–43	312
22	Authenticity in the new temple—Ezek. chapter 44	334
23	Dining with a royal host—Ezek. chapters 45–46	348
24	Christ makes all things new—Ezek. chapters 47–48	358
	Endnotes	370
	Select bibliography	400

List of Bible abbreviations

THE OLD TESTAMENT

		1 Chr.	1 Chronicles	Dan.	Daniel
		2 Chr.	2 Chronicles	Hosea	Hosea
Gen.	Genesis	Ezra	Ezra	Joel	Joel
Exod.	Exodus	Neh.	Nehemiah	Amos	Amos
Lev.	Leviticus	Esth.	Esther	Obad.	Obadiah
Num.	Numbers	Job	Job	Jonah	Jonah
Deut.	Deuteronomy	Ps.	Psalms	Micah	Micah
Josh.	Joshua	Prov.	Proverbs	Nahum	Nahum
Judg.	Judges	Eccles.	Ecclesiastes	Hab.	Habakkuk
Ruth	Ruth	S.of S.	Song of Solomon	Zeph.	Zephaniah
1 Sam.	1 Samuel	Isa.	Isaiah	Hag.	Haggai
2 Sam.	2 Samuel	Jer.	Jeremiah	Zech.	Zechariah
1 Kings	1 Kings	Lam.	Lamentations	Mal.	Malachi
2 Kings	2 Kings	Ezek.	Ezekiel		

THE NEW TESTAMENT

		Gal.	Galatians	Heb.	Hebrews
		Eph.	Ephesians	James	James
Matt.	Matthew	Phil.	Philippians	1 Peter	1 Peter
Mark	Mark	Col.	Colossians	2 Peter	2 Peter
Luke	Luke	1 Thes.	1 Thessalonians	1 John	1 John
John	John	2 Thes.	2 Thessalonians	2 John	2 John
Acts	Acts	1 Tim.	1 Timothy	3 John	3 John
Rom.	Romans	2 Tim.	2 Timothy	Jude	Jude
1 Cor.	1 Corinthians	Titus	Titus	Rev.	Revelation
2 Cor.	2 Corinthians	Philem.	Philemon		

Preface

Why read or study the book of Ezekiel? Does it have any relevance today? Have you ever taken the time to read through this lengthy book? If so, did you enjoy it? Perhaps more importantly, to what extent did you understand it? The fact that it is among the longer books in the Bible and yet also among the least understood, is ample reason for encouraging you to take a more careful look at the prophecy of Ezekiel.

My own experience is that having read through the book many times and having read several commentaries by notable authors, I felt that I was beginning to understand the prophet's message. As a pastor I wanted to preach from Ezekiel but always found an excuse for avoiding it. I quite simply found it intimidating. In the course of my ministry in Albania some years ago I had the great good fortune to host one of the authors cited in the select bibliography of this book. During conversation with him about his commentary I shared my hesitation about teaching from Ezekiel to which he simply responded 'Why?' That gentle response was the encouragement I needed to get on with the task of teaching my congregation something of the richness of Ezekiel. What I quickly came to realise is that this message, although written more than 2,500 years ago, is as relevant to our times as it was to the exiles in Babylon. Ezekiel's teaching spans the centuries and addresses the issues that arise in a world where people need to know the meaning and purpose of life, but reject biblical absolutes.

At the time of writing I have been serving in the Royal

Army Chaplains Department for almost nine years. In 2007 when I was re-evaluating my role in Albania and considering the Army as a potential area for ministry, I was struck by the words of the then Chief of the General Staff, General Sir Richard Dannatt (now Lord Dannatt), to the effect that our soldiers need better preparation for life after death.[1] Indeed, at a time when we were losing young soldiers in both Iraq and Afghanistan, his words were the catalyst to me joining the department. It is my firm conviction that the greatest need young soldiers have is the same as that of society in general: that is, a saving relationship with the Lord Jesus Christ, so that when the end comes, as it inevitably comes to us all, they can know the truth of those inspiring words of the Apostle Paul, 'For to me to live is Christ, and to die is gain' (Philippians 1:21). To put that in Ezekiel's terms, the greatest need people have is a restored relationship with God.

Ezekiel's message emphasises the restoration of God's name through the restoration of his people. To put it another way, it is a message that calls for the restoration and exaltation of God's glory through the salvation and spiritual growth of his people. In our day too the Lord's name is abused, treated with contempt, and brought into disrepute by the language and behaviour of people made in his image, who want to live without accountability to God.

Ezekiel's message emphasises the restoration of God's name through the restoration of his people.

My aim in this book has been to cut to the heart of Ezekiel's message and hopefully bring some clarity and practical application from his gospel to this postmodern (or post-postmodern) generation. The title of this series is Opening Up and I have tried to open up and make accessible the teaching of Ezekiel. If you have questions relating to Ezekiel's message that are not addressed here then I heartily commend to you the works cited in the select bibliography at the end of this book.

My prayer is for the restoration of God's glory in this generation, where necessary beginning in the church. If you put in the effort to study the book of Ezekiel, I believe that, like me, you will soon come to benefit from, and enjoy, the word pictures and antics of this rather enigmatic individual. More importantly you will learn much of the mind of God that is as relevant to today's people of God as it was to those in captivity in Ezekiel's day.

Introduction

'Truth has gone the way of the toaster review.' This was the title in the Comment section of The Times newspaper in which journalist Hugo Rifkind addressed what he termed 'the growth in alternative facts.'[1] The article drew attention to the preposterous extreme to which postmodernism has taken us in its refutation of truth claims. It is inconceivable, even laughable, to think that a fact can be challenged by an alternative fact. Yet that is where we are and if enough people believe something then it becomes true, it becomes fact. This is the essence of populism and postmodernism. To quote Rifkind once more, 'For the populist, there can always be alternative facts, because there are no facts. Not anymore. There are only reviews.'

He relates all of this to the process of buying a toaster from a popular internet site. The best toaster is very quickly assumed to be the one with the 738 five-star reviews. Little thought is given to the possibility that there might actually be an even better toaster for sale at a similar or better price, but which simply is not as popular or, for whatever reason, has fewer reviews. The point of all this talk about toasters and populism and alternative facts is simple really. Often the 'truth' of a matter is determined by its popularity! In our day, if enough people say it then it must be right, it must be true.

In 2016 the Oxford Dictionaries Word of the Year was post-truth. They defined it as an adjective 'relating to or denoting circumstances in which objective facts are less influential in shaping public opinion than appeals to emotion and personal belief'.

But what has all of this got to do with Ezekiel? What can a book that was written some 550–600 years before Christ have to say to the postmodern, post-truth times we live in today? Well, when you consider the Oxford Dictionaries definition of post-truth and compare that with what was going on in Ezekiel's day, it is hard to see what has changed! Though he was living in very different times, many of the issues people were facing were not much different. The Israelites had in many ways turned their backs on God, and public opinion seems to have been shaped more by appeals to emotion and personal belief than by God's revealed truth. All kinds of religious practice were found acceptable because they were popular. If truth was not being challenged by 'alternative truth' it was certainly being ignored in favour of the popular view. Truth claims were being refuted in Ezekiel's day, and truth claims are being refuted today. The way in which Ezekiel addresses this speaks clearly to his contemporaries in Babylon and reaches down through the corridors of time into our day.

Ezekiel shows us how to preach with authority without being authoritarian.

We are told that our post-truth society is non-authoritarian and therefore does not respond well to authoritarian preaching. Ezekiel shows us how to preach with authority without being authoritarian. His faithfulness to what God calls him to do illustrates that the word of God has an authority all of its own. Ezekiel appealed to the people simply by obeying God's word himself and passing on God's message to the people, keeping it true to God's meaning.

It has been remarked that postmodern people respond well to storytelling. The book of Ezekiel deals with narrative history, offering theological perspective on historical events. It addresses a turbulent time in the history of Israel just before Jerusalem was finally destroyed by the Babylonian army. It tells the story of the exiles by the Chebar canal and of those still living in Jerusalem at the time of his ministry. It recounts in detail the historical and practical reasons for God's judgement against Judah. But more than that, it tells of the wonderful future God has for his people despite their failings. It is a story of hope to any generation that feels a sense of hopelessness. Since Nietzsche's cry that God is dead our world has certainly been plunged into despair and hopelessness.

Authenticity is another one of those words that keeps popping up in discussions about postmodernism.[2] If we expect people to listen to what we have to say then they must be able to see the difference God's Word is making in our own lives. Ezekiel could certainly not be charged with being inauthentic. His whole life of obedience to God, including dealing with the traumatic death of his young wife, is played out in the public gaze. Even if the people did not listen to him, they certainly could not accuse him of hypocrisy.

All of this also ties in with the postmodern emphasis on community. We live in what has been described as a global village and postmodern people are passionate about international issues. Ezekiel's message is not only for his own people but reaches out across borders. His message emphasises the concern of God, reiterated in the New

Testament, to make his name known among the nations. Christians of all people should be those living in authentic community; that is to say, our churches should not simply be what Francis Schaeffer described as 'preaching points and activity generators'[3] but rather communities in which the unsaved can see God's word being authentically lived out.

But perhaps the greatest message that Ezekiel has to offer this postmodern generation is his message of redemption. If postmodern people do not respond well to moralistic preaching then Ezekiel has the answer. God's message through Ezekiel addresses not simply moral decline but their acute spiritual need and how to redress that. His message is one of redemption and hope. It is not simply about changing behaviour but of trusting in God who alone can change their hearts. This is a message borne out in the life and ministry of Jesus, the one who encompasses the entire grand narrative of the Bible from Genesis to Revelation, and the one in whom authentic redemption is found.

Overview

Ezekiel's prophecy covers a period of approximately twenty-three years (from 593–571 BC) during which the political landscape in the Ancient Near East was changing quite dramatically. Egypt, which had enjoyed superpower status for some time, was now in decline as was Assyria to the north. Babylon was the rising new power in the region.

This was to have a devastating effect on Jerusalem—resulting in the city's destruction, the temple being burned, many of its inhabitants being carried off into slavery in Babylon, and the end of the monarchy which had started with King Saul some 500 years earlier (around 1050 BC).

Ezekiel was among those exiled to Babylon during the second of three deportations (597 BC). Assuming that the reference to the 'thirtieth year,' (Ezek. 1:1) is actually Ezekiel's age, then he would have been twenty-five years old when taken captive and thirty when he began his prophetic ministry among the exiles by the Chebar canal in Babylon. His ministry is sandwiched between, and overlaps with, Jeremiah's in Jerusalem, and Daniel's in Babylon.

The dating and historical chronology within Ezekiel, including fourteen date references, leaves us in no doubt that his ministry took place in what Francis Schaeffer describes as historic space-time events.[1] Because his prophetic pronouncements are grounded in these specific dates, Ezekiel cannot be charged with simply interpreting history after the event.[2] He is a proven prophet of God. His prophecies came in the context of historic space-time events and were later fulfilled in historic space-time events.

Judgement and hope

The forty-eight chapters of Ezekiel fall into two main divisions, which can be summed up in the words judgement and hope. The turning point is the fall of Jerusalem (Ezek. 33:21–22).[3] Although it may be among the more difficult books, Ezekiel's message will be somewhat easier to understand when we see it in that light. I therefore suggest the following outline:[4]

1 Declarations of Judgement: Chapters 1–32
   -judgement on Israel (3:22–ch. 24)
   -judgement on the heathen nations (25–32)
2 Declarations of Salvation and Hope: Chapters 33–48
   -redemption for Israel (33–39)
   -redemption in the Final temple (40–48)

There are, of course, many subdivisions within these,[5] and the twin themes of judgement and hope appear throughout the chapters of this book.

The glory of God

If the book of Ezekiel is divided into two main sections as noted above, then we must draw attention to the overarching theme—the glory of God. From the opening chapters, which are dominated by visions of the glory of God, to the glory departing the temple in Jerusalem (10:18 and 11:23), then manifest in his judgement on the nations (39:21), and then the glory returning to the temple (43:1–5), this theme dominates throughout.[6]

Ezekiel is full of imagery and allegory which can be difficult to understand. However, as we shall see, Ezekiel does not leave it to our imaginations to work out what they mean, nor how such visions of God's glory affect those who truly witness them (1:28). If we keep in mind that all these images and allegories and symbols in one way or another represent the glory of God in these two great acts of judgement and hope, then the basic meaning and message will become clearer.

God's concern for his name

Closely aligned with the theme of God's glory in Ezekiel is a concern for his holy name. Indeed, some suggest that in Ezekiel Yahweh's name is more important than his glory.[7] In the past God had withheld his wrath for the sake of his name, but Israel's repeated sin had brought his name into such disrepute that God can no longer allow it to continue. However, even the Exile had caused God's name to be despised among the nations, prompting further concern leading to the restoration of Israel (36:16–22). Much of God's concern throughout Ezekiel is that his holy name might be made known among both Israel and the nations of their exile (e.g. Ezek. 39:7). That brings us to God's mission.

Some suggest that in Ezekiel Yahweh's name is more important than his glory.

The mission of God

The glory of God and his concern for his name are the

overarching theme not simply of Ezekiel's prophecies, but the mission of God himself. Much ministry and evangelism in our day is focussed on the needs of the people to whom it is addressed. Ezekiel's pronouncements of judgement and hope also show God's love for his people, and his desire that they might return to him with all their hearts and be saved (33:11). But more significantly Ezekiel's declarations and bizarre enactments have at their root God's own mission—that his glory and the honour of his name be restored. The people are being judged because God is being ignored and his name dragged through the mud. Likewise, the people are given hope and offered salvation so that God's reputation might be restored. The mission of God is the restoration of the glory of God through the restoration of the people of God. 'For the earth will be filled with the knowledge of the glory of the LORD as the waters cover the sea,' says Habakkuk (Hab. 2:14). This '... is God's will and purpose. Such is the mission of God.'[8]

The mission of God is the restoration of the glory of God through the restoration of the people of God.

This mission continues to the present day. The Apostle Paul, in his letter to the Corinthian church, talks of the '... glory of God in the face of Christ' (2 Cor. 4:6). This verse reminds us that the Christian's mind is enlightened by knowing Christ so that we might see clearly the glory of God. The glory of God is seen in Christ. He and no other is the express image of God (Heb. 1:3). It is through Christ and Christ alone that the divine perfections and divine glory are known today. 'He and he alone declares, represents, and makes known, unto angels and men, the essential glory of the invisible God ...'[9]

Table 1

JUDGEMENT			HOPE
Babylon Ezekiel's vision, call, and commission	**Judah** BEFORE SIEGE Key moment is when God's Glory departs 11:22–23	**Nations** DURING SIEGE Judgements against the nations who gloat over Judah's demise	**Future of Judah** AFTER THE SIEGE Key moment is when God's Glory returns to the temple 43:1–5
Chapters 1–3	Chapters 4–24	Chapters 25–32	Chapters 33–48
7 YEARS ⌛ 593–586 Ezekiel prophesies JUDGEMENT			15 YEARS ⌛ 586–571 Ezekiel prophesies HOPE
THEME The restoration of God's name via the judgement and restoration of God's people			

Table 2													
What's being said	Ezekiel's Vision Master and Ministry	Siege of Jerusalem acted out	Idolatry condemned (High places and Hearts)	Idolatry condemned (Going's on in the temple)	Selective hearing and false teachers condemned	Parables and a sad song (Shocking images)	Bad habits, pain and presumption	Judgement on the nations	The Watchman	The King of Love victorious (New heart, new Spirit, new life)	The final temple	Regulations for worship (Christ makes all things new)
Ch.	1–3	4–5	6–7	8–11	12–14	15–19	20–24	25–32	33	34–39	40–43	44–48
Main Theme	JUDGEMENT								HOPE AND RESTORATION			
	On Judah Before the siege of Jerusalem							On the nations				
Period	7 years 593–586								15 years 586–571			
	Before the siege of Jerusalem							During siege	After the siege of Jerusalem			

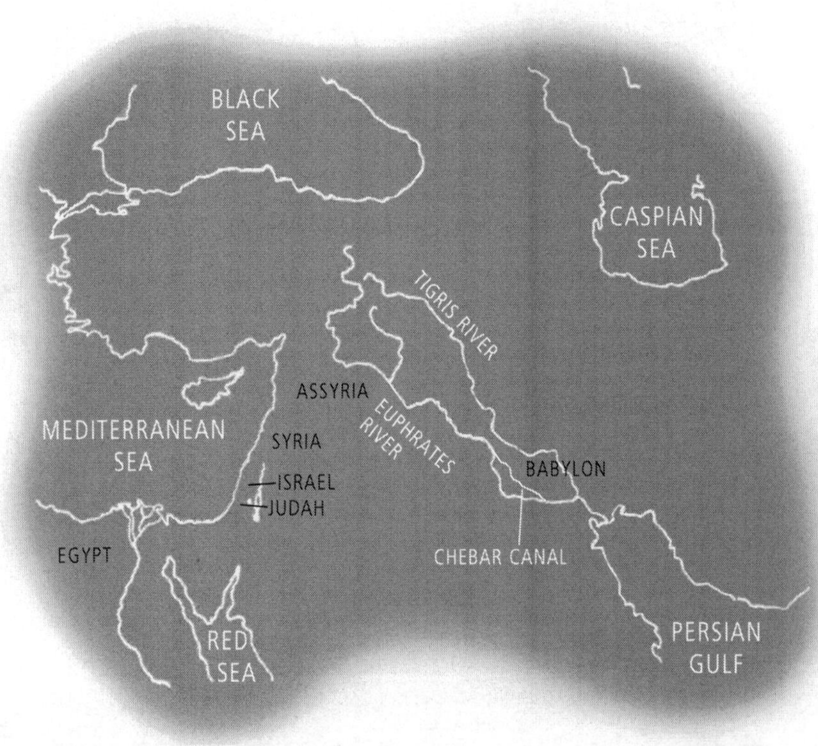

740 BC — DEATH OF UZZIAH

722 BC — ISRAEL TAKEN INTO CAPTIVITY BY ASSYRIA

716 BC — HEZEKIAH BECOMES KING OF JUDAH

701 BC — THE ASSYRIAN SIEGE OF JERUSALEM

608 BC — FIRST EXILES TO BABYLON

586 BC — JERUSALEM FALLS TO THE BABYLONIANS

539 BC — BABYLON FALLS TO THE PERSIANS LED BY CYRUS

538 BC — CYRUS'S DECREE ALLOWS THE JEWS TO RETURN TO JERUSALEM

Background and summary

Ezekiel 1:1–3 and 2 Kings 23:4–27

Ezekiel was born into turbulent times.[1] The weight of political power was shifting and as a result Ezekiel found himself called to preach to the community of Jews who were strangers in a foreign land.

We will come back to this a little later but for now I want to look at Ezekiel himself, the man whom God called to ministry. We will do this by drawing on Ezek. 1:1–3 and other relevant passages of Scripture that will help us to understand the prophet and his book.

The man whom God called

Ezekiel's name is made up of two words in Hebrew[2] and is either a statement—'God strengthens' or a prayer—'may God strengthen.' In either case it would appear that the desire of his parents in giving him such a name was that God would strengthen their newborn for whatever lay ahead. Ezekiel was certainly going to need God's strength for the ministry that he was called to.

We are told that Ezekiel was a priest, the son of Buzi (1:3). We do not know anything about this man Buzi but in all likelihood he too was a priest which would account for Ezekiel also having been prepared for the priesthood. As a priest we find Ezekiel living among the exiles (1:1). We discover early on that he was a long way from home, and a long way from the temple where he would have served as a priest. The temple was of course in Jerusalem, but Ezekiel was in Babylon by the Chebar canal, a journey of some 900 miles.

Most commentators take the reference to 'the thirtieth year' in verse 1 as indicating Ezekiel's age. This would place the events around the year 593–592 BC, which is significant for a couple of reasons. Firstly, it was the year that Ezekiel would have entered into his priestly ministry in the temple in Jerusalem but, as noted above, he instead found himself stuck in a foreign land far from the work he had trained to do. Secondly, if the dating is correct, it means that Ezekiel was born the year that the Book of the Law was found in the temple—an event that led King Josiah to begin wide ranging reforms in Judah (2 Kings 22–23). Josiah was one of the few good kings of the period. We are told that he threw out all idols from the temple (2 Ki. 23:4); got rid of the ungodly priests (2 Ki. 23:5); reinstated the Passover feast (2 Ki. 23:21–22); and turned to the Lord with all his heart (2 Ki. 23:25). Yet, with all these reforms we find that God remained angry with Judah (2 Ki. 23:26–27). It would seem that despite Josiah's personal example and his concerted efforts to bring the people back into a right relationship with God, most of the people preferred to live their lives in denial of their accountability to God. There is a tremendous challenge in this for the people of God in every age. Just how much do we truly search out God's word for our lives, and how much do we turn a blind eye to it because it does not suit our present frame of mind?

The times in which he ministered

As noted above, despite Josiah's reforms, and despite the

fact that Israel (the Northern Kingdom) had ceased to exist as a political entity in 721, some 128 years earlier, Judah (the Southern Kingdom) continued in idolatry and disobedience. They failed to read the signs that wilful disobedience led to God's chastisement. Now they too were facing God's chastisement, with their country collapsing under the threat of a foreign power and their people being carried off into captivity. In the history of Judah there were three different deportations. The first was in 605 BC when Daniel and his three friends were taken to Babylon (this initiated the beginning of the 70 years of captivity prophesied in Jeremiah 25: 11–12; 29:10; and Daniel 9:2). The second deportation took place eight years later in 597 BC during which Ezekiel himself was taken to Babylon. The third was in 587 BC when Judah's puppet king Zedekiah rebelled against the Babylonian Nebuchadnezzar. This resulted in the final sacking of Jerusalem including the temple, the palace and much of the city being burned to the ground.

Judah had fallen so low that she was no longer aware of her sin. Instead of turning to God in her troubles she turned to the world.

Despite all the evidence that disobedience brings God's chastisement, and despite Ezekiel's and Jeremiah's warnings, Judah continued unabated in her sinful rejection of God's rule in their lives. Judah had fallen so low that she was no longer aware of her sin. Instead of turning to God in her troubles she turned to the world. We see this very clearly when Zedekiah made an ally of Egypt in an attempt to defeat Nebuchadnezzar (2 Chr. 36:12 cf. Rom 12:1–2).

The ministry he was called to

Ezekiel was trained as a priest (Ezek. 1:3), called as a prophet (Ezek. 3:1), and deployed as a watchman (Ezek. 3:17). In other words, he was a priest, a prophet, and a pastor.

As a priest he would have been well trained in both God's law and the history of Israel. He had a worldview with God at the centre. He therefore would have understood that Israel's trouble was due to their disobedience and sin. He knew that what they needed was not further alliances with other ungodly nations but rather repentance, a heart-felt turning to God.

God would speak clearly through his servant Ezekiel, challenging the people and challenging the religious establishment of the day in the way that Jeremiah had done when he spoke against the false prophet Hananiah (Jer. 28:1–17). The glory of God is at stake as his people fail in their holy calling to make him known among the nations.

As a watchman, pastor and evangelist, Ezekiel would watch out for the people. He would challenge and rebuke the backsliders and the arrogant, and comfort the despairing and broken, in everything leading them according to what God said. At its heart all pastoral ministry and mission should aim to hold in perfect harmony the primary motive of a passion for God's glory, and genuine concern for our neighbour's spiritual needs.[3]

First would come the hard lesson of judgement, until such times as the people finally recognised and accepted their sin and inability to change the situation themselves. Then the message of hope, showing them the way of salvation.

FOR FURTHER STUDY

1. Read Isaiah 48:1–11 (esp. v.11). What parallels do we find between this passage and Ezekiel's overarching theme?
2. Read 2 Corinthians 5:17–21. According to this passage, in what way do Christians have a similar calling to Ezekiel's?
3. Read Romans 12:1–2. What similarities can we see between the Apostle Paul's words to Christians and Josiah's reforms in 2 Kings 22–23?

TO THINK ABOUT AND DISCUSS

1. Why is it so important to recognise that Ezekiel's prophecies were made in what Francis Schaeffer describes as historic space-time events?
2. What do you make of Ezekiel's emphasis on judgement before hope?
3. Do you recognise any areas in your own life or in your church's life that need reforming according to God's word? In what ways might you or your church inadvertently turn to the world rather than turning to God or his word for help?

1 Ezekiel's master and ministry

Ezekiel Chapters 1–3

Ezekiel is about to experience a bitter-sweet encounter with God. He will see a vision of cherubim carrying a crystal-like sea upon which is a throne representing the jaw-dropping glory of God. Following this incredible vision Ezekiel is told to take God's message to a people who will not listen to him, and to remain faithful even when all around him are unfaithful.

God is not confined to any space or place. No matter where we find ourselves there is great comfort in knowing that God is with us. Given his distance from his beloved temple in Jerusalem, at a time when he should have been entering the ministry, Ezekiel must have wondered if he would ever fulfil his ambition of becoming a priest. But God had something even more special in mind for him.

As he sat by the banks of the Chebar canal the very heavens opened up before him and he saw visions of God. The visions that follow are intricate, but the opening verse tells us exactly what they are, so we are not left to second-guess. Sometimes there is a temptation to get bogged down in the details of such a vivid description, but we must be careful to start with the big picture and that is explained to us right at the outset—it is a vision of God's glory.

The Master he is called to serve 1:1–28

Even Calvin[1] admitted that he could scarcely understand this vision. Yet he saw great value in studying it so that in having a better understanding of God's glory we might better understand the authority with which his servant spoke. In turn Ezekiel's aim is that this hard-hearted and rebellious people might fear God and return to him. Such is God's love for his people in every age. If we are to learn anything from the very outset of this prophecy surely it is that among God's people are those who want to do things their own way by turning their back on the clear teachings of God's word, but also that God loves them too much to allow it to continue. In every generation we need a fresh vision of the glorious God we are called to serve. If we can but recapture something of this glory then so many other issues will fall into place. So long as we put our own selfish desires first, then the glory of God will be obscured.

All-powerful 1:4

Storms are often used in the Bible as a symbol of God's power and judgement (Jer. 23:19; Jer. 25:32). The fact that it is coming from the north is probably emblematic of God's judgement on Israel. The great northern powers of Assyria and Babylon have already been used by God to chastise his disobedient people. God often speaks from the cloud, as when he spoke to Moses at Sinai and delivered to him the Ten Commandments, or when our Lord was transfigured in the presence of Peter, James, and John (Matt. 17:1–13). A mass of fire can be seen within the cloud and bursting forth in bolts of lightning,[2] perhaps representing God's powerful agitation at his people. Fire is often symbolic of God's presence, or of purification. We can see this vision as implying that an all-powerful God was coming to purify his people.

Fire is often symbolic of God's presence, or of purification.

All knowing 1:5–14

The four living creatures of v5 are identified for us in chapter 10:20 as cherubim, that is, attendants of God or angels. The way they are described and used in this vision serves the purpose of expressing certain attributes or characteristics of God.[3]

Each had the appearance of a man but with four faces. Douglas Stuart suggests that the faces may represent the four most impressive of God's creatures on land and in the air: the face of a man representing the highest intelligence; the face of a lion the greatest ferocity; that of a bull the greatest strength; and the eagle freedom.[4] Each creature had four wings (cf. Isa 6:1–3), and four human hands, and we are told that they did not turn. With four faces there is an implication that these creatures were able to see in every direction. They did not need to turn their bodies to see in opposite directions, which would mean they saw everything all the time. This is perhaps indicative of God's all-knowing character. Nothing is hidden from his sight; nothing can take him by surprise. This is both a challenge and a comfort for the child of God. Israel would come to know that their secret sins were no secret to God, and whilst God would not tolerate that sin, yet he would forgive his children if only they would turn back to him.

Always present 1:15–21

Ezekiel moves on to describe the wheels within wheels, with rims full of eyes, and containing the spirit of life which was their driving force.[5] In ancient times many peoples believed that gods had authority only over their own country. This part of the vision seems to contradict such thinking. God is not limited to one place, such as the temple in Jerusalem. He was moving here right among the exiles in Babylon. Our God is the God of all the earth. Despite their history[6] the people of God need reminding of this foundational teaching. They have been too long among those of differing beliefs and have allowed themselves to absorb too much of their neighbour's practices—a salutary lesson to the children of God in every age.

Majestic 1:22–28

The next part of Ezekiel's vision describes an expanse apparently hovering above the cherubim, whose wings were making a tremendous noise. This noise is given three descriptions including a noise like the voice of the Almighty.[7] It is important to note the word like. The prophet is trying to express as best he can something that he himself is probably struggling to understand. This noise which stops when the cherubim put down their two wings seems to be a precursor to the voice of God. After hearing the voice (v. 24) Ezekiel goes on to describe something that looked like a throne and seated above the throne the likeness of a man. The prophet seems to struggle with how to describe this part of the vision. The grammar is clumsy and the imagery mixed. It is the appearance of a man who glowed like fire or amber and a glow of brightness all around him, and he is seated above the likeness of a throne (v. 26). Who sits on a throne but royalty? In this instance the King of Kings in all his majesty. 'The prophet has witnessed the incredible—far away from the temple, among the exiles in the pagan land of Babylon, Yahweh has appeared to him!'[8] Ezekiel is in no doubt about what he has just seen. This is a vision of God in his all his glory. In fact it is only an expression of that glory, an appearance of the likeness of the glory, because the full glory of God could not be explained in either words or pictures. What a majestic, all-glorious God we have!

Humbling 1:28, 3:23; 43:3; 44:4

Ezekiel is so overawed by this vision of the glory of God that we see a two-fold reaction. Firstly, he is not exactly speechless, but close to it. He struggles to find the words to describe the glory of God. Just consider how many times he uses the word appearance and likeness. It seems that even with his extensive vocabulary as an educated man he is still stuck for words to explain this incredible God. What a contrast to those in our day whose view of God simply suits their own lifestyle or philosophy!

Secondly, Ezekiel is so overawed that he falls down upon

his face and God has to help him to his feet again (2:2). Ezekiel responds appropriately with an instinctive gesture of homage to the divine King.[9] What a picture of true humility. What an expression of his own sense of unworthiness, and his fear and reverence for God. What a counter-balance to the casual way that many today come into the presence of this same majestic, glorious, all-powerful God!

Empowering 2:2 and 3:14, 24

The God who humbles him by his majestic presence, also infuses Ezekiel with the power of the Holy Spirit and raises him to his feet in readiness for the task at hand. This is the same power from the same Spirit that drove the wheels within wheels in chapter 1, and it is this power that will accompany Ezekiel throughout his ministry among the exiles. Not only does God call his servants to ministry and provides them the words or message they are to speak, he also equips them with the power of the Holy Spirit to make their ministry effective in a way that mere human agency can never do. This is the Master Ezekiel was called to serve and this is the master we are called to serve.

The God who humbles him by his majestic presence, also infuses Ezekiel with the power of the Holy Spirit and raises him to his feet in readiness for the task at hand.

The Ministry he is called to fulfil 2:1–3:27

In chapters 2:1–3:27 we find what theologians have described as Ezekiel's five-fold calling. In other words the Lord's call contains five parts, each with a different emphasis. The first three parts of Ezekiel's calling can be summed us as follows. Firstly, he is called to speak to what God describes as a nation of rebels who are impudent and stubborn (2:3–4). Secondly, he is to speak even though they will not listen (2:5). Ezekiel is being sent out like a lamb amongst the wolves. There is anticipation that not only will the people refuse to hear the message that Ezekiel is given, but they will treat him with scorn (2:6). No one enjoys being on the receiving end of a disdainful look. We naturally want to be liked and take care not to say things that might bring the disapproval of our peers. But often in the service of God things need to be said that do not meet the approval of our audience. Thirdly, he is to ensure that regardless of how this rebellious and stubborn people respond to God's word, he is to pay attention to it himself (2:8). There is nothing more hypocritical than a preacher who does not practise what he preaches to others. The scroll (3:3) that Ezekiel is given to eat, representing the word of God, proves to be as sweet as honey to him. Such is the word of God to his children even when it pricks our conscience, challenges our failings, and leads us down paths we would otherwise fear to tread.

There is nothing more hypocritical than a preacher who does not practise what he preaches to others.

Bitter sweet 3:14

What is Ezekiel's response to all of this so far? He is embittered

(3:14). Why is it that having eaten a scroll that was as sweet as honey Ezekiel becomes embittered? Most of us who are called to serve God in a full-time capacity consider it a real privilege and blessing. We are not naïve to the possibility of the occasional disappointment or painful experience, but in general we enter upon our ministry with enthusiasm and the expectancy of God working through us. So why would this man, who has prepared for most of his adult life for the priestly ministry, now be embittered that God has called him to go and preach? The answer is in the people to whom he is called to minister. God's people! And why would that upset him? Because of their predicted response—they will not listen! They are not interested in being reformed or transformed by God's word.

Could this be a perennial problem among the people of God? In Romans 12:2 the apostle Paul exhorts believers not to be conformed to this world, but to be transformed by the application of God's word to their hearts and minds. Ezekiel himself found the word of God as sweet as honey; but when he thinks of preaching it to people who will not listen, it is a bitter thing. Matthew Henry sums up how Ezekiel must have felt and indeed how any minister of the gospel must feel when their ministry is not heeded. He writes, 'It is a great grief to faithful ministers, and makes them go on in their work with a heavy heart, when they find people unmovable and hating to be reformed.'[10]

Overwhelming 3:15

We read that Ezekiel is emotionally exhausted by what he has just witnessed and is asked to do. Indeed, he sat down among the exiles by the Chebar canal (3:15), those to whom he is called to minister, and remains there feeling overwhelmed for seven days. We picture Ezekiel sitting there looking around him and wondering what on earth he is getting into. He is overwhelmed and embittered and we have only arrived at point three of his five-point calling! He probably needs time to ponder all that he has just witnessed and heard. And God gives him seven days to do just that.

However, God has not simply left Ezekiel to deal with his fears on his own. When God calls any of his children to a specific role he does so in a manner and timescale that they can cope with. God's advice to Ezekiel is that he is not to take to heart the people's rejection of his message because their rejection of him is fundamentally a rejection of God himself. Ezekiel is to draw encouragement from the fact that ultimately the reason the people will not listen to him is because they are not willing to listen to God (3:7). What an indictment on the people of God to be told that even the ungodly pay more attention to his word than they do (3:6). Surely this ought to be a catalyst to drive God's people back to the Bible so that we can better know and understand the mind of God, especially given the postmodern influence on our society and pressures on our churches. It should also encourage church leaders to be faithful to the Lord by drawing close to those we are called to serve and sitting where they sit in their distress and suffering, even if they do not always or immediately take our advice or see the relevance of God's word to their lives.

Pastoral 3:17–21

After seven days God introduces Ezekiel to the fourth part

of his calling. He has been made a watchman (3:17–21). The role of the watchman is to guard and protect. It involves keeping watch at all hours in all sorts of weather, for the benefit of both the wicked (3:18) and the righteous (3:20). This is the language God uses to describe Ezekiel's pastoral ministry. Even rebellious people with selective hearing need a pastor. As Calvin succinctly points out,[11] what is expected of Ezekiel is what is expected of all teachers in the church, that they should keep watch by instructing the people in the things of God, warn them of any wrong practices, care for them as a shepherd cares for his flock, and be prepared to do so at any time of the night or day.

It is a weighty matter to be held to account for the souls of others, but this is the calling of a pastor and should not be entered upon lightly. At the heart of this ministry is a two-fold mission of glorifying God by seeing people turn from their wickedness or sin. The language of sin and rebellion is not popular in our day. I sometimes get the distinct impression that if Ezekiel were to preach on our streets today some local church leaders would be embarrassed by the language he uses and conspire to have him stopped. But in any age when God's own people are more influenced by the society in which they live than by the eternal word of God, Ezekiel's bluntness may well be necessary. What is at stake is life and death (3:18–20), not just physical

If Ezekiel were to preach on our streets today some local church leaders would be embarrassed by the language he uses and conspire to have him stopped.

death but eternal death and separation from God. And this is not simply Old Testament doctrine. 'For the wages of sin is death …', Paul tells the Roman Christians (Rom. 6:23). This is no trifling matter and has very little to do with the latest trends in philosophy. As a pastor to the people Ezekiel will be compelled to speak only what the Lord tells him to say (3:27). We err when we think that we have a better way than God of identifying our neighbour's needs.

Theatrical 3:22–27

For the second time we read that Ezekiel is confronted with such a vision of God's glory that he falls on his face (3:23). This time it is in a valley, where once again the Spirit of God actively raises Ezekiel to his feet and infuses him with power for what is about to come—the first of a series of dramatic enactments. He is to shut himself up in his house (3:24) and when the time comes speak only what God tells him to say. God is very specific about this. Ezekiel is not simply to go expressing his own views but is to preface his pronouncements with 'Thus says the LORD God.' Ezekiel is a man so possessed by the Spirit of God that he will be unable to form a word in his mouth without God's prompting. Ezekiel is to preach whether the people listen or not. It is often difficult to understand the ways of God, and yet we must believe that God's plans will not fail, that his word will not return empty but that it will succeed in the purpose for which God sends it out (Isa. 55:11). Preachers, Sunday School teachers, and parents take encouragement that the power of redemption and restoration lies not in the hearts of the hearers but in the Spirit of the living God.

God never expects more from us that we can cope with but feeds us our duties in bite-size pieces. Christians are called to serve the same Master that Ezekiel is called to serve. We are called to be ambassadors as God makes his appeal through us (2 Cor. 5:20). We are to go to a rebellious people, to go to a people with selective hearing and say things to them that they will find distasteful, to speak to those who may disdain us or abuse us. But we do so in the knowledge that the same God who infused Ezekiel with power for the task will also empower us as we speak to people in great need of God's restoring love.

For further study ▶

FOR FURTHER STUDY

1. Read Matt. 24:30; 26:24; 1 Thess. 4:17. What parallels do we find between Ezekiel's vision of God coming in the clouds and the second coming of the Lord Jesus Christ in the passages you have just read?
2. Read Exod. 25:18–22; 1 Kings 6:24–27; and Isa. 6:1–3. What further can we learn from these passages about the nature and role of the cherubim? Are there any practical lessons we can learn from them?
3. Read Rev. 1:17. John has a very similar experience to Ezekiel. What practical lessons can we learn from the response of these two men when they encounter the living God?

TO THINK ABOUT AND DISCUSS

1. The people of God in Ezekiel's day seem to have been greatly influenced by those they were living among. In what ways, if any, are you or your church in danger from ungodly influences? What can you do to avoid this danger?
2. What plans have you made that have not been fulfilled? Can you see how God has redirected you in life? Do you find this exciting or frightening?
3. Pastoral ministry in Ezekiel's day had lost much of its authority and the people were living as they saw fit. Is pastoral ministry today in danger of losing its authority? If so what reasons would you give for this? Drawing on Ezekiel's experiences, how might a proper biblical authority be returned to pastoral ministry?

Judgement against Israel

2 Mimes and models

Ezekiel Chapters 4–5

Ezekiel begins his ministry with a four-scene mime act involving some model building depicting the coming destruction of Jerusalem. This will undoubtedly be an uncomfortable experience for Ezekiel, lasting over a year, but not half as uncomfortable as the reality he is illustrating. Any among the exiles who were still looking to Jerusalem for salvation are in for a bitter disappointment. The people must learn that salvation is from the Lord not man.

When I was a child growing up in West Tyrone in Northern Ireland I was fascinated by stories of World War Two. Like so many of my generation, one of the things I loved to do was spend the money I earned on Airfix models such as the Spitfire, Hawker Hurricane, Fokker, and Messerschmitt aeroplanes. I have to confess that I was not very good at building these models, with as much of the plastic cement ending up on my fingers as on the models. Nevertheless, the process brought me a tremendous amount of enjoyment and it was followed by hours of amusement as I re-enacted scenes from the Battle of Britain. In this chapter we find Ezekiel building a model and delivering a performance directed by God. Bearing in mind that for most of this Ezekiel was mute (3:26), it was in fact more of a mime. Mime is a fascinating art and wonderful skill, although I have to confess to not always understanding exactly what the actor is trying to communicate. However, by the time Ezekiel is done there will be no doubt as to what his message is—even if it all seems a little bizarre to those watching.

Having been confined to his home in a state of enforced silence, Ezekiel is now to take a brick and engrave upon it a picture of Jerusalem. With this as his centrepiece he is then to build his model around it. It is a scene of war. Siege mounds are put around the city, as well as battering rams and even enemy camps (4:1–2). Next he has to lie down on the ground beside the model every day for over a year in a very elaborate and somewhat disturbing mime that involved holding an iron griddle or frying pan between him and the model. During this performance, Ezekiel is told to live on a strange diet of bread cooked over burning human dung, and finally following fourteen months of this bizarre behaviour Ezekiel is told to shave off all his hair and beard and to dispose of it in three symbolic actions.

What does it all mean? It is not left to our imaginations. Ezekiel tells us what it all means. It concerns the reality of, and reasons for, biblical discipline.

The reality of biblical discipline

The reality of God's discipline upon Israel is expressed here in four acts held in open theatre by Ezekiel's new home on the banks of the Chebar canal.

Act 1 Divine displeasure 4:1–3

In the first act he takes a brick, probably a soft unfired brick, and draws a sketch of Jerusalem on it. Then he sets up siege ramps and towers against it and finally takes a steel pan and hides his face behind it. The meaning of this model building is explained very clearly in chapter five. God is against (5:7) his own people and will discipline them. 'Jerusalem had rebelled against the one who had chosen her and set her apart. Instead of being a light to the nations and demonstrating before them the righteous character of Yahweh's revealed will, she had taken her cues for her own conduct from them.'[1]

> Instead of being a light to the nations and demonstrating before them the righteous character of Yahweh's revealed will, Jerusalem had taken her cues for her own conduct from them.

In this first act of Ezekiel's drama he is playing the role of God. By hiding his face behind the steel pan or placing it between himself and the model of Jerusalem he is signifying that there is a barrier between God and his people, and that barrier is their disobedience and waywardness (5:6). During the actual siege of Jerusalem, which would take place less than five years later, it would be the Babylonians who would build the real-life siege towers and ramps. But behind the Babylonians there is God, using them to discipline his people. Jerusalem has rebelled against God and brought upon herself his divine displeasure. Indeed she is so bad that God considers his own covenant people worse than the nations around them (5:5–6) and he will not allow such wanton disobedience to go unchallenged.

Act 2 Diligent discipline 4:4–8

If in Act 1 Ezekiel was playing the part of God in Act 2 he takes on the role of Israel. Ezekiel is to lie on his left side for 390 days and on his right side for 40 days symbolically bearing the sin of the nation.[2] He may have wrapped himself in rope (4:8) possibly symbolic of his being bound to declare the firm and unalterable decree of God. At one point he bares his arm. Rolling up the sleeves was the usual behaviour of an army preparing for the fray so that they might better wield their weapons. The possible meaning of the phrase could be to show how ready and diligent the Babylonians would be in carrying out the siege of Jerusalem five years later.[3] However, we must not forget that behind the bared arm of the Babylonians was the bared arm of God exacting discipline upon his wayward people. The same phrase is used of God in Isa. 52:10 to signify his power to deliver his people.[4] How merciful God is—not only does he bare his arm in readiness for discipline but does so in preparation for deliverance. Ezekiel symbolically bears the sin of the nation, but the sins of all God's children are dealt with once and for all in the ultimate deliverance of Christ's atoning sacrifice on the cross of Calvary. Here we again see God punishing sin but also bearing sin to deliver his people.

Act 3 Defiled food 4:9–17

Ezekiel evidently did not have to lie on his side 24 hours each day as we read that he had to prepare his own food. The weights and measurements described (v. 10–11) are to show the meagre diet Ezekiel had to live on during the 390 days. This diet seems to represent two things. Firstly it is symbolic of an unprecedented famine that the inhabitants of Jerusalem would suffer during the actual siege (4:16–17). In 5:9–10 we read that this famine will be so bad that the people will turn to cannibalism. In due course Ezekiel's words would prove very accurate indeed. We are told that about two years into the siege the famine in Jerusalem was so severe that there was no food for the people (2 Kings 25:1–3). Secondly, the requirement placed upon Ezekiel to cook his food over a fire of human dung (4:12) indicates that following the siege this holy people, this people who had been chosen from among all the nations by God, will be forced to eat defiled food among the nations to which God will exile them (4:13). But even in the midst of wrath there is mercy. Note the one concession to Ezekiel in this passage. In the place of human dung God allows him to use cow dung as fuel for the fire, a common form of fuel in many parts of the world even today. However, even with this concession for the sake of his servant Ezekiel, the implication remains that God's decree against Israel stands. This nation, God's own people, will face defilement by exile among the pagan nations around them. They had trifled too long with pagan practices so now God will give them over to the desires of their hearts, something that will prove a very painful lesson indeed. The parallels with the Apostle Paul's letter to the Romans cannot be ignored (Rom. 1:24ff.) even though it is frowned upon in our day to draw attention to such matters.[5] As they had deserted God so God has deserted them. God has withdrawn his providential restraints from them and will leave them to wallow in the consequences of their own choices.

What a frightening thought that the righteous Judge of all the earth would tire of our waywardness and give us over to such an unstable judge as our own hearts.

Jeremiah issues the warning that the heart is deceitful and desperately wicked (Jer. 17:9). It is the source of all wickedness. The lusts that dwell there are many and when unrestrained can lead to all sorts of wrong behaviour. What a frightening thought that the righteous Judge of all the earth would tire of our waywardness and give us over to such an unstable judge as our own hearts. Thankfully Ezekiel's message does not end with judgement but with hope. The Lord takes pleasure in those who fear him and who place their hope in his steadfast love (Ps. 147:11).

Act 4 Demeaning haircut 5:1–17

The final act of this performance, which takes place fourteen months later, contains two scenes. If the mime to date has involved a great deal of lying down, then this final act will involve a flurry of activity designed to grab the audience's attention. In the first scene Ezekiel is to take a sharp blade and shave both his head and beard, and then carefully divide it into three equal piles whilst tucking a small amount into the hem of his robe. You can almost imagine the lights going down briefly to allow the people to ponder what this wretched soul has just done, only to be raised again to put the spotlight on him throwing a third of the hair on the fire, chopping at a third with a sword, and scattering the final portion to the wind. The first is a scene of humiliation, the second one of hopelessness. If the people were befuddled by this bizarre behaviour, their befuddlement would not last for long. As always Ezekiel brings a very clear explanation of the performance. It was a symbol of what would happen to the people of Jerusalem once the city had capitulated to its attackers (5:5). The nail is being driven home one painful heart-wrenching blow after another.

Chris Wright in his commentary points out a threefold humiliation involved in Ezekiel shaving his head and beard. Complete shaving of the head and beard was prohibited to priests;[6] it was associated with mourning or military defeat;[7] and forced shaving was sometimes inflicted to cause deep shame and humiliation.[8] Without doubt this was a humiliating exercise for Ezekiel and it represented the humiliation that the inhabitants of Jerusalem would experience when the city fell (5:15). The third of the hair he cast on the fire indicating that a third of the population of Jerusalem would die in the burning city (5:12). The third thrown around the model and hacked at with his sword until it was decimated and lost in the dry earth, representing the many who would flee the city only to be cut down by the sword as they fled. The final third would be scattered to the four winds to live among the pagan nations they had for so long emulated.

Even the remnant (the small amount tucked away in the hem of his robe) will not escape God's discipline. Some of them will also perish (5:16–17). It is a scene of utter hopelessness. Jerusalem has failed to fulfil its God-given role of being a light to the nations around her. Instead she has courted the nations and adopted their sinful practices, and God will chasten her for her unfaithfulness. The church is under constant pressure to adapt to society's norms and adopt its ways of doing business. We are told we need to come out of the dark ages. In some ways this may well be true. On the other hand, church leaders and indeed all Christians must be extremely careful not to adapt to society in ways that contradict God's eternal word or lower his standards and thereby fail to fulfil our God-given role.

The reasons for biblical discipline

Within Ezekiel we find reasons for discipline that have a wider application in the rest of Scripture.

To challenge disobedience 5:6–9

The first reason for God disciplining the people of Jerusalem is clearly established by Ezekiel. It is quite simply because of their disobedience (5:6–9). It is because they have rejected God's rules and have not walked in his statutes. This is a plain and simple point that carries immense ramifications for the children of God in every age.

To make an example 5:15

The second reason mentioned by Ezekiel is that God intends to make an example of Jerusalem so that others might learn from and avoid her mistakes (5:15). They are to be a reproach and a taunt, a warning and a horror to the people around. There is a very clear parallel here with the Apostle Paul's reasoning in his first letter to Timothy. He tells Timothy to rebuke those who persist in sin and to do so publicly, so that the rest might understand that open and persistent sin is not acceptable behaviour in the church (1 Tim 5:20). No one is perfect. Even those whose calling it is to lead the people of God have their flaws. But church leaders fail in their God-given role when they allow open and persistent sin to go unchallenged in the church. It is no easy task for one sinner to confront another about their wrong behaviour or lifestyle. It reeks of hypocrisy. But it is not hypocrisy to follow God's directive by recognising one's own faults whilst at the same time rebuking another for their open sin. The church is made up of sinners, and if we wait for a perfect person to come along before we challenge sin then we will wait until the Lord himself returns for he alone is perfect in all his ways. But God challenges us to root out sin in our own lives and in the corporate life of the church. Therefore, as imperfect as we are, we must follow God's

It is not hypocrisy to follow God's directive by recognising one's own faults whilst at the same time rebuking another for their open sin.

directive lest we fall under the same criticism, and dare I say condemnation, as Jerusalem. Recognising our own sin should make us much more compassionate when faced with challenging another for their faults, but challenge we must if we are to live as God desires.[9]

To confirm sonship

This principle is found elsewhere throughout the word of God and underpins the discipline inflicted on his children in Jerusalem. Moses writing in Deuteronomy 8:5 tells us that 'as a man disciplines his son, the LORD your God disciplines you.' The clear implication is that God disciplines his children, not as punishment for their wrongdoing but rather as an expression of his love. This is the essence of Hebrews 12:5–11 'For the Lord disciplines the one he loves and chastises every son whom he receives.' Discipline, the writer to the Hebrews tells us, is for our good so that we might share in God's holiness. Is not this what is behind the discipline inflicted upon the children of God in Ezekiel's day? Was not the purpose of his divine displeasure to prompt his children to return to him with all their hearts? (Ezek. 33:11). 'By his discipline God frees us from the attraction of the world and the attentions to self that keep us distant from him and his purposes.'[10]

For further study ▶

FOR FURTHER STUDY

1. Read Romans 1:18–32. What parallels do we find in the Apostle Paul's letter to the Romans and this passage in Ezekiel? What implications can we draw from these two passages that relate to the church today?
2. 1 Timothy 5:17–25. What comparisons do you find here to Ezekiel 5:1–17? What are the challenges for your church?
3. Read Matthew 18:15–20. What are the implications of this passage for church discipline?
4. Read Hebrews 12:5–11. How does this passage complement the teaching about discipline in Ezekiel? How might this teaching be applied in your family or church?

TO THINK ABOUT AND DISCUSS

1. When you think of the word 'discipline' what comes to mind? Does it make you uncomfortable when you think of it being applied in the church? Is this a good thing or a bad thing?
2. What do you think of the reasons for discipline outlined above? How can discipline be carried out in the most compassionate way?
3. How do the ideas of discipline mentioned in this chapter compare to the practice in your church?

3 High places and hearts

Ezekiel Chapters 6–7

Not everything is acceptable in worship. God had been very specific with Israel about what he found acceptable when he delivered his laws through Moses. But God's people have allowed ungodly practices to creep in. Their hearts are far from God, idols abound in their worship and daily lives, and God is about to exact his jealous judgement against this idolatry. There is irony in the people seeking a fresh vision from God whilst ignoring his law. God will reassert himself and the people will be in no doubt that he alone is the Lord of all, and that he is the ultimate director of worship.

The Lake District is a wonderful place to holiday. Windermere certainly has its attractions and draws an international crowd, but it is good to get away to the quieter spots and simply revel in

God's beauty in creation. Anyone who has spent some time in the Lake District will no doubt have seen the storm-clouds gathering over the mountain tops. Because of its westerly position and height above sea-level the area is prone to thunderstorms which can be quite dramatic. But even in the midst of such a storm there is often a glimpse of hope as a magnificent ray of sunshine breaks through the black clouds, casting its light across the dramatic terrain and illuminating the white sailboats on the waters. In the passage before us the storm-clouds are gathering over the mountains of Israel and God is about to unleash a terrifying tempest. However, even in the midst of the darkness and despair there is a ray of hope and evidence of God's grace.

Ezekiel chapters 6–7 is a clear prediction of God's judgement on a nation that was so caught up in doing things their own way that they had effectively pushed God aside and ruled him out of their planning. You could be forgiven for thinking that this sounds a little repetitive given what we found in Ezekiel chapters 4–5. It is essentially the same message of doom from another perspective. Sometimes though a little repetition is necessary. People simply do not pick up on things first time around. So God is about to give them a sharp reminder so that they will once more give God his rightful place and recognise the practical implications of his Lordship. If I were to choose just one phrase that sums up this segment it would be God's own words used seven times in these two chapters: 'Then you will know that I am the LORD.'[1]

For now however, it would seem that even after all this time of attending Ezekiel's theatre of drama and model building, the people are still not listening and still not embracing God's rule. They still do not seem to accept the possibility that Jerusalem might fall. Selective hearing can affect most of us and we need to hear the same thing more than once before the message gets through.

It is not as if God has not spoken clearly enough in the past! God's eternal word is very clear on many matters that some, even among his own people, still choose to ignore or find ways to explain away.

> God's eternal word is very clear on many matters that some, even among his own people, still choose to ignore or find ways to explain away.

It is not difficult to imagine the Jews in exile sitting by the Chebar canal where, perhaps, from a particular vantage-point, they could see the mountain tops of their own beloved land. Perhaps they entertained thoughts of hope and restoration. Would those left behind would find a way of defeating the Babylonians and bringing the exiles back home? God is about to dash any such hopes as he tells Ezekiel to face those mountains and prophesy, not in their favour but against them, not to comfort them but to confront and discipline them. What a blow that must have been to the exiles (Ezek 6:2). Perhaps they are still waiting for a change in Ezekiel's message, a change in tone, a word of encouragement. What they get instead is further clarity on Ezekiel's mime act. Ezekiel moves from mime to preaching a sermon of judgement against idolatry and the discipline that God's own people will be subjected to because of their idolatrous worship.

The reason for God's discipline must have had something to do with Israel's selective hearing or their sheer obstinacy. It seems that those left behind following the exile were not moved to change their wrong religious practices—either by the exile of their friends and neighbours or by their own calamities. It seems that nothing so far has been enough for them to turn away from whatever forms of idolatry they had allowed to infiltrate their worship and embrace the true and pure worship of God.[2]

The reason for God's discipline must have had something to do with Israel's selective hearing or their sheer obstinacy.

So let us now take a closer look at what Ezekiel is called upon to do in order to awaken this people from their false hopes and fake religion. There are three natural divisions within these two chapters but also a fair amount of overlap. I am going to use these three divisions and at the same time pull together the common threads that overlap into each section. What are these divisions? They consist of three more symbolic acts. In the first Ezekiel is told to face the mountains (6:1–10); in the second he is told to clap his hands and stamp his feet (6:11–7:22); and in the third he is told to make a chain (7:23–27).

Facing the mountains 6:1–10

Ezekiel is told to stand up in the midst of his contemporaries as they watch his antics by the Chebar canal in Babylon, look towards the mountains of Israel, and prophesy against those mountains. As usual, the meaning of Ezekiel's behaviour becomes clear as we read on. In verse three God says that he is going to bring his sword on Israel's high places. High places is a term used in the Bible for places for worship offered to the pagan gods since the nations around Israel tended to establish their altars on the tops of high hills or mountains. Some suggest that it simply represented an attempt to get closer to their god before making their offerings. Unfortunately Israel had adopted much of the practice of their pagan neighbours and integrated it into their worship, and in so doing had moved away from worship that was acceptable to the true God. To put it simply, the reference to high places here means that Ezekiel was to prophesy against the idolatrous worship that had become commonplace among the Israelites. Idolatry can take many forms, and although high places in this passage refers literally to these altars erected on mountain tops to false gods, yet there is evidence of other high places in these two chapters, that transcend the practices of the ancient Israelites and can be seen even in our society today. So what are these high places? What are these other idols or false gods that had become such an integrated part of Israel's life, and that exist even among God's people today?

The majority view

In Ezekiel's day it would seem that what eventually led Israel into forms of false worship was that they were bringing outside influences into their religious life. It is clear from Ezek. 6:3–4 that Israel had adopted much of the practice of their pagan neighbours by erecting altars on high places. Associated with this form of worship was prostitution and adulterous behaviour. In 6:9 God talks of being 'broken over their whoring heart' (ESV). Now that is pretty strong and unsavoury language. But God uses these terms to emphasise that the Israelites' behaviour in setting up these high places is akin to having committed adultery against him. They have breached their covenant relationship with God. It is the same principle as betrayal in a marriage. Marriage is elsewhere in the Bible described as a covenant, and any betrayal of that covenant relationship is considered adultery. Two passages make this point very clearly. In Proverbs 2:16–17 we read, 'It will save you also from the adulteress, from the wayward wife with her seductive words, who forsakes the companion of her youth, and forgets the covenant of her God.' Furthermore, in Malachi 2:14 we read, 'Yet you say, "For what reason?" Because the LORD has been witness between you and the wife of your youth, with whom you have dealt treacherously; yet she is your companion and your wife by covenant.' The covenant of marriage in the Bible is a reflection of God's covenant with his people.

Simply stated, a covenant in Scripture is the most solemn and binding arrangement that two people can enter into. According to the first passage mentioned above, God warns against the adulteress who flatters with her words and leaves her husband. In leaving her husband she is accused of forgetting and breaking the marriage covenant. Likewise, when God's people turn their backs on him, and turn away from the sort of worship that is acceptable to him, they are guilty of adultery. The moment they set up the first high place, emulating the nations around them, they were guilty of breaking that solemn promise and binding arrangement that was theirs as the people of God. And this attitude to worship did not stop on the mountain tops. What was happening outside soon found its way into the temple itself and led to further corruption of worship in the house of God. It would appear that the worship being offered in the temple in Jerusalem, his treasured place (Ezek. 7:20–22), had also become corrupted and unacceptable. The Israelites have desecrated the temple ornaments by making them into such 'detestable things' (Ezek. 7:20) as images like the pagan idols around them. The temple ornaments have been moulded and shaped into something, and given a meaning, that God never intended. We shall see more on this in Ezek. 16:17 but for now Ezekiel points to the use of the temple treasures for making images as the height of arrogance and pride.[3] The Israelites were going with the flow of contemporary opinion, allowing outside influences to enter and dominate their worship. They were embracing the religious practices of the pagan nations around them.

Secular humanism—the current majority view?

> Secular humanism suggests that new ideas should be tolerated in the name of pluralism.

Ralph Martin contends that secular humanism is having a much more profound influence on the church than perhaps many recognise.[4] He suggests that affluence and an increasingly secularised higher education system have contributed to what he calls moral lukewarm-ness in the church. He draws attention to the influence of mass media on the church in pressing home a false understanding of tolerance. Secular humanism suggests that new ideas should be tolerated in the name of pluralism.[5] What you find firstly is that equality is enforced between old and new ideas, then there is an assertion of the new over the old, often leading finally to the total discrediting and rejection of what had previously been orthodox. Such a view of tolerance is superficial. 'Its apparent neutrality masks secular imperialism, imposing its views as powerfully as any religious tradition and intolerant towards any who challenge its assumptions.'[6] Tolerance is not a two-way thing here, but a ramrod pushing aside what does not fit with this new ideal. True tolerance is the ability or willingness to allow the existence of behaviour or practices that one dislikes or disagrees with, and encourages dialogue.

True tolerance is the ability or willingness to allow the existence of behaviour or practices that one dislikes or disagrees with, and encourages dialogue.

But in current use it seems to go beyond this definition, to mean we have to like and agree with that practice or behaviour. Dialogue is stifled because we dare not say that we consider another point of view to be wrong. In practice this means that if a Christian says that salvation is found in Christ alone, he is labelled intolerant and a fundamentalist. As Don Carson puts it, '… if any religion claims that in some measure other religions are wrong, a line has been crossed and resentment is immediately stirred up: pluralism has been challenged.'[7] True tolerance is a good and positive and commendable thing, although tolerance may be altogether the wrong word to use. As Christians we are called to *love* our neighbour no matter how they differ from us. Love is a deep-seated respect of people made in the image of God, even though we may differ radically with them on points of principle and practice. 'Love your enemies and pray for those who persecute you,' Jesus tells us in Matt. 5:44. But love does not mean we have to embrace or accept any teaching or behaviour that is contrary to God's standards. Without doubt we see the influence of false tolerance in the church, not least with a dumbing down of the gospel message to make it more appetising, and in an attempt to make the offence of the cross a little less offensive. Paul writes in this vein to the Galatians: if we were to become friends of this doctrine of pluralism (for Paul the issue was circumcision), then the offence of the cross would soon be removed. In other words, if we preach only what is acceptable to pluralism then we must of necessity stop preaching Christ crucified.[8]

I think it is a fair reflection on our times when I say that compared to a generation ago the church has a very different view on issues such as sexuality; alcohol consumption among Christians and even as part-and-parcel of church-organised events; roles within the church; the programmes or films Christians watch; modesty; and attitudes towards divorce; and even keeping Sunday special. Now, if the word of God is unchanging then what has changed? There seems to have been a shift from a God-centred Christianity to a religion that places the worshipper at the centre. The underlying premise seems to be that we should be free to behave as we wish and worship as we wish and still be accepted by God. Of course some old practices need looking at and perhaps some change is needed. Sharing and adopting best practice in church life is no bad thing. We can all learn from others. We certainly should not be slavishly tied to practices of the past. But we also need to be cautious in our expectations and cautious about what we seek to integrate into the life of the church.

I say this because there seems to be the underlying implication that by adopting a growing church's management style or format of worship, blessing and growth will follow. Worse still perhaps is the danger of applying the latest secular management styles with a view to promoting growth, or the more casual approach to life today leading to an overtly casual approach to God. The real danger is that the format becomes more important than the content and tone of our worship. Worship should be a joyous experience, but should it be over-familiar? We should be able to call God our loving Father, but in the context that he is also our sovereign, our Lord, our judge and our law-giver. God is a God of grace, but he is also a God of standards. Ezekiel draws attention to the absence of God's standards and the encroachment of outside influences in the lives and worship of the people in his day. Are these simply old covenant matters? Not at all. Implicit in the teachings of both Old and New Testament authors are patterns of belief and behaviour that equip us for holy living and exercising suitable worship in the church.[9]

Often pressure is brought to bear upon church leaders to submit to the latest popular fad. But caution is needed. In the words of Mark Twain's Widow Douglas in *The Adventures of Huckleberry Finn*, 'Just because an idea is popular, don't make it right.' Of course churches must take seriously the culture in which they minister, and likewise the philosophies that permeate and direct that culture. But we must be careful not to allow that culture to direct how we go about serving and worshipping the Lord in his church. By not adapting, some church leaders may be left feeling ostracised. They are viewed as out of touch with the modern world, not keeping up with the times. It is never easy being in the minority.

It seems clear from Ezekiel's situation that the high places or the idolatry of which the Israelites were guilty, came about by their acceptance of the majority view. They probably did not want to seem odd or different and so, turning their backs on God's clear directions, they adopted the practices of their neighbours. Indeed they had a track record of wanting to be the same as the nations around them.[10] These practices probably started with a few individuals or families who chose to set up their high places, but in time their influence could be seen in the gathered assembly also.

The superficial tolerance of secular humanism which is having such a profound influence on church life in many areas ultimately leads to a denial of parts of Scripture.

The superficial tolerance of secular humanism which is having such a profound influence on church life in many areas ultimately leads to a denial of parts of Scripture. So how can we be truly tolerant of and loving towards those who differ from us in so many respects? Perhaps a starting point is a quality that has found expression historically in such movements as the Quakers and English Baptists—

the principle of religious liberty. These groups held to this principle, not because their own beliefs and convictions were unimportant but quite the opposite—they were too important to be imposed. 'Religious liberty treats convictions seriously, accepts faith communities hold divergent views, respects their freedom to make competing truth claims, encourages exchanges of views, identifies secular-humanism as another faith position, rejects inducement and coercion and develops ways to protect minorities from oppression.'[11]

True Christian love respects all men and women made in the image of God, yet, it seeks to persuade them of the need for reconciliation with God through Christ alone.

If we take God at his word, then we can encourage such religious liberty safe in the knowledge that it is God who transforms hearts, bringing people into a saving relationship with him in the power of the Holy Spirit and through Christ alone. We can enjoy the rich experience of cultural diversity that pervades western society today without compromising on the truth claims of the gospel. True love for our neighbour, whatever their faith system, is not a false or superficial tolerance that pretends we have no differences. Rather, true Christian love respects all men and women made in the image of God, yet, it seeks to persuade them of the need for reconciliation with God through Christ alone. The Apostle Paul writing to the church in Corinth states that as Christians, 'knowing the fear of the Lord, we persuade others' (2 Cor. 5:11). John Gill in his commentary on this verse talks of Christians endeavouring to persuade others by the best arguments they can master from the word of God, and the need to show others that outside of a saving relationship with Christ they are on a pathway to eternal destruction. The Bible is clear that salvation is by Christ alone, indeed Christ himself makes this assertion when he says, 'I am the way, and the truth, and the life. No one comes to the Father except through me' (John 14:6). Whatever tolerance may have come to mean in a secular society, in God's economy it can never mean a denial of this fundamental life-changing truth. If we are to love our neighbours then we must seek to persuade them and encourage them to turn to Christ and believe in him so that they might be saved.[12] Ezekiel is clear that in judging their adulterous behaviour towards him, it is God's desire not simply to punish but rather to show the people just how far they have wandered from him, so that they will turn to him again and recognise him as the Lord (Ezek. 6:7, 10, 13, etc.).

Self-sufficiency

Another idol is self-sufficiency. Our modern western society is relatively affluent. Keeping a close eye on current market trends and investing accordingly can be handsomely rewarded. Of course wealth is not inherently wrong, but it brings the danger of the people becoming flabby and apathetic.[13] God's people should beware of becoming too comfortable and of believing in themselves and their own ability more than trusting in God. Judah's trust in their business practices and accumulation of material wealth has become a stumbling block. As far back as Moses, God's children were warned not to become conceited. They were reminded that it is God who gives them the strength to prosper and increase their wealth (Deut. 8:17–18). This warning has clearly gone unheeded. The people have become self-sufficient and God has been pushed to the sidelines. However, God is about to bring this self-sufficiency to an end: 'Let not the buyer rejoice nor the seller mourn' (Ezek. 7:12). The seller will not enjoy any benefits from his latest must-have purchase (Ezek. 7:13). Even today it is usual for the buyer of a house or land to rejoice as he increases his estate, and often a seller mourns because the sale may have been necessitated by personal economic downturn. Ezekiel will drive home the message that there will neither be time to rejoice nor mourn since all will be carried off captive, or worse. Their possessions (Ezek. 7:12–13), their financial status (Ezek. 7:19), not even their plans for survival (Ezek.7:14), will be of any benefit. All such self-reliance will fail miserably. In telling Ezekiel to face the mountains of Israel and prophesy against them God is clearly rebuking Israel for their idolatry; their acceptance of the majority view; their overt self-sufficiency seen in their possessions, finances, and plans for future survival. We will consider these things again a little later in this chapter. In the meantime we need to ask, What is God's response to all of this? What is God's response to Israel's adoption of the majority view, seen in their high places and their overt self-sufficiency?

Clapping hands and stamping feet 6:11–7:22

What strange behaviour! It is as though God says: 'Ezekiel, in response to Israel's covenantal adultery, and their adoption of the majority view and pagan practices; in response to their overt self-sufficiency, clap your hands and stamp your feet!' What can it possibly mean? There are several suggestions. Douglas Stuart suggests it indicates a form of taunting; Albert Barnes in his Notes on the Bible suggests it is an expression of grief; John Gill in his Exposition of Ezekiel suggests it is an expression of distress and agony; whilst Matthew Henry suggests that '… he must make it to appear that he was in earnest in what he said to them, that he firmly believed it and laid it to heart. Thus he must signify the just displeasure he had conceived at their sins …'

Any one of these suggestions makes good sense of the context. The expression is followed up by emphasising that God has become their enemy—so whatever the expression means it is most certainly designed to grab the attention of Ezekiel's hearers and make them know that God is Lord. It precedes a dire warning that contains two parts.

God will show the sheer folly of his people's idolatry, as the slain will be found at the feet of the very idols they put their trust in.

Firstly it contains repetition. There are echoes of chapters four and five (Ezek. 6:11–12) that the people will be struck by the sword of the Babylonians, or by famine during the siege, or by plague and disease resulting from the abhorrent conditions during the siege. There is further repetition in 6:13 (cf. 6:6–7) of God's displeasure with his people's sinful practices. God will show the sheer folly of their idolatry, as the slain will be found at the feet of the very idols they put their trust in.

Secondly Ezekiel's warning contains rebuke. In the first instance this is for their arrogance or pride (7:10). The reference to rod in these two verses is somewhat obscure but seems to be a play on words. 'When we note that the Hebrew for "rod" (*matteh*) can also mean "tribe", the allusion to Judah's arrogance becomes apparent. God "will put an end to the pride of the mighty" (7:24).'[14] But rod in 7:11 could well be a reference to Nebuchadnezzar. 'He was the rod, with which the Lord smote his people, as the Assyrian monarch is called the rod of his anger, Isaiah 10:5.'[15] So the rod that is proud Judah will be struck by the rod of God's anger. God's seven-fold use of the phrase, 'then you will know that I am the LORD,' has a significant difference in 7:9 with the addition of the Hebrew word *makkeh*, 'who strikes'. The people of God had been used to hearing of God as *Yahweh Yireh*—the Lord will provide (Gen. 22:14); or *Yahweh Nissi*—the Lord my banner (Exod. 17:15). But *Yahweh Makkeh*—the Lord who strikes—is a further emphasis that the fall of Israel is the work of God.

Yahweh Makkeh—the Lord who strikes—is a further emphasis that the fall of Israel is the work of God.

In the second instance Ezekiel's prophecy contains a rebuke for Judah's self-sufficiency (7:12–19). As noted above this encompasses their dependency upon possessions (7:12–13); finances (7:19); and plans for survival (7:14). None of these will be of any benefit. All such self-reliance will fail miserably. They shall cast their silver into the streets (7:19) because it will be of no use to them. It will not help them one iota against the famine and disease that will come upon them during the siege. They will not be able to buy their way out of their predicament nor will they be able to exchange their wealth for food to satisfy their increasing hunger. As John Gill points out, their gold and silver cannot be eaten and will not satisfy the craving appetite, nor fill the hungry belly.[16] Money certainly has its uses, but beware the danger of allowing it to bring a false sense of security leading you to marginalise God in your life.

The reference here to blowing the trumpet (7:14) has echoes of Joshua and Gideon (Judges 7:18), and even Nehemiah (Neh. 4:18–20). Blowing the trumpet as a warning system had been common practice among the people of God for many centuries. The difference was that in the times of Joshua or Gideon or Nehemiah, the people were not simply depending on their own ability to prepare for battle. Rather, the sound of the trumpet was a reminder that God was the one who would deliver the enemy into their hands—the battle was the Lord's. In Ezekiel's day they have blown the trumpet and made everything ready but on this occasion the Lord is against them and not against their enemies. Their best made plans were of no use without the Lord at their side. The plans in themselves were not wrong; it was planning without utter dependence upon God that was the problem.

In the third instance the people are rebuked for their procrastination (7:25–26). Now at last they will look to God for peace and a vision from his prophet (7:25–26). But it will be too late! They have waited too long to bring God into the picture and into their planning. They have procrastinated too long. The irony is, they have always had the law of God for direction but have chosen to ignore it. Yet still the people seek a vision from the prophet because the priest's ministry is perishing in their midst, and the elders have no more counsel to offer (7:26). People look for fresh expressions in worship and fresh visions to lead them, whilst at the same time turning their backs on clear guidance God has already given them in his law. When the children of God take their direction from the society they live in rather than from the word of God, they have no sure foundation when difficult times come. There are clear echoes here of our Lord's teaching in Matthew 7:24–27: And everyone who hears these words of mine and does not do them will be like a foolish man who built his house on the sand. And the rain fell, and the floods came, and the winds blew and beat against that house, and it fell, and great was the fall of it. These words are clearly a warning of the danger of being swept away in judgement, to the unsaved and all those who think that they are right with God but are not. Although the child of God is forever secure in the salvation that has been purchased by Christ (Rom. 8:1), yet surely there is wisdom here for building the church. The foundations of contemporary opinion simply will not stand, but the word of God lasts forever.[17] According to Ezekiel, when anguish comes the people will seek peace but there will be none. For them it was too late. Beware the danger of procrastination. Do not put off living God's way or doing what God clearly expects of you.

> The Lord has ways of undermining all the supports on which we may base our security. Under his judgement the wealth of the rich turn to rubbish, the futility of idolatry is exposed, and the resources found in human institutions are annulled

... and those who seek shalom from their leaders will be disappointed.[18]

We do not like to think about such fun-spoiling subjects as discipline. Discipline suggests legalism, a slavish pandering to rules and regulations. Grace on the other hand sets us free from any such rules. Grace suggests fun and 'spontaneous and unstructured living, and most of all, a God who loves us unconditionally regardless of our sinful behaviour.'[19] However, as Jerry Bridges points out, such thinking reflects serious misunderstandings of both discipline and grace. The Bible is full of exhortations as to how we ought to live as the children of God. This is not legalism but rather grace in action. In a similar vein, the Apostle Paul writing to the church at Ephesus tells us to walk as children of the light (Eph 5:8). Dealing with this very issue of legalism he tells the Christians of the church in Galatia that if we live in the Spirit then we ought also to walk in or by the Spirit. In other words, if we live a life of faith in Christ, and of holiness and communion with him, then by the power of the Spirit of Christ in us we should expect to be influenced by him according to the rule of his eternal unchanging word. This is not legalism. Living according to the Spirit must not become some postmodern excuse for living as we please, setting our own standards, establishing our own set of rules. Living in and enjoying the fullness of

Living according to the Spirit must not become some postmodern excuse for living as we please, setting our own standards, establishing our own set of rules.

God's grace is not about marching to our own tune but rather keeping in step with the Spirit! (Gal 5:25). We must remember that God's Spirit never contradicts God's Word.

Make a chain 7:23–27

So far Ezekiel has faced the mountains and prophesied against them. He has grabbed the attention of the exiles by clapping his hands and stamping his feet. He has shown the Israelites their guilt, and God's displeasure with them. He has further highlighted the sheer futility of their own efforts to change the situation. Now as he stands on the banks of the Chebar canal he is told to make a chain. The chain represents the fetters that will bind the population of Jerusalem as they too are led off into captivity, just as the others were before them. Everyone will be affected, beginning with the religious leaders (7:26). There will be no more visions from the prophets since God has abandoned them, nor any direction from the priests or counsel from the elders. Similarly, no help will come from the civil authorities as they together with the people will also be bound in chains and taken off into captivity. The king will mourn, the prince will despair, and the people will be paralysed with fear. And yet in the midst of all of this there is mercy. Once again we see the twin themes of judgement and hope.

A ray of hope 6:8–10

Not all will perish. Some will survive to tell the story, regret their part in bringing about the downfall of Jerusalem, and speak of how God is true to his word (Ezek. 6:8–10). These few verses teach us that despite men's failings God keeps his covenant. Men may break their side of the covenant relationship by going after other gods and forms of worship, but God is faithful even when they are not.

Remember that the mission of God is the restoration of his name and honour, through the restoration of his people. God continues to show his mercy to an obstinate people by preserving a remnant who will remember him among the nations (6:9). His great desire is not to punish his people, but that they might turn from their wayward practices and embrace his Lordship over their lives. They will know that I am the Lord, he repeats seven times in these two chapters. The people will recognise God's Lordship; either in the proper expression of God's covenant through worship that is acceptable to him, or they will recognise his Lordship through the discipline of those who fail to keep covenant with him. There are echoes here of Paul's teaching in Philippians[20]: '… so that at the name of Jesus every knee should bow, in heaven and on earth and under the earth, and every tongue confess that Jesus Christ is Lord, to the glory of God the Father.' The parallel passage in Isaiah refers to the homage that God's own people will pay towards him; but there is also a clear sense in which one day all people will bow before our Lord and Saviour—either in fear as those who face his judgement, or in adoration and worship as those saved by his wonderful grace. Either way, as the Lord himself puts it—'They shall know that I am the Lord' (6:14).

As God's children it should be our heart-felt desire to promote a vision of the God who cares enough to discipline, and a vision of humanity, which though fallen retains profound dignity because it is made in God's image. Such a high view of God and humanity should spur us to gentle yet robust persuasion that the greatest need our neighbour has is to turn from their ways and embrace Christ as Saviour and Lord.

FOR FURTHER STUDY

1. When Jesus invites sinners, 'Come to me, all who labour and are heavy laden, and I will give you rest,' he immediately adds, 'Take my yoke upon you, and learn from me' (Matt. 11:28–29).[21] What does this teach us about Christ as both Saviour and Lord?
2. Read John 4:24. What are the practical implications for our personal devotions and corporate worship?
3. Read Ephesians 5:6–10. What does it mean to walk as children of light? Drawing on the experiences of the Israelites, how can we know that we are walking in the light?
4. Read Philippians 2:10–11; Romans 14:10–12; and Isaiah 45:23. What are the practical implications of these passages for your life and worship?
5. Read Romans 12:1–2 and James 4:4. In what practical ways might these passages have a bearing on the content of your worship services? What parallels with Ezekiel do you see in these New Testament passages?

TO THINK ABOUT AND DISCUSS

1. Why was it necessary for God to discipline his people in Ezekiel's day? Under what circumstances do you think God might discipline his church today?
2. Derek Thomas in his commentary[22] says we are prone to forget God and refers to spiritual amnesia as a deadly disease. Discuss the implications of this for your life and the life of your church.
3. To what extent is God our director of worship?
4. God is a God of grace but also a God of standards. How might this affect the worship in your church? How might this affect your life day to day?

4 The glory of God departs

Ezekiel Chapters 8–11

Ezekiel is carried by means of a vision from the company of Judah's elders in his home by the Chebar canal in Babylon to the temple in Jerusalem. There God reveals to him his reasons for inflicting such severe discipline on his people. His holy temple has become the melting pot for all sorts of false worship and the pollution of God's house can no longer go unchallenged. God's executioners are sent in to mete out his judgement on young and old alike. No hope is to be found within the city walls, as is symbolised by the departure of God's glory. Rather, hope is found only in God giving a new heart and a new spirit. This is the Gospel according to Ezekiel.[1]

It has been fourteen months since Ezekiel first encountered God (Ezek. 1:2) and 420 of the 430 days of lying down beside his clay model of Jerusalem have passed.[2] The beginning of this portion finds Ezekiel in his home in the company of the elders of Judah, who may have been there to try and make some sense out of Ezekiel's behaviour over the past year. Whilst in their company Ezekiel is transported to the temple in Jerusalem in visions of God[3] by the Spirit (Ezek. 8:3). There he is shown a series of goings-on which show that God's people have not only strayed from the faith but have made the house of God into what Chris Wright describes as '… a melting pot of religious pluralism'.[4]

Goings-on in the house of God 8:1–18

Image worship 8:3–6

It is important to remember throughout these events that Ezekiel is not physically in Jerusalem but rather taken there in a vision. He remains physically in the presence of the elders in his home in Babylon. The first vision he is confronted with at the North Gate to the house of God is described by Ezekiel as an image of jealousy (Ezek. 8:3–6). There are a variety of suggestions as to what this image may have been. Some suggest it was an image of Baal;[5] others suggest perhaps an image of Asherah.[6] Both suggestions have good biblical support, but the bottom line is that the prophet does not tell us. Rather than satisfy our curiosity on the matter, Scripture leaves us to ponder the fact that any image, whatever it may be, is a clear breach of the second commandment (Exod. 20:4–6), is offensive to God, and provokes his righteous indignation and jealousy. More significantly, God describes the practice of using idols as a great abomination, and something that will drive him far from his sanctuary (Ezek.8:6). In other words, by bringing into their worship the practices of the cultures around them, the people of God are driving God out! What a warning against the pluralistic leanings of any church in our day. Such a church may well end up with a novel form of worship, and may well experience numerical growth, but it will risk the absence of the true and living God! Again, this is not simply an Old Testament matter. Revelation 3:20 portrays Jesus excluded from his own church. But, God goes on to say to Ezekiel, worse is yet to come!

Animal worship 8:7–13

Having taken Ezekiel from the North Gate to the entrance of the court, God tells Ezekiel to dig into the wall. The purpose of this visionary exercise is to reveal an entrance to a hidden chamber. Within that chamber he finds seventy elders of the house of Israel worshipping a series of pictures or engravings on the wall. The engravings include every form of creeping things and loathsome beasts and idols. Wright suggests these images represent Egyptian gods being prayed to by Israel's political leaders in the hope of engaging the help of Egypt's armies against the Babylonians.[7] At its simplest, this is yet another form of idol worship. The striking thing here is that it is the elders, including a man called Jaazaniah,[8] who are engaged in it. They conduct their idolatry in the darkness (8:12), possibly thinking that hidden in the dark recesses of this room God will not see them and perhaps, they reason, God has already abandoned them. Not only had the elders adopted the practices of the nations around them, but they seem to have adopted the belief that the god of the conquering people is the greater than the Lord. According to their reasoning, the God of Israel has been defeated; therefore they must summon a god that is greater than that of their conquerors if they are to have any hope of restoration.

They are missing the point all together! It is not God who is weak but they themselves. It is not that the true and living God has been defeated by the lifeless gods of the nations around them, but rather that the people have weakly capitulated to those lifeless gods and turned their backs on the sovereign God of all creation. People engage in their sinful practices in the shadows, believing they remain anonymous, unseen by anyone including God. But as we saw in chapter one God is all-knowing and all-seeing. A man or woman may be able to hide their indiscretions from those closest to them, but God sees what happens in the shadows. In teaching his disciples against hypocrisy Christ himself declared that nothing is covered up that will not be revealed, or hidden that will not be known (Luke 12:2–3), and the Apostle Paul tells us that God will judge the secrets of men (Rom 2:16). Christ's disciples were among his most faithful followers and yet Christ deemed that they should be warned against hypocrisy—an exhortation that remains valid for all God's children but especially for leaders in the church. Former Archbishop of Canterbury William Temple remarked that 'religion is what you do with your solitude.'[9]

A man or woman may be able to hide their indiscretions from those closest to them, but God sees what happens in the shadows.

Cultic worship 8:14–15

God now takes Ezekiel in his vision to the North Gate of the temple where he witnesses still greater abominations. This time it involves a group of women crying for the Sumerian-Babylonian god Tammuz. Tammuz is reputed to have been an ancient King who was banished to the underworld to be mourned by his wife, mother, and sister.

> His death is supposed to typify the long, dry summer of Syria and Palestine, when vegetation perishes, and his return to life the rainy season when the parched earth is revivified and is covered with luxuriant vegetation, or his death symbolizes the cold, rough winter, the boar of the myth, and his return the verdant spring. Considering the disgraceful and licentious rites with which the cult was celebrated, it is no wonder that Ezekiel should have taken the vision of the women weeping for Tammuz in the temple as one of the greatest abominations that could defile the Holy House.[10]

Sun worship 8:16

The final abomination revealed to Ezekiel on his visionary travels is found in the inner court of the house of the Lord. Here he is shown twenty-five men with their backs to the temple, facing east and worshipping the sun. Though it was expressly forbidden by God (Deut. 4:19) the Israelites have succumbed to sun worship on more than one occasion (2 Kings 21:3), thereby corrupting themselves and, in this case, the very house of God. Turning their backs on the temple is indicative of having turned their backs on God himself to worship what God had created, and which was at that time one of the most prominent gods in the Babylonian Empire.[11]

God's verdict 8:17–18

When the glory of God is insulted then God must act. He cannot allow such insulting behaviour to continue unchecked. 'Have you seen this?' God asks Ezekiel. Then his rhetorical question continues—can such dreadful abominations as those committed here in the temple, be considered light things? The answer is clearly they cannot! But as bad as these things are, there is more. The sinful behaviour of the priests, elders, and women in the temple runs throughout the whole land. The land has been filled with violence. God's holy standards are ignored. Worship that tickles the fancy—rather than scratching the itch—prevails.

God's response to the goings-on 9:1–11 and 11:1–13

God is patient but when his name is dishonoured he will act—and act decisively. And this is not simply an Old Testament notion. The writer to the Hebrews tells us that it is a fearful thing to fall into the hands of the living God (Heb.10:31). God is love, but he is also to be feared should we continue to turn our backs on him. Ezekiel is no doubt rooted to the spot as God cries out for his executioners to enter the city each with a destroying weapon in his hand.

The executives of God's judgement 9:1–4

Seven men appear, six of them with a weapon ready to mete out God's judgement, as we shall see clearly in 9:5–6. But there is one clothed in linen and carrying a writing case, with a significantly different role. In fact he has a dual role. Firstly the man with the writing case is to scour the city for signs of repentance (v. 4). He is to put a mark on anyone who shows signs of a broken heart over the despicable idolatry taking place in the temple. They alone are to be spared. This is without doubt a picture of God's justice and mercy. He will deliver the innocent, keeping them safe through the judgement. But it is also an encouraging picture of godliness in a context that is predominantly godless. What a challenge for us! When was the last time you felt yourself 'sigh and groan' over the godless man-centred condition of the society that you live in? When was the last time you felt the burden of that humanistic philosophy weighing in on your church? When was the last time you mourned the fact that many among God's own children consider God's holy and righteous law as irrelevant to the church, and who dismiss the keeping of the Lord's Day as legalism? Just as in Ezekiel's day, are we in danger of destroying God's house from within? We will catch up with the linen-clad man again in chapter 10.

> When was the last time you felt yourself 'sigh and groan' over the godless man-centred condition of the society that you live in?

The recipients of God's judgement 9:5–7

God's instructions to his executioners is that old and young, men, women, and children are all to be killed. The slaughter is to begin in the sanctuary (9:6), referring specifically to all those whom Ezekiel has just witnessed carrying out their abominations in chapter 8. In the New Testament Peter echoes this thought when he says that judgement must begin at the house of God (1 Peter 4:17). Some suggest Peter is referring to the temple at Jerusalem, but the context seems to suggest the Christian church. 'And if it begins with us,' he goes on to say, 'what will be the outcome for those who do not obey the gospel of God?' The clear meaning is that judgement begins with God's people. Of course, we must be careful to discern the correct meaning of judgement in this context. For true children of God it cannot mean punishment for our sin as Christ has already taken that punishment upon himself (1 John 2:2). However, as noted in chapter 2, God does discipline his children with fatherly chastisements[12] which differ greatly from God's judgement on the world. Nevertheless, God does hold his children accountable for their behaviour. In Ezekiel, God's judgement begins in the sanctuary against those guilty of the abominations revealed in chapter 8. But then it extends to all who have shown no remorse for the abominations that were openly carried out in the house of God.

The nature of God's judgement 9:5–7; 10:1–8; 11:1–13

As noted in the preceding paragraphs, God's judgement involves punishing the wicked with death at the hand of his executioners. Some will fall by the sword within the city limits when it is taken by the Babylonians, but God has a particular punishment in store for the wicked counsellors (11:1–13). It all revolves around a phrase first used by the counsellors themselves in 11:3—'This city is the cauldron, and we are the meat.' At a first reading this almost sounds as though they recognise their dire position in a city that has become a cauldron of death. But that is not the meaning of this expression. Rather, these wicked counsellors consider themselves the 'cream of the crop', providentially left behind to plan and initiate the rebuilding of the city. The most likely meaning of 11:3 seems to be 'There is no need at this time to worry about building houses.' As Block points out, the expression reflects a 'complacency and smugness characteristic of those who think they have everything under control.'[13] They see themselves as the prime cuts of meat, or the newly emerging leaders of the city, and they see Jerusalem as the storage vessel or crock[14] in which they are protected and which they can rebuild all in good time. However, the city is far from being a place of safety and the wicked counsellors will face the one thing they fear (11:8). They will be dragged out of the city as exiles, just as others before them, but rather than end up in exile in Babylon they will be killed by the sword on the borders of Israel (11:10). The city will afford them no protection (11:11). God takes their own proverb and turns it against them.

We need to return to chapter 10 and mention a significant part of God's judgement on Jerusalem. Ezekiel witnesses again the original vision that he had by the Chebar canal in chapter 1, identifying the winged creatures now as cherubim (10:15 and 20). This vision which was initially an expression of the character of God (see again chapter 1) has a specific role to play in the judgement on Jerusalem. The linen-clad man (9:3ff) is also given a further role to play. He is to take some of the burning coals or fire from between the wheels within wheels that carried the crystal-like sea and throne of God, and scatter them over the city (10:2). In chapter 1:4 we considered how fire is often symbolic of God's presence, or of purification. Now we see this coming to a head as the throne of God becomes the bearer of judgement and purification.[15]

The intercessor of God's judgement 11:13

The nature of God's judgement is clearly seen in the expressions of death and exile and purification by fire. And it all becomes too much for Ezekiel to bear. As he sees all of this death and destruction in his terrifying vision, he finally reaches breaking point when he witnesses the death of Pelatiah son of Benaiah (v. 13). The names mean 'Yahweh has delivered', son of 'Yahweh has built up.' The two names symbolized the hope of Jerusalem, but with Pelatiah's death the hope of the nation vanishes.[16] Ezekiel saw in the death of Pelatiah a kind of prelude to the slaughter of the entire city.[17] In response to this death, with its loss of hope, he falls to the ground in grief and despair, fearing that God might well destroy everyone and that even a remnant would not remain after the destruction of the city. We can learn much from these few words in v. 13. There is a vivid sense of urgency in Ezekiel's plea. He is desperate that some might survive. And his prayers are no doubt based on his knowledge of God's promises to this nation throughout its turbulent history. Surely a remnant must survive?

In the depths of Ezekiel's despair God offers some hope that he will not abandon his covenant with Israel. The true essence of this distressing vision is not to portray

God as vindictive and all-consuming but rather as the God of grace that he has always been. Despite Israel's unfaithfulness, God's purpose is not to wipe them out but rather to restore them to himself. The only hope of a proper relationship with God involves some radical surgery—a heart transplant.

The promise of a return to Jerusalem with one heart and a new Spirit 11:14–20

There is yet hope for this doomed people, but not in the way they had anticipated. It will not be revival through power or might or political means, and certainly not through ungodly alliances with other nations. Rather, the hope that God promises to his people is inward and of the heart, the very seat of their affections. This promise is not for the choice meat citizens who still remained in the city, those who would take advantage of their exiled neighbours' misfortune. Rather, it is for the exiles themselves—and the promise is incredible. Firstly, in place of their beloved temple, God himself will be a sanctuary to them in the countries of their deportations (11:16). The lesson must surely be that the presence of the living God far outweighs any physical building. Many of those in exile were the true children of God and no matter where they found themselves God has remained their sanctuary. Secondly, there is a promise that he will once again gather them out of those countries and restore them to their own beloved land. This is in fact what happened following the collapse of the Babylonian Empire when the Israelites eventually returned to Jerusalem and rebuilt its walls under Ezra and Nehemiah. Thirdly—and most significantly—he promises them unity of heart and a new Spirit (11:19–20). So long as the people of God were divided in their loyalties by serving many gods, no unity of purpose was possible. But when God restores them to Jerusalem they are to put aside all the detestable practices about which we read earlier. Only then can they experience unity of purpose in restoring God's name among the nations. In addition to this, God promises them a new Spirit and a heart of flesh. This is something that will find its fullest expression in Christ under the new covenant. Ezekiel deals with this in more detail in chapter 36.

This act of grace—the giving of a new Spirit and new heart—will give the people of God a greater propensity to walk according to his standards and obey his commandments. Living in God's grace does not negate the need to learn from God's law (11:20), especially given that the law written on tablets of stone will then be written on the believer's heart (see Jer. 31:33). With the words they shall be my people, and I will be their God, Ezekiel introduces us for the first time to what is commonly known as the covenant formula, which appears throughout the Old Testament and even into the New Testament.[18] God's covenant with Israel which has been broken will be renewed. By their idolatry Israel has cast God aside, and by their captivity it seems that God has cast them aside. But a time is coming when this unique relationship will be

Living in God's grace does not negate the need to learn from God's law.

renewed as Israel puts off their idolatry and God delivers them from their captivity.[19]

The glory of God departs 11:22–23

But the restoration of their relationship with God is something for the future. For the present, the worst thing of all is to befall this once glorious city; the glory of God is about to depart. Throughout Ezekiel's vision God has been moving towards this moment. In 8:4 the glory of God is clearly present among his people in Jerusalem. But as the Lord takes Ezekiel through the increasingly detestable practices in the city his glory moves ever closer to departure. Firstly the glory of God went up to the threshold of the temple (9:3 and 10:4) from where he directed his executioners. His glory then went out to the east gate where Ezekiel witnessed the musings of the wicked counsellors (10:18–11:4). Finally, in 11:22–23 the glory of God goes up out of the city towards the east and stood on the mountain. The glory of God has departed. Surely the greatest punishment that can come upon man is that God should leave us to our own devices.

> Surely the greatest punishment that can come upon man is that God should leave us to our own devices.

This chapter began with Ezekiel sitting with the elders in his home by the Chebar canal (8:1), from where God whisked him off on a visionary tour of the corruptions taking place in Jerusalem. It concludes with his return to the elders to report to them all that he saw (11:24–25). Surely one lesson we must draw from all the events in Jerusalem is that misdirected worship, no matter how sincere it may be, is unacceptable to God. Are we in danger of idolatrous worship in our churches when we place the desires of the worshipper above God's self-revelation in his word? 'True worship is driven by God's Spirit and focuses on the reality of his person.'[20]

For further study ▶

FOR FURTHER STUDY

1. Read Exodus 20:1–7. What bearing does this passage have on God's reaction to the goings-on in the temple in Ezekiel's day? What about its relevance for your church?
2. Read 2 Corinthians 6:16. How does the Apostle Paul take teachings from the Old Testament Law and apply them to the New Testament church? What can you learn from this for worship that is acceptable in your church?
3. Read John 4:23. Why is it important to get the balance between worshipping God in spirit and in truth? What defines our truth for worship purposes?
4. Read Ezekiel 11:19 and compare with Luke 22:20. How can God's discipline, as seen Ezekiel chapters 8–11, be seen as an act of grace?
5. The Apostle Paul in 1 Corinthians 6:19 tells us that as children of God our bodies are temples of the Holy Spirit. What bearing does this have on how we worship God?

TO THINK ABOUT AND DISCUSS

1. What do you understand by religious pluralism? Can you identify subtle ways in which this might affect your worship of God?
2. Those whom God denounces to Ezekiel in chapter 8 were clearly sincere in their worship. Why is sincerity a poor measure of true worship? What ought to be our measure and why?
3. 'False worship leads to false morality. Where people presume to define the character of God they also redefine their own ethical standards' (Block p359). Discuss the implications of this for your own life and the life of your church.
4. The child of God must realise that they cannot go on sinning so that grace might abound (Romans 6:1–2). Discuss the relevance of Paul's teaching in the light of Ezekiel's visionary experience.
5. 'Perhaps we have seen the idolatry in our drive for security, the flirtation with sexual licence that we call maturity or freedom, the arrogance, complacency and false security that feed off our relative wealth and comfort' (Wright p126). Discuss.
6. 'Religion is what you do with your solitude' (William Temple). Prayerfully consider the potential implications of this statement in your life.

5 Pay attention

Ezekiel Chapter 12

One of humanity's shared needs is that of approval. Often when we cannot find relief from our fear of rejection in one place we seek it elsewhere. The accusation that Ezekiel is told to address over the next three chapters is that God's people simply were not listening to what he was saying, and were seeking approval for their actions from other quarters. They will learn that it is God's approval that really matters and that even the difficult parts of God's word are true and will not fail.

Captain Mainwaring of *Dad's Army* fame is constantly heard rallying his befuddled platoon with the words 'Pay attention …' The implication is that in listening to what is about to be said they might just learn something. To date Ezekiel has grabbed the attention of his audience by the Chebar canal in several lesson-ridden emotional dramas. But they still refuse to heed the lesson that God is teaching them (12:1–2). The inhabitants of Jerusalem are described as people who '... have eyes to see, but see not, who have ears to hear, but hear not.' They are not paying attention. Their inability to see and hear is not a medical ailment but a sign of rebellion (12:2). It is not merely a weakness but a wilful hardening of the heart against God. They simply refuse to listen, and despite all the evidence before them they still refuse to see where their rebellion is taking them. What an affliction. Ezekiel is told once again to address this rebellious people in the form of another drama. This time the drama contains two acts which involve preparing for a journey and not enjoying a meal. In contrast to the procrastination of the people, verse 7 talks of Ezekiel's obedience. There is no hint of hesitation in Ezekiel's response: he simply does what God tells him to do. And so we find ourselves once again waiting in anticipation as the curtains are drawn back in the theatre of Ezekiel for the latest instalment.

> The inability to see and hear of the inhabitants of Jerusalem is not merely a weakness but a wilful hardening of the heart against God.

Act 1 Scrambling through a wall 12:1–7

As a family we enjoy sitting down to watch Bear Grylls' Mission Survive. In the first episode of season 2 Bear Grylls sends the two groups off to find supplies with the express directive that they are only to choose those items that they consider absolutely necessary for their upcoming challenges of survival. Unsurprisingly, a four-kilogram hammer was subsequently removed from one of the contestants as not essential to survival in the South African bush. Here Ezekiel is told to pack a bag that is suitable for a long journey. It is described as an exile's baggage (12:3) and was probably a common item for those already in exile by the Chebar canal—simple bag of some sort loaded only with items necessary for a difficult journey. He is then told to carry the bag out in daylight in the sight of the people, presumably leaving it in open view all day. His behaviour is designed to intrigue. Having gained their attention Ezekiel was to return to the bag in the evening but not by the conventional route. Rather than go out through the door he is told to dig his way out through the sun-dried bricks of his exilic home (12:5). No doubt the chiselling and scratching attracted further attention until, having climbed out through the hole in an undignified scramble, he picks up the bag and walks off a short distance, all the while covering his face so as not to see the land (12:6). Characteristically in Ezekiel, neither the exiles nor we are left to ponder the meaning of his behaviour. The next morning Ezekiel receives another word from God telling him to explain all to those who were asking 'What are you doing?' (12:9).

What it all means 12:8–16

If the people thought that the packed bag meant that they would soon be packing up to return to Jerusalem, they were in for a disappointment. The display was not about them but about those remaining in Jerusalem. It is describing how the prince—a reference to King Zedekiah[1]—and all the people will be forced to leave in disgrace. The whole story is recounted in 2 Kings 24:17–25:7 and 2 Chronicles 36:11–21. Some historians believe that Zedekiah received a copy of Ezekiel's words but seeing a contradiction between Ezekiel 12:13—'he shall not see Babylon,' and Jeremiah 24:8–9—declaring he should be carried to Babylon, he believed neither. Zedekiah's response is just another example of ears to hear that do not hear, and eyes to see that do not see. It is another example of not paying attention. It seems likely that he had received God's message from both Ezekiel and Jeremiah but refused to listen. He certainly could not have missed the siege mounds being built against the city walls over a period of almost two years. Yet he still does not pay attention to God's word. Despite burying his head in the proverbial sand, 2 Kings recounts how he eventually attempted to escape from the city under the cover of darkness through a breach in its walls. But he was pursued, captured, and put through the horrendous ordeal of watching his sons slaughtered before being blinded and taken to Babylon in chains. There are no contradictions in God's word. 'Seeming discrepancies in Scripture on deeper search prove to be hidden harmonies.'[2]

It is interesting how people interpret the same information in different ways. I want to suggest four common responses to God's revealed judgement. The first is scepticism or unbelief—it is all a lot of old nonsense! The second is procrastination—putting it off as irrelevant, or at least not urgent. The third is obedience to what God says, taking seriously the claims of God upon our lives and walking in the light of God's revealed truth. The people of Ezekiel's day were certainly guilty of procrastination if not outright unbelief. A fourth response to the hard bits of God's word is to make the reader's opinion more important than the author's intent. In other words, what you think is more important than what God is actually saying. Many evangelicals seem to interpret God's ways and God's word in keeping more with their own desires than God's original intention. Such a subjective approach to God's word has led many of God's children away from a proper understanding of the Bible and towards adopting practices in the church that have more to do with expediency than exposition. In Ezekiel's day the King and the people did not want to believe that proud Jerusalem would fall so completely. We are told that they simply mocked the messengers of God (2 Chr. 36:16). No doubt they played with God's warnings through his prophets, searching for an alternative understanding. But God's word proved true to its original intent. The proud city fell, the proud king was so humbled as to have to clamber out through a breach in the wall by night, and with him the people are carried off into exile. The purpose of it all is clearly stated 'they shall know that I am the LORD.'(12:15–16) What a warning to church leaders. AS Block notes, 'As the king went, so went the nation.'[3] The calling to leadership in any church is a high calling with wonderful opportunities and immense responsibilities. When a leader and especially a teaching elder goes off the mark in his understanding of God's word

Many evangelicals seem to interpret God's ways and God's word in keeping more with their own desires than God's original intention.

he potentially misleads an entire congregation. But what if, as seems to be the case in Jerusalem, the people are only too willing to follow such a leader? Even if that involves them personally ignoring God's word in favour of what they want to hear? Then they too become personally culpable, and it is to the people that the second act is squarely directed.

Act 2 Shuddering through a meal 12:17–28

If the King gets it in the neck in the first act, it is the people of Jerusalem that are on the receiving end in the second act. Here we read that Ezekiel is told to eat his meal with quaking and drink his water with trembling and anxiety (12:18). What a sight that must have been! This poor wretch Ezekiel, no doubt a dishevelled and pitiful sight anyway given all that he has already been through, is to tremble through a meal in the presence of the Jewish exiles. This haggard man has to deliberately shiver and shake as he draws the spoon and cup to his mouth, no doubt spilling food and water down his chin and clothes as he does so. Again Ezekiel quickly spells out what it all means. The answer is found in verse 19—They [the inhabitants of Jerusalem] shall eat their bread with anxiety, and drink water in dismay. The Jews in Jerusalem, who despite everything seem to think that nothing or no one can touch them behind their fortified

> Where there is a tendency to reinterpret God's word without due attention to God's intended purpose, people become spiritually weak and their senses become dull.

walls, will eat in trembling as they finally realise that they are living in false hope. The city will be laid waste and the land shall become a desolation (12:20). Where there is a persistent refusal to hear and obey God, and a tendency to reinterpret God's word without due attention to God's intended purpose, people become spiritually weak and their senses become dull. When passages of God's word are twisted to fit the latest theological fad even the faithful can become lax in their observance of God's standards. The unsaved world around us is certainly not impressed by the people of God conforming to its standards. Furthermore there are those who do not simply want the church to conform to the world, they actually want to consume it, just as Babylon consumed Jerusalem.

The dangers of popular proverbs 12:21–28

Many of us grew up with popular proverbs like 'cleanliness is next to godliness' or 'God moves in mysterious ways'. Whilst such proverbs have a semblance of biblical authenticity they are nowhere to be found in the Bible. It seems that in Ezekiel's day there were popular proverbs doing the rounds and bringing false hope to a desperate people. One of these is challenged by God: Son of man, what is this proverb that you have about the land of Israel, saying, 'The days grow long, and every vision comes to nothing'? The idea behind this is that God's true prophets are to be rejected as it seems that their prophecies are failing. Perhaps it was the listeners' way of convincing themselves that even if these prophecies are to come true, it will not be in their generation (12:27). As we shall see in the next chapter, part of the problem is that other so-called preachers of their day were preaching nice comfortable messages, and they had become used to hearing messages that pleased them. Such messages neither challenged them nor provoked them, but rather lulled their consciences to sleep. Ezekiel is to counter this popular proverb by making clear that such flattering men-pleasing teaching will come to an end (12:23–24). Furthermore, the prophecies from such men as Ezekiel and Jeremiah will come to pass, and very soon (12:28).

The same scepticism is seen in the way that some over the years have responded to teaching about the second coming of Christ. Peter faced just such a challenge (2 Peter 3:1–4). Perhaps many of us are guilty even today of failing to live in the light of this wonderful teaching. Perhaps many of us have our doubts that it will happen in this generation. But whether or not Christ returns in our lifetime this incredible teaching was given so that we might live in the light of it. This is the emphasis of Peter's letter (2 Peter 3:1–11). Peter's response to the scoffers—and perhaps even just the doubters—is simple. God's time is somewhat different to ours and he will fulfil his promises. If he delays it is so that others might repent and be saved. His timing is an act of sheer grace not procrastination, and we should be living in the light of that wonderful grace, using our time to exhort others with the gospel.

Incarnational mission

The rebellious house of Judah is once again challenged. King, people and—as we shall see over the next two chapters—prophets, fortune tellers, and even the elders in exile are challenged for seeking approval in the wrong quarters.

I cannot help but wonder if there are lessons here for the contemporary church specifically in relation to its valid but excessive emphasis on incarnational models of mission. Care is needed in the use of the term incarnational. The doctrine of the incarnation is unique and explains how the God of all eternity came into the world as a man and lived among us. Many draw from this that Jesus Christ the eternal Son of God is our model for incarnational mission. There is truth in this. We do, and indeed should, live among the people we are trying to reach with the gospel and express the love of Christ in practical ways. We should be open to exploring new ways of reaching out to an increasingly secularised community. However, the term incarnational as understood by many goes too far. It so emphasises the experience of living among those we are trying to reach, that truth statements of the gospel are deliberately avoided. It is a mission of being rather than telling. It necessitates a non-offensive form of the gospel to the point where collective experience and shared community service replace any talk of the need for regeneration or new birth or repentance. In practice the offence of the cross is removed. It is a case of process over content. Individual and collective stories become central. Often incarnational mission involves more emphasis on our story than God's story.

Often incarnational mission involves more emphasis on our story than God's story.

There is much to be commended in the concept of incarnational ministry, and it may well be used as a means of inspiring a new generation of Christian workers to take the gospel to the lost and outcast and poor by going to live among them and seeking to meet their needs. But the incarnation is about the divine becoming human. Ultimately this is not something we can do! In living out the story of God's love in the incarnate Christ, it must not be at the expense of telling that story with all its indelicacies regarding sin and repentance. The two went hand in hand for Jesus. Therefore, the two should go hand in hand for all involved in incarnational ministry. As Kostenberger notes, Christians are sent into the world '… not the way in which Jesus came into the world (the incarnation), but according to the nature of Jesus' relationship with his sender (one of obedience and utter dependence).'[4]

> In living out the story of God's love in the incarnate Christ, it must not be at the expense of telling that story with all its indelicacies regarding sin and repentance.

Ezekiel certainly lived among the people and, in the best sense of the word, his ministry was incarnational. Yet he never for a moment shrank from the unpleasantness of addressing his audience with the hard-hitting messages that God gave him to deliver. Did this show a lack of love? On the contrary! It showed that his love for his fellow Israelites was greater than a love of his own dignity. He was prepared to do whatever it took to shock his countrymen into repenting of their wicked ways and turning back to God. But not at the expense of biblical truth or the authority of God's eternal word! The Apostle Paul likewise lived among the people to whom he was called to minister. He goes as far as to say, 'I have made myself a servant to all, that I might win more of them ... I do it all for the sake of the gospel' (1 Cor. 9:19 and 23), and Paul's gospel involved acknowledging and repenting of sin.[5] For Ezekiel, and the Apostle Paul, and even the Lord Jesus Christ, serving in an incarnational ministry involved declarations of biblical truth including the need for sinners to repent and live lives in keeping with repentance (Matt. 3:8).

As those who would follow Christ's example we must be prepared, as Ezekiel was, to move out of our comfort zones and live and serve among the poor and needy, sharing the only hope that exists for humanity—the love of God as expressed in the sin-defeating work of the cross where Christ died as the propitiation for our sins. Propitiation means that the wrath of God against our sin was appeased by the Saviour's offering of himself. The very idea is offensive and will not meet with everyone's approval. But '... It is the combination of God's deep love for the sinner with His uncompromising reaction against sin which brings about what the Bible calls propitiation.'[6] In the words of the Manila Manifesto, we should '... determine to give no unnecessary offense in anything, lest the name of Christ be dishonoured. However, the offense of the cross we cannot avoid'.[7]

Furthermore, whilst it is important to leave our comfort zones to reach out to people relationally as God reaches out to us relationally, and to help the needy, more is needed: there are clear biblical reasons for challenging people in cases where sinful lifestyles and habits have contributed to their condition in the first place.

For further study ▶

FOR FURTHER STUDY

1. Read 2 Timothy 3:16–4:5. What parallels do you see between these verses and the lessons brought out in Ezekiel chapter 12? What are the implications for your church and your choice of leaders in particular?
2. Read Hebrews 5:11–6:3. How are the warnings here related to what we see happening in Ezekiel chapter 12? What practical measures could you put in place in your church to ensure that people do not remain on the milk of God's word or become dull of hearing?
3. Consider Paul's address before Agrippa in Acts 26 and especially Festus' response in verse 24. Consider the similarities with Ezekiel 12:22. Why do you think people are so disparaging of God's faithful servants?

TO THINK ABOUT AND DISCUSS

1. What do you understand by Incarnational mission? What are the strengths and weaknesses of this as a model for mission?
2. 'Searching preaching is either divinely inspired or intolerably insolent. What but a warrant from God could justify one mortal in provoking, probing, piercing the consciences of other and in public too!' W. E. Sangster, 'The Craft of Sermon Construction' p.25. Discuss this statement in the light of 2 Timothy 3:16.

6 False teachers and fortune tellers

Ezekiel Chapter 13

In every age there are people who prefer to surround themselves with those who will tell them what they want to hear rather than face a truth they may have to act upon. False teachers have been a problem for the children of God from earliest times. From heretics within the community of God's people to fortune tellers and demonic black magic, many vie for our attention. They may gain a hearing and a following for a while but in the end God will bring both them and their falsehoods under his judgement.

As Peter Jeffery writes, 'There is now no such thing as right and wrong, because there are no recognized absolute standards.'[1] He is lamenting the condition of a society that has turned its back on the standards upon which it was built.

Whilst it is understandable how such philosophies enter into and influence society, it is more disconcerting to see the ease with which they enter the community of God's people. But it seems that even in the church there are those who prefer to have their own ideas reinforced than to submit to the authority of God's eternal word. Whether it is the result of the postmodern mindset, or the age old problem of proof-texting,[2] or deliberately avoiding the bits of Scripture that contradict the preacher's theory, there are too many individuals gifted with natural eloquence and the art of rhetoric who simply do not teach God's word as God intended. The great misfortune is that sometimes natural eloquence is mistaken for spiritual gift.

It is evident from Ezekiel chapter 13 that such people existed in Ezekiel's day. There have always been young men who desire to be teachers. I am sure that in most cases they sincerely want to and indeed go on to serve God faithfully. But perhaps, as suggested above, some desire recognition for their ability. Perhaps they are career driven, or perhaps they start out well but are overtaken with a fault and find themselves craving popularity or enjoying some sense of power that comes from declaring the very Word of God. There are many reasons why men desire to teach and preach and unfortunately some of the reasons are self-centred or consumer driven. That is, fulfilling their own perceived needs or trying to provide what the people want as opposed to what they need. Whether through false prophets within the church, or popular fortune tellers, or astrologers in the glossy magazines, people are led astray by false teaching, and in

Ezekiel chapter 13 we find God rebukes and condemns such false teachers and fortune tellers.

What a load of old whitewash 13:1–16

God's complaint against the false teachers 13:1–7

False prophets in Jerusalem are the first to come under scrutiny. They are charged with several closely-related faults. Instead of delivering God's message they are prophesying from their own hearts (13:2) and following their own notions or spirits (13:3). Although they seem to have plenty to say, they have in fact seen nothing from God (13:3). If they have seen anything it is false visions and lying premonitions (13:6). But the fact that they have not really heard from God does not stop them talking with self-induced authority, and that in the name of the Lord (13:7). They are scavengers. God describes the false prophets as jackals among ruins (13:4), fitting imagery given the devastation Jerusalem was experiencing. He considers them scavengers, foxes or jackals that scour the ruins of old buildings searching for what they can use for themselves. They are guilty of feeding off others rather than feeding God's sheep.

> God describes the false prophets as jackals among ruins, fitting imagery given the devastation Jerusalem was experiencing.

They are negligent.

They neglect to make the necessary repairs to the decaying

walls of Jerusalem (13:5). This phrase should be taken both literally and figuratively. Jerusalem's fortifications have fallen into disrepair and need rebuilding. But also the false teachers have not taught the people as they ought to have done. They have neglected to build up and edify the people of God with sound doctrine.

They are superficial.

Instead of building up walls of sound teaching to protect and educate the people they have instead whitewashed over the cracks in the weak walls that the people have brought to them (13:10). Note carefully that it is the people who build their own walls here. Ezekiel is of course using figurative language. The walls referred to here are a synonym for teaching. The people are coming to these false teachers with their own ideas and thoughts and the false teachers are essentially telling them that their ideas are as valid as the next man's. Is it going too far to suggest that these false teachers are consumer-driven, giving the people what they want rather than what they need? Hungry for power, enjoying having the people flock to them for their advice? They certainly give the impression of being popularity seekers. Wanting the people to like them, they simply gloss over the weak walls or ideas that the people bring to them. Specifically they have misled God's people in Jerusalem by preaching a message of peace (13:10 and16), when in fact God has already declared very clearly through both Ezekiel and Jeremiah that there will be no peace until the city is overpowered by their enemies and the inhabitants either slain or carried off into exile. They are guilty of being men-pleasers instead of being faithful to God's word, whitewashing the people's weak walls (13:10). The people in Jerusalem wanted to hear that peace was just around the corner and so that is what the false teachers told them.

God's reaction to the false teachers 13:8–16

God has had enough of them using his name to shore up their ignorance. He condemns them for their falsehoods and lying visions (13:8–9). The people may love them for now, but God is against them and will remove them. God will tear down their whitewashed 'peace' walls (13:14–16), and even the people will turn against them blaming them when their ideas come to nothing (13:12).

The Apostle Paul warns against such teachers in the church. Writing to Timothy he says: For the time is coming when people will not endure sound teaching, but having itching ears they will accumulate for themselves teachers to suit their own passions (2 Tim. 4:3). It is always handy to have someone else to blame. Is it possible that when people come to a pastor for his approval of their own ideas it is really their way of passing the responsibility to him? Whether it is seeking the pastor's approval for a relationship or a lifestyle that goes against God's Word; or justifying all sorts of activities on the Lord's Day rather than meeting regularly for worship as God wants us to do; people want their choices rubberstamped. But sooner or later God will judge the practice of giving divine authority to private opinion. He will judge the practice of proclaiming messages that the people want to hear. And he will judge those who would so mislead his people. This is no doubt behind James' teaching when he says, Not many of you should become teachers, my brothers, for you know that we who teach will be judged with

Contrary to the postmodern mantra, there is still such a thing as absolute truth and that truth is God's wonderful gift to us.

greater strictness (James 3:1). Care is needed in handling the word of God. It is too easy to turn a deaf ear to what the Bible teaches. This can happen as a result of cultural conditioning—'this is the way it is here'; or peer pressure—'my friends do it'; or personal desire—'it feels right'. Be careful that you are not building walls smeared with whitewash. Contrary to the postmodern mantra, there is still such a thing as absolute truth and that truth is God's wonderful gift to us.

My heart is filled with thankfulness
To him who reigns above,
Whose wisdom is my perfect peace,
Whose every thought is love.
For every day I have on earth
Is given by the King;
So I will give my life, my all,
To love and follow him.[3]

Trapped in a web of lies13:17–23

God's complaint against the fortune tellersFortune cookies, fortune tellers and astrology: a harmless bit of fun or a dangerous lie? Ezekiel moves on from addressing the false teachers in Jerusalem to addressing 'the daughters of your people who prophesy out of their own minds' (13:17). Interestingly, although the term 'prophetess' is used of five women in the Old Testament 'Ezekiel refuses to dignify his target audience with the title.'[4] The implication is that they were probably more like fortune tellers. What is absolutely clear is that God is against them (13:17 and 20). Whatever method these women were using for reading the future, it involved them making and selling superstitious trinkets in the form of wristbands and veils to be worn on the head (13:18). Perhaps these were symbolic of control over the recipient's behaviour and thinking. Perhaps the veils and wristbands were an attempt at a female version of the traditional Hebrew phylacteries. In any case, they appear to have been used as something akin to good-luck charms.[5] But this was not a bit of harmless fun. The fortune tellers are accused of hunting down the people as a hunter stalks his prey (13:20–22). Note the play on ideas with the fortune tellers selling their veils enslaving their victims like birds caught in nets. Their 'ministry' has a definite bias. They are guilty of disheartening God's children and encouraging the wicked (13:22). They are guilty of profaning God's name among his own people by telling outright lies—which unfortunately God's people were only too ready to believe (13:19). They are guilty of leading people to their death by encouraging the unsaved not to turn from their sins (13:22). Is it cynical to suggest that otherwise they would have put themselves out of business? Their momentary gain was more important to them than the eternal wellbeing of those upon whom they preyed. Nothing much has changed in that respect. How many men and women today in search of real answers to the pain they are experiencing are trapped by the web of lies spun by the fortune teller? The false teacher or fortune teller exploits people when they are at their weakest. This is certainly not harmless fun. It is deadly serious. People's very souls are at risk of being lost for all eternity.

God's reaction to the fortune tellers

He is against them (13:20). He will remove all their trinkets (13:21). He will bring an end to all their lies (13:23). By an act of his sovereign grace he will set free the souls trapped in their web of lies (13:21). Once again he will make himself known to all (13:21 and23). Fortune tellers, witchcraft, and the occult may still lead people astray, but a time is coming when God will free his people from their snare.

Both the false prophets and the women had set themselves up as leaders of the people, as shepherds, but they were false shepherds and God would tear them down just as he would tear down their weak walls of false hope. We must learn to discern between the true and false teacher, between natural eloquence and genuine gift. In contrast to the false teachers, the true teacher is one who is called by God and equipped with the necessary gifts to be a true shepherd and pastor. The true teacher is one who feeds and protects God's people, challenging them when necessary; one who will risk unpopularity for the sake of truth and to see those under his care grow in holiness. Be discerning in who and what you listen to. Beware of false teachers and fortune tellers. And do not put you own ideas before the eternal wisdom of the word of God.

FOR FURTHER STUDY

1. Read Lamentations 5:18. In what way does this verse reinforce the fact that Ezekiel's prophecy was given and later fulfilled in historic space-time events?
2. Read 2 Timothy 4:3 and James 3:1. What are the parallels between these verses and what Ezekiel is saying in chapter 13?

TO THINK ABOUT AND DISCUSS

1. What do you know about fortune tellers and good luck charms? What are the dangers of viewing them as a harmless bit of fun?
2. 'With endless curiosity, and an insatiable desire of variety, people get their ears tickled with the language and accent of the person, abandoning the good and faithful preacher for the fine speaker.' Discuss the possible ramifications of this statement in the light of Ezekiel chapter 13.
3. It is good for gifted preachers to train up the next generation of teachers, but what are the potential dangers of allowing someone who feels 'called' to the ministry to preach and teach in the church? How can we encourage gifts and yet not expose the people to error?

7 Idols of the heart

Ezekiel Chapter 14

Many feel uneasy that a loving God could condemn anyone. But God is clear that we are all responsible for our own actions. Any judgement on his part is just. So far we have seen that both prince and people in Jerusalem are denounced for their selective hearing, along with the false teachers who were only too willing to lead them astray. Now God turns his attention to the elders by the Chebar canal who have embraced idols in their hearts.

Jeeves and Wooster have certainly had many an adventure together. In a letter described by Jeeves as a 'rummy communication'[1] we find the intrepid heroes invited to the country to take part in what was to be known as The Great Sermon Handicap. The general idea behind the scheme was to pit a number of unsuspecting preachers, from hamlets within a six-mile radius, against one another in a covert race to see who preached the longest on a particular Sunday morning. 'Each parson is to be clocked by a reliable steward of the course, and the one that preaches the longest sermon wins', reads the directive sent to Bertie Wooster. The humour is simply splendid, and I can imagine the air of anticipation and feigned propriety that accompanied the 'stewards' as they entered each church and took their place in the pews. But the humour points to the reality that not all who turn up to church on the Lord's Day are in the right frame of mind for meeting with God.

The issue of heart idols diagnosed 14:1–5

We are back in Ezekiel's home by the Chebar canal with the elders once again coming to him to enquire of the Lord (14:1). But something is not right. Before the elders can even speak God pre-empts them and gives another word through Ezekiel (14:2). God gets straight to the point. Although the elders have an outward appearance of propriety in coming to him, yet their hearts are not in the right place. They are accused of having idols in their hearts that are a significant hindrance to any possible communion with God (14:3). So serious is their condition that their hearts are home to a multitude of idols (14:4). So repulsive is their condition that God questions whether he should even take time to listen to what they have to say (14:3). This is not simply an issue of propriety. It is a matter of unfaithfulness, betrayal. In coming to consult God through Ezekiel they are showing the outward signs of devotion to God. Yet their hearts are devoted to a multitude of things that are more important to them than their relationship with God. Those things, whatever they are, are described as stumbling blocks of iniquity (14:3, 4, 7). It is no small thing to claim to be coming to meet with God, all the while devoting your heart to other matters. Calvin talks of the impudence of the elders. They did not hesitate to come to God's servant with an air of piety when they had none.[2] It is for this very reason that God's purpose is to lay hold of the hearts of the house of Israel (14:5). There is no point in dealing with externals when the problem lies deep within. Superficial change will avail little while the heart remains unchanged. The Preacher in Ecclesiastes puts it like this, 'Guard your steps when you go into the house of God. To draw near to listen is better than to offer the sacrifice of fools.'[3]

What constitutes idolatry of the heart? We are not told what the idols are in the hearts of the elders. Given the situation we can speculate that they may have been related to their home in Jerusalem, or the politics of returning there. They may have now wondered if they were not the bad guys after all. They may be thinking that even though they had been carried off in exile, the real reason for God's chastisement upon the nation rests with those still in Jerusalem—a form of pride perhaps. As we have already seen in chapter 3, idolatry had become a problem of some magnitude in the temple at Jerusalem, and the elders in Babylon were very much aware of this. Yet, they seem quite happy to feign their own piety. If not related to the politics of Jerusalem, perhaps the idolatry of the elders may have had more to do with the customs and practices of their exilic home. It may well be that as they reflected on how well the Babylonians were doing they felt inclined to adopt some of their religious practices. Whatever form the idols in their hearts took, the problem is aggravated by the fact that it was to this special people that God had delivered the directive of

Exodus 20:3–5. In God's economy idolatry is not just about tangible alternative gods. It can be a matter of what takes first place in your heart.

We may be inclined to play this down as more of an Old Testament issue, but the Apostle Paul simply will not allow us off the hook that easily. In writing to the Ephesian church he points out that idolatry included covetousness (Eph. 5:5; Col. 3:5). It would be too easy to apply this only to the worship of money when in reality it can apply to just about anything that dominates our hearts and draws on our energies to possess. It can be any desire that is more important to us than our love of God (Matt. 6:24).

In God's economy idolatry is not just about tangible alternative gods. It can be a matter of what takes first place in your heart.

So what might those idols be in modern society? One could certainly be money, although it could also be such legitimate objects as work or career, success, status, power/influence, family, relationships, material possessions, appearance, and pleasure in general. To that we could add a further manifestation of idolatry—putting personal opinions before God's revealed truth and pursuing our own agenda rather than God's. We live in times when matters of opinion are confused with matters of truth, and the church is not exempt from its consequences. No doubt you could to add to the list. The point however should be clear. As Comfort writes, 'Those who make their desires their object of devotion, are as much idolaters as are any of those who bow before an idol in a pagan temple.'[4] If this is true, and the Bible says it is, then the worrying thing is just how many in the church are guilty of idolatry?

It is not that these things are wrong in themselves. For example, money is not the root of all evil, but rather the love of money. It is not the thing that is the problem. Anything may become an idol depending on the response it evokes in the individual's heart, and the extent to which they become defined by it. If the loss of something is akin to your life losing meaning—for example the breakdown of a relationship—then that may have become an idol in your heart because it is your relationship with God that should give you true meaning and worth. I am not playing down the pain experienced with the loss of someone special. I am simply making the point that even something as precious as a personal relationship can become an idol. Let us explore a few other areas.

> Even something as precious as a personal relationship can become an idol.

How important is your work or career to you? How important is your family, or your appearance, or possessions? I believe that if we are open to giving an honest answer as opposed to the right answer, we will confess that these things are very important to us. These are the things that give us a sense of identity and purpose and achievement in life. They are part and parcel of God's gift of community to us. But we must be careful not to allow them to so dominate our lives that they take on idolatrous proportions.

Our society is affected to a large extent by the philosophies of men like Nietzsche, who declared God is dead in his book

Gay Science (1882). Pete Lowman in his book *A Long Way East of Eden* points out that when God is dead people have an emptiness or a void that they try to fill in other ways. Losing their sense of identity in God, people have tried to replace God with other identities. This pseudo-identity may take the form of a political ideal or community projects. It may take the form of work or achievements. The busier I am then the more valuable I am. Or, people will respect me because of the position I hold at work. Power is another identity. The classic Nietzsche will to power can be seen in many quarters: identity gained by being in a position of influence, whether politicians or civil servants, those who love to hold power over others. These are things that I witnessed almost daily during my nine years in Albania but are far from missing in Western society. It could be the desire to love or to be loved by someone else; or possessions; or the success of my children. Any one of these things, many of them legitimate and certainly not unimportant, may become idols in our hearts.

In answering the question of what constitutes idolatry of the heart we might answer, anything that we allow to take, what Lowman calls, the God position in our lives. That is, putting anything other than God in first place in our hearts is a form of idolatry. These things may not of course be gods before whom we actually bow down and worship, but they are the next best thing to it.[5] They are the things that matter most to us, the principles that dominate our lives, and which determine our sense of worth and identity. The disturbing thing is the extent to which Christians allow society to direct what they consider important in life. It is possible for us, just like the elders who came to Ezekiel to consult with God, to be guilty of coming to God on the Lord's Day, or any day, with hearts full of idols. Our spiritual growth will be hindered by allowing legitimate things to take a wrong place and a wrong emphasis in our lives.

The cure for heart idols described 14:6

God has raised the question as to whether he should even listen to the elders who have come to consult with him through Ezekiel (14:3). They do not deserve a hearing, but God declares that he will answer them (14:4), although perhaps not as they were expecting. God is simply not into rubberstamping our perceived needs. So in responding to the enquiries of the elders he points them to their real need. He wants those that are estranged from him through their idols (14:5) to repent and turn away from those idols (14:6). The starting point for ridding ourselves of idolatry is so simple—repent and turn away from it. In his grace God answers us even when we do not deserve a hearing. And if God's answer is not what we were expecting, you can be sure that it is better for us than what we wanted. Repentance, and not seeking approval, is the only way to deal with sin. Just like the Israelite elders we can be guilty of coming to God for approval of our decisions rather than coming to him for the help or direction we truly need.

The judgement against heart idols is deserved 14:7–23

Anyone who is affected by idols of the heart can expect God's displeasure. Whether it is one of the house of Israel or strangers living among them, God will not allow them to dabble in a superficial religion. Like all sin, superficial religion separates people from God (14:7). That is too serious a matter for God to dismiss. When anyone harbouring such a stumbling block in their heart comes to God's prophet, God will answer them in order to expose that which they thought was hidden (14:5). But God's motives are not simply to punish. He wants to remove that which is a hindrance to a meaningful relationship with him (14:11). He wants those who are estranged from him to be restored. For those who choose not to turn away from idolatry it is a different matter. Whether it is the idolater or the prophet who glosses over the idolater's own opinions, God has declared that he will set himself against that person (14:8–10). God's judgement against heart-idols is deserved but it is merciful for those who repent and turn away from the practice. God is merciful, and when he expresses his anger at people for their sin it is not simply to punish them but to restore his relationship with them (14:11). God will judge sin in its many disguises and his judgement is always with a purpose (14:23). Either he will make an example of the one who persists in their sin (14:8) or embrace with forgiveness the one who turns his back on his sinful ways (14:11). God wants to undo the separation that we cause by our sin.

God is merciful, and when he expresses his anger at people for their sin it is not simply to punish them but to restore his relationship with them.

There is a paradox here for the Christian. Our sin has already been forgiven in Christ and yet even as Christians we can, and often do, separate ourselves from God in the sense that our sin hinders our personal communion with him. It is not that we are not safe and secure in Christ—we are! Nevertheless sin remains a very real problem for us. This is the meaning of Paul's discussion in Romans chapter 7. Thankfully as Christians we have God's law both in our hearts and in our hands (Bible) so that our consciences alert us to our sin and we can confess it to God. If I allow idols to fill the God position in my heart, then the sooner I recognise the problem and repent the sooner I can enjoy an uninterrupted relationship with my heavenly Father. The answer is so simple. It is no great mystery.

If I allow idols to fill the God position in my heart, then the sooner I recognise the problem and repent the sooner I can enjoy an uninterrupted relationship with my heavenly Father.

But are we as Christians recognising this idolatry for what it really is? Or are we allowing our postmodern opinions to enslave us in heart idolatry and keep us away from a transforming loving relationship with God? Israel as a nation lived with their heart idols for too long before God finally intervened, but when he did the consequences were devastating. As individuals saved by God's redeeming grace we may face his loving discipline but not his righteous anger against sin. Christ has already taken that upon himself. As church communities however, I think we too often presume on God's grace. God will not allow heart idolatry to go on indefinitely and any church that is guilty of putting their personal opinions before God's eternal word will not remain a place of God's presence for long. God simply will not condone a superficial religion.[6]

Too late for Jerusalem Ezekiel 14:12–23 sounds in some ways similar to 6:11–7:22. What with his references to the judgements of God in the form of sword, famine, plague, and the addition here of wild beasts (14:15and21), the sentiments are essentially the same as those we viewed in the earlier chapter. This passage mentions three men—Noah, Daniel and Job. The idea seems to be that even if one of these three godly men should go and preach to those remaining in Jerusalem and warn them of the impending disaster, even then they will not escape God's judgement. The issue has already been decided by God.[7]

Hope

And yet there is hope. As is the pattern in Ezekiel's pronouncements of judgement, it is once again succeeded by a pronouncement of hope. We are told that God will not leave himself without a witness (14:22). There will be survivors of his judgement who will be brought to Babylon, as indeed they were as part of the third exile. When these survivors arrive in Babylon and recount all that has been going on in Jerusalem (their ways and deeds) the exiles will understand that God's judgement has not been without good cause (14:23). It is not always comfortable to think of a loving God condemning anyone. But God is clear that we are all responsible for our own actions. Any judgement on his part is well-founded and just. True hope is to be found only in repentance.

For further study ▶

FOR FURTHER STUDY

1. Read Ephesians 5:5 and Colossians 3:5. According to the Apostle Paul what sorts of practices can become idols in the heart? What does Paul say is God's response to this in the next few verses? What is Paul saying that applies to today, but which people often view as an Old Testament theme?
2. 'Mammon' is a Syriac word or name given to an idol worshipped as the god of riches. Jesus uses it in Matthew 2:24 and Luke 16:9–11. What lessons can we learn that are relevant to Ezekiel's message in this chapter?

TO THINK ABOUT AND DISCUSS

1. Personal opinion can too often become more important than Biblical truth. Are there any opinions or practices in your church that are in danger of becoming heart idols? How might these be dealt with?
2. Can you identify anything in your life that has become or could easily become an idol in your heart? How can you put this right?
3. Mercy is all about being quick to encourage people towards restoration after they sin. Mercy does not gloat over someone's failures but shows a deep longing to see the offender renewed in their spiritual health. How can we see this reflected in God's dealings with the elders by the Chebar canal? How can we put this into practice today?

8 Shocking images

Ezekiel Chapters 15–17

Another series of powerful pictures are used to describe Israel's condition. The pictures highlight the depths to which human nature can plummet, and man's tendency to break his promises and trample underfoot the favour with which God has looked upon him. And yet there remains hope! Hope in God's unmerited grace and undeserved love.

C. S. Lewis addresses the dangers of subtly turning our backs on God in his wry and satirical portrayal of human life in *The Screwtape Letters*. Throughout the book the character Screwtape (one of Satan's senior demons) is writing to his nephew Wormwood offering advice on how best to corrupt the patient's (Man's) soul and lead him away from God. In chapter 12 we find the following devilish instruction:

> He [the patient] must never be allowed to suspect that he is now, however slowly, heading right away from the sun on

a line which will carry him into the cold and dark of utmost space.

For this reason I am almost glad to hear that he is still a churchgoer and a communicant. I know there are dangers in this; but anything is better than that he should realise the break he has made with the first months of his Christian life. As long as he retains externally the habits of a Christian he can still be made to think of himself as one who has adopted a few new friends and amusements but whose spiritual state is much the same as it was six weeks ago. And while he thinks that, we do not have to contend with the explicit repentance of a definite, fully recognised, sin …[1]

Religious observance can mask a cold and detached heart in our day just as it seems to have done in the days of Ezekiel.

It is possible for a man or woman to be regular in church attendance and to maintain an outward display of religion and yet be moving slowly and almost unknowingly away from God. Religious observance can mask a cold and detached heart in our day just as it seems to have done in the days of Ezekiel. Octavius Winslow expresses the problem like this: 'If there is one consideration more humbling than another to a spiritually minded believer, it is that, after all God has done for him, after all the rich displays of his grace, the patience and tenderness of his instructions, the repeated discipline of his covenant, the tokens of love received, and the lessons of experience learned, there should still exist in the heart a principle, the tendency of which is to secret, perpetual, and alarming departure from God.'[2]

There is no sense of impropriety or unease, and yet the people must surely know that much of what was celebrated as worship was in fact a smokescreen for hearts that had drifted away from the very God to whom they claimed to be close. In their state of self-imposed ignorance the Israelites still fail to recognise that much of the pain and anguish that has come upon them is the direct result of their misdirected affections. They still do not seem to see that the reason for their dire circumstances is their unfaithfulness. Their predicament—slavery in Babylon and impending final destruction of Jerusalem—is their own fault. In the early years of the exile the Israelites still tended to think that they were being treated unfairly, that perhaps the exile was a mistake and perhaps God would soon come to the rescue and restore them. After all, they did not really deserve this treatment did they? In response to this misdirected mind-set God speaks to them so graphically that they should be left in no doubt as to their contribution to the fall of their nation. They have failed to produce fruit in keeping with their privileged position.

The useless vine 15:1–8

The Jews at Jerusalem would have been well acquainted with the metaphor of a vine. The image is used throughout the Old Testament[3] representing the nation of Israel as '… planted and cultivated by God for his delight and the produce it should yield.'[4] According to the Jewish historian Josephus, the area directly above the temple gates in Jerusalem was decorated with a gigantic golden vine and clusters of grapes as large as a man.[5] It was a constant reminder that Israel was the vine that God had taken out of Egypt and planted in a new land. God speaking through Jeremiah says, Yet I planted you a choice vine, wholly of pure seed. How then have you turned degenerated and become a wild vine?[6] Jeremiah is bringing God's charge against this backsliding people. Israel had been planted by God as a choice vine all true[7] but the vine is not producing good spiritual fruit.

Christ is the True Vine John 15:1–17

It is possible that Jesus was alluding to Ezekiel's prophecy when he calls himself the true vine in John 15:1. In other words Jesus is not just a faithful vine but the true vine. The parallels between Ezekiel 15 and John 15 are striking in that Israel is said to have degenerated, that is they did not abide in God and did not bear fruit. Therefore, God was going to 'cut them off' by sending them into exile. In a similar vein Jesus talks of fruitless branches being removed, thrown into a fire, and burned. The central thrust of Jesus' teaching is that if we as the branches are truly attached to him as the vine, then our attachment will be evident by the fruit we bear. To put it simply, from a vine we expect to find grapes and from a Christian we expect to see the fruit of a Christian life as exemplified in the Saviour himself and in the teachings of his apostles.

'Branches' who are not true branches

The text mentions 'two characters who are in some respects exceedingly alike ...'[8] both appear to be branches but evidently one is not in Christ effectually or savingly. One is truly attached so that the life-giving and fruit-producing sap courses from the vine to the branch; the other lacks that life-giving attachment and so will be cast aside. As Spurgeon puts it, such teaching calls for serious self-examination.[9]

The metaphor is designed to teach us two things that the Father does:

> One is that God takes away fruitless branches, and the other is that God prunes fruitful branches. He cuts away the lifeless, and he cultivates the living. He destroys and he disciplines.[10]

Not all who believe are true believers, and not all disciples are true followers. In John 2:23–25 we read that some believed but Jesus remained wary of them. Similarly in John 6:60–66 we read that many disciples turned back and no longer walked with him. Judas is perhaps the clearest example. He was numbered among the twelve and walked with Jesus for three years, but he was not a true believer. In Ezekiel's day the people of Israel had been in a privileged position with God, just as Judas had been in a privileged position with Jesus, but neither Israel as a nation nor Judas as an individual were truly in God. Our identity in God can be seen, at least in part, in the fruit we bear of obedience to his teaching. As one who came not to abolish the law but to fulfil it, Jesus himself taught us that if we love him we will keep his commandments (John 14:15). Obedience to the law of God is not the basis of our salvation or justification; it is rather the fruit our salvation, expressed in love towards God and our neighbour (Rom. 9:6).

Not all who believe are true believers, and not all disciples are true followers.

The sinner's only hope

On the other hand, we must not look for perfection in the true branches. No one except Christ possesses such perfection. Even the fruit-bearing branches need pruning (John 15:2) so that they might be even more fruitful. Jesus is not looking for perfection and neither is he asking us to do more than he did himself. These words are preceded with Jesus telling us, I do as the Father has commanded me, so that the world may know that I love the Father. He simply wants us to abide in him and show his love, as he abided in the Father and reflected his love.

Jesus is not looking for perfection and neither is he asking us to do more than he did himself.

This teaching is not designed to cause a sensitive believer to live in fear of being cast aside. That is not Jesus' intention. In fact much of the teaching of Jesus in the Gospel of John is designed to give the true believer great comfort and a deep sense of security. Whoever comes to Jesus in saving faith will never be cast out (John 6:37); Jesus will lose none that the Father gives him but will raise them up in the glorious resurrection on the last day (John 6:39–40). As Christians we are not perfect and can never be, but then it is not our perfection that secures us a place in God's presence for all eternity, but rather the perfection of our Lord and Saviour. That is why our only hope is in abiding in him, and when we do we will produce the fruit of love and obedience—however imperfect—that shows our attachment to the true vine.

The central meaning[11]

In Ezekiel chapter 15 the main point is that the vine is useless because it is fruitless. It is for emphasis that he talks of the wood being too flexible even to make a peg for hanging cooking vessels on (Ezek. 15:3, 5). The point that it is of even less worth when half burned refers to the fact that since Israel has already experienced two deportations it is worth less than previously (Ezek. 15:5) and will therefore face a further deportation and be utterly consumed (Ekek. 15:6–8).[12] According to Ezekiel 15, when compared to other trees (other nations) the vine (Israel) has no value except for its fruit. The sole purpose of the vine is to produce fruit and Israel was failing in this purpose. Historically they had been chosen by God from all the nations,[13] but 'the claim to divine election is no substitute for covenant faithfulness.'[14] There are many ways in which true believers can be fruitful but all true fruit begins in the heart, a heart that has been transformed by the Spirit of the living Lord. We have seen time and again throughout Ezekiel that God's name and reputation have been tarnished by the exploits of the Israelites. The result of spiritual fruitfulness, on the other hand, is that God's name and reputation are exalted, believers enriched in their faith, and unsaved people are won for Christ.

The adulterous wife 16:1–63

In this the longest chapter in Ezekiel we have a rags to riches story, to make essentially the same point as the story of the vine. An abandoned child is taken in and nurtured (Ezek 16:1–7). As she grows she is lavished with love and gifts and raised to the status of queen (Ezek 16:8–15). But it all goes horribly wrong when she turns her back on her loving benefactor and begins to trust in her own beauty and fame (Ezek 16:16–52).

What embarrasses you? It is interesting how little it takes for some people to become embarrassed, whereas for others nothing seems to faze them at all. I must confess that I feel uncomfortable watching some television talent shows whose format often depends on a performer doing poorly. I feel a sense of embarrassment for the individual who is standing in the limelight before a panel of judges and millions of viewers, singing their hearts out, but in a tune that seems to come from another planet. I feel embarrassed for them and yet they remain totally unfazed by their lack of talent and poor performance. It seems that they see the world in a totally different way; they see themselves and their behaviour in a way that does not reflect reality.

In Ezekiel 16 we come across some very explicit and somewhat embarrassing language.[15] It makes for an uneasy read in private, never mind reading it aloud in the church. It talks very explicitly about things like the blood-stained new-born child; the naked young woman; the unfaithful wife who is so promiscuous that she opens a love nest on every street of the city and has many lovers from many places. What are we to think of such graphic language? God does not often use such lewd or shocking imagery, but sin must be seen for the shocking evil that it is.[16] Despite all that has happened to date, the Israelites still see themselves and their behaviour in a way that does not reflect the reality.

The rejected child / Israel's past 16:1–14

God's grace is displayed as Ezekiel recounts how God took in the rejected child, Israel (Ezek 16:1–7), and although she was nothing more than any other nation God clothed her and nurtured her and entered into a covenant relationship with her (Ezek 16:8–14). One cannot fail to see the parallels with Ruth and Boaz as Ezekiel talks of God spreading his cloak over the now beautiful young woman. He washes her (v. 9), clothes her (v. 10), and gives her many beautiful gifts (v. 11–13). The young woman becomes known for her beauty. Israel became known for her splendour, especially in the time of Solomon—see for example the Queen of Sheba's visit recorded in 1 Kings 10). It is important to remember that this beauty—and anything of true worth that Israel possesses—is from God and not from herself. Indeed, Scripture recounts how she was smaller and less significant than the other nations (Deut 7:7). But despite God's gracious dealings with Israel she turns her back on him.

Anything of true worth that Israel possesses—is from God and not from herself.

The Bride rejects her benefactor / Israel's present 16:15–34

Ezekiel now recounts how the beautiful bride who has been lavished with gifts, betrays her benefactor and begins to trust in her own beauty (v. 15). Her unfaithfulness is seen in several ways—in relationships with other nations (v. 15); in making idols from the gold and jewels that God had given her (v. 16); in engaging in worship of the idols that she has crafted (v. 17). There is a clear progression in her unfaithfulness, beginning on the high places (v. 16), and then coming closer to home she displays her unfaithfulness in the city squares and streets (v. 24–25). She even adopts the pagan ritual of child sacrifice (v. 21). How sick is your heart, declares the Lord (v. 30). When we pine after those things that God knows are not good for us, our hearts become weak and sick and, it would seem, unable to resist temptations and lust. According to the Apostle Paul God sometimes gives us over to those sinful desires (cf. Ezek 16:27 with Rom 1:24).

The main idea here seems to be that Israel gave away so much of what God had given to her. She had been rich in her relationship to God but she became gradually poor and finally bankrupt as she flirted with the other nations. Surely a lesson to be drawn from this is the spiritual bankruptcy we experience when we turn our back on God for the pleasures of this world.

Loves that destroy / Israel's future 16:35–43

It is no secret that often in life the things we most long for and depend upon can become our downfall. This section opens with the word therefore (Ezek 16:35), an indication of the direct causal link between what the bride—Israel—has done, and the punishment she will face. We are told that God will turn her lovers against her (Ezek 16:38); those lovers—those who were apparently so promising—will totally destroy her (Ezek 16:39–40). Furthermore, God will judge her (Ezek 16:38), and God's anger will be satisfied (Ezek 16:42). The warning is a reminder of the holy hatred with which God views sin. But God's judgement of sin is never erratic or temperamental. His punishment is always appropriate to the offence. God does get angry with sin, and punishment will be meted out. The penalty of sin will be paid for either by the individuals themselves or, if they will but accept the free gift of grace, Christ pays the penalty in their place (Rom 3:25; Heb 2:17; 1 Jn 2:2; and 1 Jn 4:10). As always, God's hatred of sin must be seen in the context of his grace and the fact that he has provided the perfect payment for the debt accrued.

Like mother like daughter 16:44–52

The main idea here seems to be that Israel has been worse than the Hittites, Sodom, Samaria, and the other nations around her (Ezek 16:47 and 52). The nations are less guilty than Israel since Israel enjoyed greater benefits from the hand of God. It is a sad reflection that on occasions the ungodly are more righteous than the children of God (Ezek 16:51). As Block points out so challengingly, '... the test of one's spiritual parentage is not one's confession but one's life.'[17] But even though we may break our promises, God remains faithful to his. Even though we would rather turn a blind eye to our failings, yet God will expose them to us so that we will once again turn to him.

Hope for all 16:53–63

Even though discipline will be carried out, God promises that the captivity will end. Not only will he restore Israel's fortunes, he will also bless the surrounding nations (Ezek 16:53). The idea here seems to be that as God's people enjoy fresh blessings so the ungodly will also benefit. A brief look at history shows that in times of spiritual revival crime rates fall and not only those who come to faith are blessed but all of society benefits from the outpouring of God's Spirit. It is suggested that during the Welsh revival of 1904–1905 an estimated 150,000 people were saved. Thousands of lives were transformed and whole communities turned upside down. 'The police force reported that they had little more to do than supervise the coming and going of the people to chapel prayer meetings, while magistrates turned up at courts to discover no cases to try.'[18]

Time and again in Old Testament history God promises to establish an everlasting covenant with his people (Ezek 16:60, 62). The nation of Israel will enjoy a degree of restoration, but the ultimate fulfilment of this wonderful promise of God to his people will come to pass with the redemptive work of Christ, as we will see in later chapters of Ezekiel. For now we see a glimpse of the gospel of grace, good news to all mankind beginning in Jerusalem and all Judea and Samaria and to the end of the earth (Acts 1:8). To quote Kenneth Martin, 'This was a wonderful promise, but a promise that was followed by a clear-cut command, a command to be witnesses of the risen Lord Jesus Christ. They [the disciples] were to tell the whole story—a story that would shake legalistic Judaism to its very

God's promises may be delayed due to the failings of his people but those promises will find their fulfilment in ways greater than man could ever imagine.

foundations and penetrate the darkness of paganism causing even Imperial Rome to take fright.'[19] God's promises may be delayed due to the failings of his people but those promises will find their fulfilment in ways greater than man could ever imagine. Israel's fall into sin was gradual, with success and prosperity giving them a false sense of security and leading them away from dependence on God. A brief look at society today reflects similar patterns of behaviour. There remains that same deep-seated need for people to experience shame for their sin[20]—shame that leads to repentance and faith in the redemptive work of Christ. What a transformation our society would go through if this were to happen!

Two eagles and a vine / The mechanics of Israel's impending downfall 17:1–24

If chapters 15 and 16 tell us what is about to happen to Israel, chapter 17 gives us an insight into how it will all unfold. God tells Ezekiel to speak to Israel in a riddle, a parable or a fable. This fable is recounted for us in verses 3–10. True to form, Ezekiel gives us an explanation in verses 11–21, and a warning is succeeded by an expression of hope as Yahweh himself intervenes and offers security in verses 22–24.

The first eagle that we read of in verse 3 is revealed to be 'the King of Babylon' (17:12) that is Nebuchadnezzar, and the 'top of the Cedar' and 'topmost of its young twigs' refers to Jehoiachin and the first exiles who were carried off to Babylon (17:3–4 and 17:12).

The seed and vine of verses 5–6 is none other than Zedekiah whom Nebuchadnezzar made a vassal king.

Zedekiah rebelled against Nebuchadnezzar and reached out to Egypt—the second eagle—for help (17:7 and 15).[21]

The parable of the vine reaching out to the second eagle seems to relate yet again that the Israelites were still looking to the remnant in Jerusalem for hope of restoration. However, when Ezekiel asks them 'Do you not know what these things mean?' he goes on to show how the allegory is about the final fall of Jerusalem. Their attempt to secure help from Egypt whilst still rebelling against God simply must fail. What is needed is not another human agency, but God's intervention (v. erses 22–24). It is God alone who can release people from their captivity, be that physical or spiritual. Douglas Stuart suggests that the cedar top of verse 22 is none other than the Lord Jesus Christ himself.[22] If he is correct then we are now living under the shade of this stately cedar that Ezekiel talks of in v23. The ultimate salvation of Israel was always intended to come about in Christ. Even though they were restored to Jerusalem under Nehemiah, this was never the final fulfilment of these promises. The ultimate salvation of Israel is now taking place along with the Gentiles (you and me) under the shade of the great Cedar.

There is much to learn from Ezekiel chapters 15–17. Let me suggest a few lessons. Firstly we are only useful when we are fruitful, and we are only fruitful when we remain in a close and obedient relationship with Jesus. Secondly, we often make the mistake of trusting in our own abilities and possessions. What we need is to develop a resilient trust in God. Thirdly, the heart is the place where coldness begins and so we should keep a constant check on it, and not allow our affections to wander to things that may bring temporal pleasure but no lasting hope. Finally, our hope in this life and the next is in Christ alone and our covenant relationship with him.

The Israelites were faithful in going to the temple to engage in acts of worship, but Ezekiel has made it abundantly clear that their hearts were far from God despite all that he had done for them. He had chosen them out of all the nations to be a special people, embraced by his special love, and held by his special covenant. He has made them a great nation from very humble beginnings, but they have rejected his affection and turned back to the very nations from amongst whom they had been rescued in the first place. Whilst man breaks his promises and forgets his covenants on a whim, the Lord God will establish an everlasting covenant. God's covenant is sure and steadfast, with God himself in Christ atoning for all the shocking betrayals of his covenant people.

For further study ▶

FOR FURTHER STUDY

1. Read 2 Corinthians 11:12–14 and compare Paul's words with those of C S Lewis at the beginning of this chapter. In what ways might these teachings affect you personally or the life of your church?
2. Compare Ezekiel 15:1–8 and John 15:1–17. Consider the different types of people in these two passages. What can we learn from them?
3. Read Romans 11:11–24 and compare it with Ezekiel 15. What does this mean in real terms for you and me?
4. Read Proverbs 23:17, 1 Peter 2:9–12, and Titus 2:11–14. How can we avoid the mistakes of the Israelites in Ezekiel's day?

TO THINK ABOUT AND DISCUSS

1. If it is possible to be a regular church-goer and display an outward form of religion, and yet be moving away from God, how can we know for sure that we are saved and that our faith is real?
2. Using relevant Bible passages, discuss the phrase 'Branches' that are not true branches. What does it mean to bear fruit according to the Bible?
3. Chopping off, pruning and grafting-in are all biblical expressions found in Ezekiel 15 and Romans 11. Discuss the difference between these terms, and in what ways they matter for your church.
4. The story of the unfaithful bride in Ezekiel 16 teaches God's grace and human ingratitude. Discuss.
5. In the parable of the two eagles and the vine in Ezekiel 17, the vine reaches out to the wrong source for help. How might we in the church be guilty of doing the same?
6. What part does shame play today in the life of (a) the unsaved; (b) the saved? What part does the grace of God play in this?
7. C S Lewis said- 'Do not put your trust in something you may lose.' Think of practical applications of this statement for you personally and how to avoid the mistake.

9 Personal responsibility

Ezekiel Chapter 18

Ezekiel here challenges another popular but misguided proverb that suggests the people are being punished for the sins of their fathers. People tend to blame others for their situation, or even blame God, but they need to take responsibility for their own actions. God makes it clear that the one who sins shall die, but his impassioned desire is that people might turn from their sinful ways and live.

From financial recession, to political uncertainty, to destructive personal habits—people tend to point the finger of blame at someone or some vague and elusive force that is responsible, either directly or indirectly, for the ills of this world and my personal hardships. Ezekiel is addressing a people who were evidently asking who was to blame for their situation, who is to blame for the fall of Jerusalem to date, and the slavery they were currently enduring in Babylon. Their answer was to put the blame firmly on previous generations.

The proverb which God rejects 18:1–4

In Ezekiel 18:2 we read a proverb that seems to summarise how the Israelites view their current political, religious, and personal situation: The fathers have eaten sour grapes, and the children's teeth are set on edge. In other words, the children are suffering for the offences of their parents. The Israelites were blaming their fathers and grand-fathers for doing things in the past for which they were now paying the price. Whether we see this proverb as consequential[1]—'That is just the way it is and there is nothing we can do about it'; or as a complaint—'It is not fair that we are being punished for something we did not do'; God unequivocally rejects this proverb (18:3). God does not condemn people to predetermined outcomes. He does not condemn people to a hopeless existence on the basis of someone else's wrong-doing. God deals with each person on an individual basis. 'All souls are mine …,' says God, the son as well as the father. Therefore the innocent son will not suffer for the father's sin but rather—the soul who sins shall die (18:4). To put it simply, each person will be held accountable for their own actions. Ezekiel's hearers need to wake up and respond personally to God's claim upon their lives. They can no longer blame others for the pickle they are in. They are accountable for the choices they have made.

A misunderstanding of Exodus 20:5?

This is not the only place we read this proverb. Ezekiel's

contemporary Jeremiah also quotes it (Jer. 31:9); so it seems to have been doing the rounds in Jerusalem as well as in Babylon. It is entirely possible that the proverb is a misunderstanding of the second commandment. God's people are told not to make any carved images with a view to worshipping them[2]—'You shall not bow down to them or serve them, for I the LORD your God am a jealous God, visiting the iniquity of the fathers on the children to the third and the fourth generation of those who hate me' (Exod. 20:5). To take this to mean that sons suffered the penalty of their fathers' sins is to misunderstand the commandment.

The principle of personal culpability was already well established in Moses' day when the law stated clearly: Fathers shall not be put to death because of their children, nor shall children be put to death because of their fathers. Each one shall be put to death for his own sin (Deut. 24:16). The point of Exod. 20:5 is not that innocent and godly children should be punished for the wrong their fathers did. Only those children who follow in their rebellious fathers' footsteps can expect a similar judgement. Now God is re-emphasising this point through Ezekiel. Jeremiah addresses the same issue. When the people come to him asking why God is treating them so badly and earnestly plead their innocence, Jeremiah responds by reminding them that not only did their fathers turn their backs on God but that they—this generation—have done even worse (Jer. 16:10–13). Each generation is accountable for its own sin. Whereas the Deuteronomy

Each generation is accountable for its own sin.

passage is dealing with legal processes, 'Ezekiel appears to be extending the concept of just punishment from the human court to the realm of the divine.'[3] Ezekiel here is not denying that often children suffer the consequences of their parents' sins. Rather, he is dealing squarely with the classification of a person before God. Each person stands or falls on the basis of their personal relationship with God. Children may suffer the consequences of their parents' sin but never the penalty. No one in the Bible, with the exception of Christ, pays the penalty for another's sin. The Israelites can no longer blame previous generations for their predicament. They are being held accountable for their own choices in life.

The Israelites can no longer blame previous generations for their predicament. They are being held accountable for their own choices in life.

The long parable of three generations cited as examples 18:5–20

Ezekiel goes to great lengths to make his point, citing three generations by way of example. In summary we can see that the man who lives a godly and upright life will enjoy life in all its fullness with God (18:5–9). It is assumed that if his son is likewise righteous then he too will live. If on the other hand the son turns from his father's righteous ways and becomes wicked in any number of ways—from murder to exploitation of the poor—that son shall die and his death will be his own fault (18:10–13). As if to emphasise the point God has Ezekiel take the allegory a generation further. If the grandson, the third generation, sees his father's sinful behaviour, recognises it for what it is and chooses instead to live an upright, honest and good life, then he will live without condemnation. The father will die for what he did and the son's life will be based on his own choices and lifestyle (18:14–18). The point could not be any clearer. The righteous shall live; the unrighteous shall die; no one shall die because of the sins of another. The Israelites are not suffering or paying for the sins of their fathers. Rather, their misfortune is on account of their own sin, and the choice they have to worship all forms of idols rather than remaining faithful to God.

Ezekiel is not concocting a new theology here. Instead, he is '... stating what he considers to be a solid, current, theological fact. God does not punish or reward vicariously: every individual gets what he or she deserves and no other factors enter into God's calculations.'[4] You would expect this to come as good news to the exiles, but on the contrary they question Ezekiel's theology. 'Why does the son not share the guilt of his father?' they ask almost in astonishment, reflecting what they consider the obvious upshot of their experience (18:19). All too often they embrace the arbitrary guide of experience in preference to God's word. Ezekiel's response is to reiterate what he has already said on the matter (18:20), but then takes it a step further, holding out hope even for the one who has sinned (18:21–23).

God wants no one to perish 18:21–23

If a person lives an upright life it will be accredited to them; if they live a wicked life, that wickedness will be charged against them. However, should a wicked person turn their back on their life of sin and live according to God's laws (18:21) then God will not hold a list of wrongs against him and he will not die on account of past sin (18:22). The person who truly turns their back on their past sinful life will experience God's rich mercy and will live with God for all eternity. There is therefore now no condemnation for those who are in Christ Jesus, the Apostle Paul writes to the church at Rome (Rom. 8:1). In Paul's day as in Ezekiel's, any Israelite who is conscious of his law-breaking and seeks God's forgiveness, finds provision for sin in God's free and unmerited grace.

This is not some half-hearted concession on the part of God. On the contrary it is God's deepest desire that they turn from their sin and live (18:23). Ezekiel's words can be understood on two levels. God would much rather the people had turned from their idolatrous ways previously and averted the just punishment they were now experiencing in the sacking of their holy city. But on an individual level also, God wants all men to be saved and come to the knowledge of the truth (1 Tim. 2:4). God's desire is that men and women will turn from their sin and experience his rich and full forgiveness so that they might live with him for all eternity.

Can a true child of God lose their salvation? 18:24

Following such a wonderful offer of hope, the tone of the prophet's message takes a sombre turn. Up to this point he has been urging the people to leave their sinful ways with the promise of pardon if they do. But now a renewed threat hangs over the heads of those who turn away from their righteousness. 'None of the righteous deeds shall be remembered ...,' he states, 'for the treachery of which he is guilty and the sin he has committed, for them he shall die.' This is indeed a sober warning. Does this mean that a true child of God can lose their salvation? To that we must answer a resounding no! In what sense then is Ezekiel saying that a 'righteous person' can fall away?

The issue revolves around what theologians refer to as the perseverance of the saints. This doctrine simply summarizes the biblical teaching that those who are truly born again by the Spirit of God will endure to the end. Calvin points out that Ezekiel is not here referring to the inward life-giving righteousness that makes a person a true child of God, but rather an outward form or appearance, or as he puts it, '… we see that the word righteousness is referred to our senses and not God's hidden judgement.'[5] Expressed on a practical level, a person cannot accrue a credit balance of good deeds. We are not saved by our righteous acts but by Christ's righteous life and atoning death. We are credited with Christ's righteousness (1 Cor. 1:30), and that is God's gift to us (Rom. 5:17). The righteousness that we need for redemption is not something that we can accrue, but something that Christ alone can provide, and it is ours through the simple act of faith. That act of faith, if it is rooted in genuine repentance, will lead to a changed life.

The righteousness that we need for redemption is not something that we can accrue, but something that Christ alone can provide.

This does not mean that the true child of God is perfect in their behaviour. King David fell very far short of God's ideal when he became an adulterer and a murderer (2 Sam. 11–12) and again when he took a census (2 Sam. 24). Yet when he was confronted with his sin by Nathan and confessed it, his relationship with God was renewed. Despite his failings, David was enduring in his faith. The Lord Jesus himself taught that it is the one who endures to the end that will be saved (Matt. 24:13). On the one hand, righteousness that saves is not our own but Christ's. All we have to do is believe. On the other hand, a profession of faith is not enough. Faith in Christ and a life of righteousness that flows from Christ's righteousness in us go hand in hand. Ezekiel is simply showing that self-generated righteousness will not benefit us if we do not persevere to the end. The true child of God will persevere, not in his own strength, but in the power of the indwelling Spirit of God. He who believes in the Son 'has eternal life' (John 3:36). Jesus himself says of those that follow him, 'I give them eternal life, and they will never perish, and no one will snatch them out of my hand' (John 10:28). The great assurance we have as Christians is that we are held secure in the hands of a triune God who will never allow us to fall from his all-consuming love and grace.

> Self-generated righteousness will not benefit us if we do not persevere to the end.

God accused of being unjust 18:25–29

Again the people object. 'The way of the LORD is not just,' they whine (18:25a and 29a). Now we see the exiles turn from blaming previous generations to blaming God. But the God of all righteousness asserts that it is their ways that are unjust

(18:25b and 29b), and reasserts the position he has already made abundantly clear through his spokesman. Here, as indeed throughout this whole passage, God emphasises the need for personal righteousness, not a salvation by personal merit, rather the fundamental element of salvation—repentance.

God's impassioned plea— 'Repent and live' 18:30–32

God does not wish the death of any sinner but extends to each one his hand of mercy. He appeals for people to turn from their life of sin and live (18:30). 'Why will you die?' he questions. There is no need. All you have to do is repent and turn from your transgressions. Calvin points out that the word turn '… refers to the renovation of the mind and heart: for this is the beginning of repentance, that we should be inwardly renewed in mind …'[6] Each person is accountable for the choices he or she makes. This is real choice; the individual must make a real decision. The choice to repent and live will be attested and felt and experienced by that individual as they participate in a whole new life and a new lifestyle. Ezekiel has already counselled the exiles that there is a causative link between new life in God and a new lifestyle reflected in a natural desire to keep God's decrees (18:21). This is the most important choice any individual can make and this is the message we must take to the lost of our generation.

Repentance is fundamental to evangelism. It is not enough to talk of Jesus waiting for individuals to open the door of their hearts, as if he were nothing more than some congenial door to door salesman. God demands repentance. A profession of faith may not be enough. Many people make a decision to follow Jesus, many make a profession of faith, but after a short while they show no signs of wanting to obey God's word. What might be the cause? A decision alone may not lead to repentance. True repentance involves both a negative action and a positive reaction. Negatively it involves a turning away from sin, and positively, it involves obedience to all God's statutes (18:21). Faith and repentance, a decision and an active turning, must come together. Grudem defines repentance as a heartfelt sorrow for sin, a renouncing of it, and a sincere commitment to forsake it and walk in obedience to Christ.[7] He goes on to suggest that repentance involves an intellectual understanding (sin is wrong), an emotional approval of what the Bible teaches about sin (heartfelt sorrow for sin and a hatred of it), and a personal decision to turn from it (a forsaking of sin and live in obedience to Christ instead).

While accepting that we remain imperfect, true repentance will lead to a changed life, and our obedience will instinctive. God's impassioned plea to the exiles is—repent and live. We must urge this generation to 'Seek the LORD while he may be found; call upon him while he is near; let the wicked forsake his way, and the unrighteous man his thoughts; let him return to the LORD, that he may have compassion on him, and to our God, for he will abundantly pardon' (Isa. 55:6–7). Peter's inspired sermon on the day of Pentecost culminates with a similar plea. When his hearers are pricked to their very hearts concerning the part they played in the Saviour's death they cried out to Peter for some thread of hope: 'What must we do?' Peter responded, 'Repent and be baptized every one of you in the name of Jesus Christ for the forgiveness of your sins ...' (Acts 2:38). Repentance involves turning your back on an old way of life. Old ways of thinking change; there is a radical turning away from sin and an earnest resolution to break with the past. In keeping with repentance there is fruit-bearing (Matt. 3:8; John 15:4).

A good works salvation?

With all this talk of righteousness and fruit-bearing one might think that these individuals were to be saved on the basis of their good works. But the Bible is clear in both the Old and New Testaments that there is no contradiction between individual righteousness and God's grace in salvation. Grace must never become an excuse to behave in an unprincipled, irresponsible, or sinful way. Likewise, we must not make the mistake of thinking that God's wonderful, saving, and transforming grace can somehow be earned by our behaviour.

Grace must never become an excuse to behave in an unprincipled, irresponsible, or sinful way.

We live in a blame-culture.

> We are not to blame—it is always someone else's fault, directly or indirectly. So we lay the consequences of our personal and collective wickedness at the door of our genes, or our environment, or government failures, or market forces, or global trends, or psychological stress, or anything else that is sufficiently vague and removed from the uncomfortable proximity to our own choices and actions.[8]

But such blame-shifting will not do. God dismisses the

misleading proverb espoused by the exiles, dismisses their complaints, and places the blame squarely in the laps of each individual. 'Ezekiel again exhorts the people to leave off complaining, and to acknowledge that there is no remedy for their evils but to be reconciled to God.'[9] God extends this hope to Ezekiel's and all subsequent generations with his plea—repent and live!

FOR FURTHER STUDY

1. Read Matthew 3:8. In what ways does John the Baptist's preaching reflect Ezekiel's?
2. How does the teaching of Galatians 6:7 relate to Ezekiel chapter 18?
3. Look up Paul's comments in Ephesians 4:22–23. What are the parallels between what the apostle is teaching here and that which we read in Ezekiel 18:30–32
4. Compare 1 Timothy 2:4 and Acts 2:38. How do these passages relate to Ezekiel chapter 18?
5. Read Psalm 24. What parallels do you find between the words of David and those of Ezekiel chapter 18?
6. In what ways does John 15:4 shed light on Ezekiel's message in this chapter?

TO THINK ABOUT AND DISCUSS

1. Ezekiel is preaching to people who were blaming others, and God, for their misfortunes. In what ways can we see this problem reflected in society today? How would you respond? Think of relevant passages of Scripture to help make your point.
2. It is possible that Ezekiel's contemporaries misunderstood the second commandment. Can you think of similar misunderstandings of God's Word today? How do you think such misunderstandings come about? How would you gently and effectively counter them?
3. The exiles were reflecting their own experience in the proverb they were using. In what ways can personal experience undermine the Word of God in the church today? How can we avoid this pitfall?
4. Read Matthew 24:13 and John 10:28–29. How do these texts contribute to our understanding of the perseverance of the saints? There are many other passages that emphasise this wonderful promise. Can you think of any? (Wayne Grudem's chapter on this subject in his Systematic Theology is very helpful reading.)

10 A funeral song with a difference

Ezekiel Chapter 19

Just as the previous chapter made the point that children would not suffer for the sins of their forefathers, now chapter 19 reflects the other side of that coin. The children cannot expect to inherit the blessings of their fathers if they fail to live a life of obedience to God.

Following Ezekiel's theatrics in earlier chapters, including model building and mime, he now adds singing to his repertoire. This is not a song of joy though. It is a lament, or a funeral song. Singing funeral dirges remains a practice in many Middle Eastern countries. David's lament for Saul and Jonathan in 2 Samuel 1:19–27 is one example. Ezekiel is commanded to compose a lament for the princes[1] or kings of Israel (19:1). Usually a funeral song is sung for one person; this however is a funeral song with a difference. God tells Ezekiel to direct the lament at two princes. Whereas such songs were usually sung to honour the dead, this one is an expression of dishonour and warning.

It is designed to show their weaknesses and flaws rather than their virtues. Its purpose is to help the exiles understand that any hope they might have in their own strength or the power of their kings or alliances is a false hope. Far from being their saviour, the princes have contributed to their downfall. In effect, this is a funeral song for the death of a nation.

A lioness and her cubs 19:1–9

We are introduced to the mother who is depicted as a lioness (19:2). It is a picture of the nation as a whole, too quick to emulate the nations round about.[2] Matthew Henry expresses it like this:

> She lay down among lions. God had said, the people shall dwell alone, but they mingled with the nations and learned their works. She nourished her whelps among young lions, taught the young princes the way of tyrants, which was then used by the arbitrary kings of the east, filled their heads betimes with notions of their absolute despotic power, and possessed them with a belief that they had a right to enslave their subjects, that their liberty and property lay at their mercy.[3]

The whole process, as we have been seeing throughout Ezekiel, led to what Calvin describes as 'a certain withdrawing of God's favour.'[4] God simply cannot countenance his people's actions when those actions contradict his revealed will and their own best interests. It is a message that should be familiar to Ezekiel's hearers by now. And surely there is a warning here to the church in our day. It is the Word of God that must remain pre-eminent when we make plans and strategies for reaching out to our neighbours. Of course we need to plan, and we must be open to change so that we can address our generation with its needs that Christ alone can meet. But we must be wary of adopting the world's philosophies and practices to the detriment of the gospel.

The gospel is 'the power of God for salvation' according to Paul in Romans 1:16, but unfortunately in many instances that gospel has been so affected by new techniques and methods of delivery as to be unrecognizable. The most significant difference is that in much of present-day evangelism the consumer reigns supreme. We try to make the gospel more attractive to the consumer, but according to God's word the gospel is actually foolishness to the unsaved (1 Cor. 1:18–23). David Wells asks, 'Why, then, has the evangelical Church arranged itself around the marketing dynamic rather than around the truth which is its birthright to proclaim?'[5] The answer is not to attempt to make the gospel more attractive to a people for whom it is foolishness, but rather to proclaim it and back up our claims by living in the light of it. To quote Wells again:

Unfortunately in many instances that gospel has been so affected by new techniques and methods of delivery as to be unrecognizable.

> It is only as the evangelical Church begins to put its own house in order, its members begin to disentangle themselves from all of those cultural habits which militate against a belief in truth, and begin to embody that truth in the way that the Church actually lives, that postmodern scepticism might begin to be overcome. Faith after all is dead without works.[6]

The first lion cub 19:3–4

Our attention is promptly redirected to the first of the lioness's cubs who, we are informed, grows up to become a strong lion. The weakness in this strong lion seems to lie in his voracious appetite for subduing the people around him (19:3). The first king referred to here is generally thought to be Jehoahaz II. He became king of Judah following the death of his father in the battle of Megiddo but reigned only three months before being deposed by Pharaoh Neco and taken off to Egypt where he died (2 Kings 23:30–33; 2 Chr. 36:1–4). Ezekiel describes this historical episode in terms of the prince being led away with hooks to the land of Egypt (19:4). Jehoahaz's reign was one of oppression and cruelty. He preyed on his subjects and imposed levies on them for his own gain, contrary to God's directives for a king in Deut. 17:14–20, where leadership is described in terms of obedience to God's laws and service towards others.

The motto for the Royal Military Academy of Sandhurst, the training-ground for young officers of the British Army, is Serve to Lead. Today, as in Ezekiel's day, the role of leaders is to serve the good of those under their command. National leaders are there to serve the people and not to be self-seekers simply lining their own pockets. As Block points out, Government exists for the people, people do not exist for the government.[7] Unfortunately history bears witness to the fact that too many leaders fail in this simple objective.

The second lion cub 19:5–9

There are a few suggestions as to who the second lion

cub represents. John Gill, on the basis of the Targum's paraphrase, suggests it is the next brother of Jehoahaz—Jehoiakim. Indeed in 2 Kings 23:31–34 we read that Pharoah Necho made Jehoiakim king in the place of Jehoahaz. However, Jehoiakim was never taken into exile and so some suggest that the second cub refers to Jehoiachin,[8] or possibly Zedekiah,[9] who was still on the throne as Ezekiel was making this pronouncement. It could be a reference to either.

Jehoiachin was appointed king by the Babylonians following the death of his father Jehoiakim. It is recorded that he ruled for three months and ten days (2 Kings 24:8–16; 2 Ch. 36:9) and he is said to have done evil in the Lord's eyes. As Wiseman states,

> According to Josephus, Nebuchadnezzar changed his mind about the appointment and returned to besiege Jerusalem and carried off the eighteen-year-old king with his mother Nehushta, his family, and fellow Jews, to exile in Babylon.[10]

This would accord with Ezekiel's pronouncement (19:9).

If, on the other hand, it is a reference to Zedekiah then the pronouncement contains an element of prediction since he was, at that time, still ruling in Jerusalem. According to Derek Thomas,

> The lament forms a prediction of Zedekiah's downfall. The fact that both Zedekiah and Jehoahaz had the same mother, Hamutal (2 Kings 24:18) further makes sense of this song with its mother lion and two cubs (19:2,3,5). The funeral dirge was then somewhat different: it was a funeral song for someone who had not yet died! Zedekiah's days are numbered. Make no mistake about it, he too will be brought to Babylon.[11]

The main point of the story of the lioness and her two

cubs is to remove from Ezekiel's congregation in exile any false hope of restoration instigated by those remaining in Jerusalem. As we have been seeing time and again in Ezekiel, he removes all hope in man and nudges his hearers ever closer to absolute dependence on the grace of God alone for their salvation. Their redemption is not going to come from one of the lions mentioned above but from one altogether different. In Revelation 5:5 we read the following: 'And one of the elders said to me, "Weep no more; behold, the Lion of the tribe of Judah, the Root of David, has conquered, so that he can open the scroll and its seven seals."' It is a reference to Christ as the only one who can open the seals and realize God's redemptive purposes for his people. The Lion of the tribe of Judah has conquered, as the book of Revelation goes on to point out, by becoming the Lamb. Christ has conquered sin on the cross and it is he alone who can set people free from the sin that enslaves them.[12]

A vine and her branches 19:10–14

The allegory now moves from a lioness and her cubs to that of a vine and her branches once again, but the reference is again to the nation of Judah and her many kings.

This time we are told that the mother was like a vine planted by the water (19:10). As a vine draws its nourishment from the water, so Israel was well cared for by God. It was fruitful and full of branches that were strong and suitable for a ruler's sceptre (19:11). Israel had 23 kings from Saul to Zedekiah of those 22 were from the Davidic dynasty. David is known as a man after God's own heart,[13] but his successors strayed far from the God who had established their royal household. As a result, despite its one-time grandeur and power (19:11), this dynasty is about to be uprooted in fury, thrown to the ground, shrivelled by the east wind, and its once-strong branches consumed by fire (19:11–12). There is some repetition of ideas as we are told that this vine is now planted in a dry and thirsty land where fire is again the dominant force that consumes it (19:13–14). What does it all mean? It signifies a fall from grace, and what a fall from grace! The vine that once produced strong sceptres (19:11), will produce no more (19:14). This once powerful nation and its kings have already been devastated by Babylon from the east. The people have been uprooted and dragged off into exile, but worse is yet to come. Precious Jerusalem will be razed with fire when the final blow comes, and from that day forward no branch is left that is strong enough to become a ruler's sceptre—this is the end of Israel's monarchy.

Some practical observations

The children of godly parents should not presume to qualify for God's blessing unless they personally embrace the Saviour and live to please God.

Once again the message that God delivers through his faithful servant Ezekiel is one that dashes misplaced hopes. False hopes must be destroyed before true hope can be found. True hope rests not in any man or institution but in the everlasting God and Saviour and founded on his eternal precepts. This is a matter for the individual. The children of godly parents should not presume to qualify for God's blessing unless they personally embrace the

Saviour and live to please God. As for leaders, especially church leaders, they should be first and foremost servants of those entrusted to their care. As God's servants within the church it is our duty to remain faithful to God's eternal and unchangeable word, diligently communicating it to our generation. As Block points out, 'Without the submission to the will of God of both leader and led, shepherd and sheep, any claim to security with God is a delusion.'[14]

For further study ▶

FOR FURTHER STUDY

1. Look up 1 Corinthians 1:18–23. Compare this passage with Matthew 16:24; Mark 8:34; and Luke 9:23. What does a comparison of these passages teach us about the Christian life in relation to the cross?
2. Read Deuteronomy 17:14–20. What light does this passage shed on Ezekiel chapter 19?
3. Consider Genesis 49:9. What light does this verse shed on the fact that Ezekiel's allegories of a lioness and lion cubs is a reference to the nation as a whole?
4. What parallels do we find between Ezekiel's song of the vine and Psalm 1:1–3? According to Psalm 1:1–3 what makes a man prosper? In what ways can we apply this in the church today?
5. In Revelation 5:1–10 Christ is called both The Lion of the tribe of Judah and a Lamb looking as if it had been slain. What principles of servant leadership does Christ display? How does this compare to the princes of Ezekiel 19?

TO THINK ABOUT AND DISCUSS

1. Much of evangelism today is focused on the needs of the individual. How can we meet those needs and at the same time ensure that the Word of God remains pre-eminent in our evangelism?
2. The gospel is foolishness to the unsaved yet it is God's appointed means of reaching them. What are the dangers of trying to make the gospel more attractive?
3. What are the dangers of a consumer-driven church programme?
4. God's design for leaders is that they should serve the needs of those under their care. How does your church reflect the concept of servant leaders? Do we have anything to offer the politicians and giant corporations of our day?
5. David was known as a man after God's own heart, but subsequent generations of his dynasty strayed far from God's word. They presumed on God's blessings to previous generations. What are the lessons for the children of godly parents today?

11 Old habits die hard

Ezekiel Chapter 20

Israel has displayed a history of bad habits many of which have passed from generation to generation. God's reputation is at stake in the lives of his people; therefore God will purge their ranks and they will come to loathe themselves for their corrupt practices.

According to the oft-used expression, old habits die hard. From nail biting to substance abuse, habits are very difficult to break and can have serious consequences. Some lead to issues ranging from minor to life-threatening health problems which are ignored at the individual's peril. Whilst recognizing that some of these habits may require professional and medical aid to overcome, at their root habits are simply repetitive behaviours, ways of thinking, things we do, and choices we make. They have been described as involuntary and unconscious acts. So if a person wants to change bad habits then they need to consciously attack them. Israel had a history of bad habits and again it is also clear that bad habits can develop among the children of God today.

Israel's history of bad habits 20:1–32

In the opening verse we are met with yet another of Ezekiel's precise dates. It is the seventh year of Zedekiah's reign and around July or August of that year. This means that this latest word from the Lord comes two years, one month, and five days after his first prophecy (1:2), and approximately eleven months since his pronouncement in 8:1. We are told that some of the elders come again to Ezekiel to enquire of the Lord (20:1). It seems likely that despite all that they have been told so far they are still hoping for some good news about Jerusalem's fate. Perhaps they are still holding on to false hopes on the basis of their history—after all, had not God delivered them before? But God will not allow them to set the agenda (20:3) and instead he has Ezekiel retell their history somewhat differently from the glory of which they learned it from their teachers or parents by the fireside at home (Deut. 6:1–7).[1] It is interesting how God often views history very differently to us. Ezekiel recounts their history but with a sting in the tail. He uses it to highlight their trans-generational bad habits.

Bad habits in Egypt 20:5–9

The history lesson takes them back to the sojourn of their ancestors in Egypt (20:5). He begins talking to them about God's gracious dealings with them and the promises he made to them to bring them into a rich and fertile land of their own (20:6). But the story recounts how they continued to sin against him despite his promises. They refused to rid themselves of the idols of Egypt (20:7–8). God's anger was so inflamed that he would have poured out his wrath on them but for the sake of his name (20:9). Had he punished the Israelites as they deserved then the Egyptians would have mocked them and in so doing mocked God. So, rather than punish them God delivers them from the hands of the Egyptians.

Bad habits in the desert—first generation 20:10–17

But their rebellion continues in the desert. It was here that God gave them one of their greatest possessions—his laws, including his Sabbaths (20:11–12). These laws were a sign to the children of Israel that God had set them apart as his own special people, in a special relationship with God himself, with a God-given purpose for their lives. But the people rejected his laws and utterly desecrated his Sabbaths (20:13). They failed to break the old habits of Egypt by remaining devoted to their idols (20:16). Again, God would have destroyed them but for his reputation in the eyes of the nations around them (20:14, 17).

> God's laws were a sign to the children of Israel that God had set them apart as his own special people.

Bad habits in the desert—second generation 20:18–26

Through Ezekiel God now refers to the next generation in the desert. God had warned them that they were not to follow the ways of their fathers by defiling themselves with the idols to which their fathers habitually turned (20:18). This second generation of desert wanderers are encouraged instead to follow God's laws and keep his Sabbaths, reflecting again their special relationship with God (20:19–20). But that generation also rebelled against God and followed in their predecessors' footsteps lusting after idols (20:21–24).

Bad habits in the land of promise 20:27–29

The scene now moves to the land that God had first promised to Abraham (Gen. 15:18–21), then later confirmed to his son Isaac (Gen. 26:3), and to Isaac's son Jacob (Gen. 28:13). God's promise of a land was at its heart an expression of his grace. The land was something that God would give the descendants of Abraham for no other reason than that he had chosen them for his own special possession. It was free and unmerited. As Wright says, 'Israel had a land to live in because, quite simply, the Lord had given it to them.'[2] But this covenant arrangement had reciprocal commitments. As he continues, 'The land was an integral part not only of the Lord faithfulness to Israel, but also of Israel's covenantal obligations to the Lord.'[3] The obligation on the part of the Israelites was obedience to God's word. Williamson notes: 'It is clear from the obligations imposed upon Israel that being in special relationship with Yahweh involved more

It is clear from the obligations imposed upon Israel that being in special relationship with Yahweh involved more than privilege; it entailed responsibility.

than privilege; it entailed responsibility. Like Abraham, Israel must "obey Yahweh's voice and keep his requirements, commandments, statutes and laws" (Gen 26:5).'[4] The land remained the Lord according to Leviticus 25:23, and the people were expected to maintain their relationship with their land Lord. The problem of course was that the Israelites were failing in their covenantal obligations. God had said to them, 'When you come into the land that the LORD your God is giving you, you shall not learn to follow the abominable practices of those nations. There shall not be found among you anyone who burns his son or his daughter as an offering …' (Deut. 18:9–10). But they had dealt treacherously with God (20:27), insisting on setting up their own high places where they offered up sacrifices to other gods. They did this so openly that they even called the high places by names familiar to the nations they were not to emulate (20:28–29).[5] God had made it clear through Moses that he was to be worshipped at the place of his choosing (Deut. 12:1–7). But, resolute in following the sinful practices of their fathers in lusting after idols (20:30) and offering sacrifices upon these illicit high places, including child sacrifice (20:31), they have robbed themselves of God's favour.

Bad habits in the land of exile 20:30–31

It is precisely because these practices were still being carried on 'to this day,' that is, even in Babylon, that God will not entertain the concerns of the elders (20:3, 31). We are brought full circle. For all the stated reasons, that is, Israel's trans-generational sinful habits, God states again as he did in 20:3 that he will not allow the elders in Babylon to enquire of him.

Not that they are being punished for the sins of their fathers, but rather that even they still so prefer to be like the nations around them as to continue the religious practices of their captors (20:31–32). Old habits die hard, but God will not allow this to continue unchallenged (20:33).

Summary of bad habits

As we have come to expect of Ezekiel, there are some recurring themes in this passage. Neglect of God's laws and Sabbaths; idolatry; and child sacrifice (cf. 16:21 and 20:26). Ezekiel here is drawing parallels between Israel's long history and their experience in Babylon. As they sit by the Chebar canal in Babylon the people are longing for their own home. They have expectations of God's deliverance, and yet they continue in their rebellion against God's laws, raising up false gods or idols and mixing with the religions of Babylon. Furthermore, they are guilty of failing to keep God's Sabbaths. Is not it interesting just how important God's Sabbaths are to him? They are mentioned in this passage six times (20:12, 13, 16, 20, 21, 24). There are many Sabbaths mentioned in the Scriptures,[6] and although these had specific application for the nation of Israel yet they embody the principle of Sabbath rest. Holyoake, the English humanist, wrote in 1857: 'Whether Englishmen know it or not, it is the English Sunday that has made and keeps England great.' If you would kill Christianity, you must first kill Sunday. This is not the place to go into a detailed study on the Sabbath,[7] but it is obvious that modern life has brought new challenges to the principle of keeping one day special to the Lord. While we debate the nuances of what it means to keep Sunday rather than the seventh day special, and all the while the special place and significance of the Lord's Day is eroded, I cannot help but wonder what God makes of it all?

Consequences of those bad habits

The first and most obvious consequence of Israel's bad habits is that they have been sent into captivity in Babylon. But perhaps a more disturbing consequence is reflected in Ezekiel's words, 'I also gave them over to statutes that were not good and laws they could not live by; I let them become defiled through their gifts …' (20:25–26). In other words, God abandoned them to their own sinful habits. Since they would not obey his commands, God allowed them to make their own statutes (20:25). He allowed them to defile themselves and make themselves unclean with the gifts they offered (20:26), gifts that God did not ask for nor want. There is an unmistakable parallel here with the words of Paul in his letter to the Roman church. In Romans 1:24–32 we read that God has given people over to a variety of vices. The result of people turning their backs on God's revealed truth is that they become unable to make reliable moral judgements.[8] As a result God at last abandoned them (24, 26, 28) to their own sinful practices, including not only wilful homosexuality (verses 24–27) but also to many other vices, twenty-one of which are mentioned in verses 29–31.[9]

The result of people turning their backs on God's revealed truth is that they become unable to make reliable moral judgements.

Some will be quick to pick up on Paul's reference to sexual impurity in this passage, but even Christians can be guilty of any number of the sins listed such as envy, greed, deceit, gossip, slander, disobedience to parents, heartlessness and ruthlessness. When even God's people turn a blind eye to God's teaching on such simple and practical matters to indulge in their own variety of unrighteousness, they too are in danger of God simply allowing them to carry on. But such sinful practices have consequences. Not least that the Christian who continues in them will not enjoy God's immediate presence but will meet with God's disapproval and discipline (Heb. 12:6–7). Many Christians want to believe that God is so loving that he will ignore what we consider small sins, those secret sins that no one else knows about. But God's eyes are too pure to look on evil (Hab. 1:13), and he will uncover them.

Many Christians want to believe that God is so loving that he will ignore what we consider small sins, those secret sins that no one else knows about.

Dare I suggest that as you read these words you ask yourself if there are any bad habits you are struggling to break? Are there bad habits that you cling to and refuse to give up? I wonder if perhaps some are trying to make a trade-off, like the Israelites, by offering God gifts or worship that he does not want, rather than giving him the whole-hearted, if imperfect, obedience and commitment that he does require. This is an area where we need to be ruthlessly honest with ourselves. Let us search our hearts on these issues and humble ourselves before God. Let us repent of those besetting sins and work with our whole being to remove them from our lives. We must learn to trust God's wisdom rather than our own. I can think of no greater penalty than that God should give us over to our own desires! Thomas Brooks would pray, Ah, Lord this mercy I humbly beg, that whatever Thou givest me up to, thou wilt not give me up to the ways of my own heart.

Today no less than in Ezekiel's day, God's people are beguiled by the subtleties of a society that no longer has an objective touchstone for morality. Everywhere we are enticed by convenient goods, convenient lifestyles, and convenient worship. We need to embrace the simple truth that our innate and essential worth is tied up with our relationship to God. The basis and obligations of that relationship are clearly spelled out in God's eternal word. Israel's failing was that they wanted to be like the nations around them, and so they turned their back on truths that God had revealed to them through the Law, the Prophets, and the Writings. How far are you prepared to go to be like your unsaved neighbours under the guise of trying to reach them with the gospel? Israel was God's channel for reaching out and making his grace known among the nations. They were supposed to be different! They were set apart as holy. That remains true for the church today. But if we become so like the people we are trying to reach that we live by their standards and evaluate our worship services more by consumer principles than biblical standards, then like Israel we are in danger of immersing ourselves in religious activity whilst failing to make God known as he has revealed himself. Ezekiel is repeating Israel's history to bring them back to their senses. God wants them to turn from their false hopes and false lives. He wants to spur them on to repentance and to turn them away from their repeated failings. Perhaps it is time for us to re-engage with our heritage as the people of God, including our understanding of what constitutes worship, and our use of the Lord's Day.

Israel's hope despite their bad habits 20:33–42

Ezekiel now turns from reviewing Israel's past to looking into their future, and in so doing he draws a parallel with their exodus from Egypt (20:36). He talks of restoration, a time when the exile is over and the people are gathered to their own land once again. But not everyone will be allowed to enter the land. Just as a shepherd allows his sheep to pass under his staff and uses that same staff to block the way for those that do not belong to his sheepfold (20:37), so God will purge Israel of those who continue to rebel against him (20:38). With a hint of irony God tells them to go off and have their fun and serve their idols because despite their waywardness the day will come when the house of Israel will worship God on his holy mountain (20:39–40). Despite Israel's failings, despite their repeated sin, God will maintain a people for himself. He will restore them. This is God's restoration of Israel based on promises in Deut. 4:27–31; 30:1–10; and Lev. 26:40–45. Israel will never be completely destroyed. There will always have a remnant who are faithful to God, despite the nation's repeated failings. As Chris Wright puts it in his commentary, 'Persistent sin is met by persistent grace.'[10]

Self-loathing 20:43–44

The internet is awash with articles and there are many books dedicated to helping people who have low self-esteem. Low self-esteem and self-loathing are destructive forces that in some cases lead to self-harm. It is important to support those with a sensitive conscience or too low an opinion of themselves. 'I hate myself' or, 'I hate my life,' and similar phrases are all too often heard from the lips of young people especially. They measure themselves against unrealistic models of what they should be like because that is what they are bombarded with day in and day out. Parents have a huge responsibility to help their children develop good self-esteem and confidence so that they can cope with the pressures they will face in a modern world. This is an extensive area in the field of psychology today and every effort to minimise the culture of self-harm is to be encouraged. Yet, here we find God telling the Israelites that there is coming a day when they will loathe themselves (20:43). In fact, he is encouraging this self-loathing. How does this tally?[11] It must be understood that when God does this it is not with a view to crushing people with a sense of hopelessness. On the contrary, he wants to show them that true and eternal hope resides in his wonderful mercy (20:44). There is hope because God does not treat us as we deserve.

There is hope because God does not treat us as we deserve.

As Christians and as God's ambassadors (2 Cor. 5:20), it our duty to extend hope to all people and give them a true sense of dignity and worth and purpose. As creatures made in the image of God, indeed as the only creatures made in the image of God, our true sense of worth and dignity are tied up in our relationship to God. Jesus told us to love the Lord our God with all our heart and soul and mind and to love our neighbour as ourselves (Matt. 22:37–40). Instead of focussing on our own shortcomings Jesus tells us to redirect our thoughts towards God and our neighbours. In Matthew 16:24 Jesus taught his disciples, 'If anyone would come after me, let him deny himself and take up his cross and follow me.' A definitive stepping stone on the way to overcoming self-loathing is to lift our eyes from ourselves and focus primarily on the Lord. In practice overcoming self-loathing involves self-denial! As Jay Adams writes,

> For a Christian, the alternative to self-love, self-esteem, self-worth, and any other kind of self-centred teaching that might appear in the future, is clearly self-denial. When you seek to gain yourself, you can only lose it; when you are willing to lose yourself for Christ, you save it. It is that simple—and that profound.[12]

Deliverance, that is to say, salvation, is not because we have somehow earned it, but it is in spite of our persistent sin and repeated failings. God does not save us because we deserve it any more than the Israelites deserved it all those years ago. Rather, he does so because of his grace and 'for his name's sake' (20:44). I wonder how we would feel today if God were to lay out before us our history. What would we find that needs addressing? Actually God does lay bare our history

Deliverance, that is to say, salvation, is not because we have somehow earned it, but it is in spite of our persistent sin and repeated failings.

today. The Word of God has an incisive and penetrating quality (Heb. 4:12–13). It lays bare not only our history and behaviour but our very intentions. Are we honestly listening to all that God is saying to us, specifically in relation to what is acceptable in worship? Because God's Word is living and active, each new day brings us an opportunity to face up to our own history of bad habits. How will you deal with such a penetrating revelation? God not only requires us to break bad habits, he gives us the Holy Spirit to make it all possible. As Calvin puts it, 'God wishes us to taste his goodness, that the remembrance of our crimes should be bitter, and also that everyone should judge himself that he may obtain pardon from him.'[13]

Grant, Almighty God, since we have already entered in hope upon the threshold of our eternal inheritance, and know that there is a certain mansion for us in heaven after Christ has been received there, who is our head, and the first-fruits of our salvation: Grant I say, that we may proceed more and more in the course of thy holy calling until at length we reach the goal, and so enjoy the eternal glory of which thou affordest us a taste in this world by the same Christ our Lord. Amen.[14]

For further study ▶

FOR FURTHER STUDY

1. Consider God's words to Abraham in Genesis 26:5. How does this equate to Paul's comments in Romans 3:31? We are saved by grace through faith (Ephesians 2:8) so what does the law really have to do with us? Consider Ephesians 2:10 in your response.
2. Evaluate the teaching of Hebrews 4:12–13 and Isaiah 49:2. These passages make it sound like truth can be painful. How can we deliver the truth with love and compassion?
3. Read Matthew 16:24. How can the words of Christ here help those with low self-esteem? What other passages of Scripture can you think of that bring real hope to those with a sense of self-loathing? How can we as a church better help the vulnerable?

TO THINK ABOUT AND DISCUSS

1. Ezekiel in this chapter is drawing parallels between Israel's long history and their ongoing experience in Babylon. He is very direct in pointing out areas in which they are failing. What do you consider the strengths and weaknesses of this approach to teaching for your church?
2. Why do you think it is so difficult to break bad habits? In what ways does God help us?
3. As children of God's covenant, what do you consider to be our covenantal obligations? How can we realistically live up to these?
4. What do you think of God's challenge to the Israelites concerning 'desecrating' his Sabbaths? What application does this have for us today? Be specific.
5. Ezekiel tells us that God gave the Israelites over to their own laws and statutes. In what ways might this apply to our church programmes?
6. 'Persistent sin is met with persistent grace.' (Wright, p. 165). Discuss this statement in the light of your own experience.

12 The painful side of leadership

Ezekiel Chapters 21–23

Christian leadership is not all about gently shepherding God's flock. Often Christian leaders are called to address very difficult circumstances and none more difficult than when any of God's children are living lives that are incompatible with God's teaching. It is not the job of leaders simply to encourage people to change their ways, but rather through God's word to point them to the God of grace who alone is sufficient for overcoming sinful behaviour.

Worship in the church is primarily about God's glory and not our pleasure. But, as so often happens, in Ezekiel's day this seems to have been turned on its head. In chapters 21–23 we find themes repeated that have been dealt with in earlier chapters of this book such as idolatry and unacceptable sacrifices. These are the very things that have brought God's judgement upon his people. Ezekiel has been given the unenviable task of preaching judgement against his own people for these sins. God has been merciful so often that the people of Israel are taking his mercy for granted. Despite his repeated warnings they fail to see their need to change and to embrace the grace that is so freely on offer. Perhaps it is because of the many second chances that God has extended to them that they still do not see punishment as imminent—perhaps it will not even happen at all. Rather than take to heart God's warnings and change their ways, they have used his mercy as an excuse to sin all the more. It is at this point that we see God making final preparations for Israel's punishment which includes a third and final deportation, the ultimate collapse of the nation, and the seventy years of captivity as outlined in Daniel.

God has been merciful so often that the people of Israel are taking his mercy for granted.

The forest fire and the sword 20:45–21:7

In another scene of amateur dramatics Ezekiel is told to prophesy against the south. It is another reference to Jerusalem, and the image of fire indicates that the final act of discipline will be all consuming, and Jerusalem will literally be set ablaze (20:45–48). The people will complain that they do not understand Ezekiel as he is speaking to them in parables (20:49). But their ignorance will be short-lived as the message is spelled out clearly over the next three chapters. More immediately, Ezekiel is told to put on another performance and speak yet another parable, the parable of the sword. He uses a parable to explain a parable, but the words accompanying the drama will leave the Israelites in no doubt about its message, as the second parable explains the first.

He is to face south and prophesy against the forest which is a reference to Jerusalem (20:46—21:1). Speaking to the forest (20:47) is paralleled with talking to Israel (21:3); the fire of 20:47 is paralleled with the sword of 21:3; and 'every green tree' of 20:47 is a reference to the righteous and the wicked in 21:4. These parallels make it clear that God is telling them the same message, but in language that they cannot claim to be unclear. They are truly without excuse. The message is further emphasised in what theologians call the song of the sword (21:8–17).

The song of the sword 21:8–17

Songs are an excellent way of teaching truth. There are for example, children's songs about Jesus, Noah, the battle of Jericho and so on. Children often remember songs when they forget lessons. Throughout the world there are folk songs, many of which refer to violent incidents in the past. They tell of victorious assaults that armies have made against their enemies; tragedies of battles lost (whilst making their exploits sound heroic); songs about the gun, the bomb, and the heroes of their cause. This song is in a similar vein except that it refers to something in the near future. The sword is sharpened and polished; it is sharpened for the massacre, and polished 'to flash like lightning.' The message is one of horror and fearful retribution against the people of God.

The sword bearer is Nebuchadnezzar 21:18–27

The next section tells us who will bear the sword for God, but this again is no surprise as we have been told in different ways before that it is none other than Nebuchadnezzar, the King of Babylon. It is a sad reflection on God's people that God chooses to use the ungodly to challenge them. In today's terms this is akin to non-Christians pointing out our failure to display Christian virtues. Another drama unfolds as Ezekiel is told to set the scene of two roads, possibly in a Y formation, with a sign pointing one way to Jerusalem, and another pointing towards the Ammonite city of Rabah (21:19). He is to enact Nebuchadnezzar standing at the crossroads, sword in hand, trying to decide which city to attack first. Although both places are probably about equidistant from Babylon, Nebuchadnezzar initially goes after Jerusalem. The wicked prince is a reference to Zedekiah who will lose his crown as the kingdom is made an absolute ruin (21:25–27). That crown will not be restored to another prince of Judah but only to the one to whom it rightfully belongs. Douglas says, This true king, further portrayed by Ezekiel in Chapter 37ff. is the Davidic Messiah—in other words it is the Lord Jesus himself who will have the throne of Israel.[1] God may be bringing to Ezekiel's mind the prophecy of Genesis 49:10, 'The sceptre shall not depart from Judah, nor the ruler's staff from between his feet, until tribute comes to him; and to him shall be the obedience of all the peoples.' See also Luke 1:32. True hope for the nation resides not in another wicked prince, but in the King of Kings who will be given the throne of his father David.

Hope, as the sword is directed against Israel's enemies—Ammon 21:28–32

Typically of Ezekiel, hope is extended even in the darkest moments. The Ammonites will not escape, nor will other enemies of Israel as we shall see in later chapters. This mention of Ammon's demise arises naturally following Ezekiel's drama of Nebuchadnezzar standing at a crossroads deciding who to attack first. The short straw fell to Israel as the first to be punished, but their enemies will not escape. This is simply a small foretaste of judgements pronounced against the nations later. Prophecies against Israel's enemies were often a way of reminding Israel of God's covenantal promise to restore them: if Israel is to be restored then their enemies must first be removed (e.g. Lev. 26:40–45 and Deut. 30:1–10). In many ways it is a simple logic of war. God extends a sliver of hope even here amidst so much horror and judgement.

Prophecies against Israel's enemies were often a way of reminding Israel of God's covenantal promise to restore them.

The reasons for the sword 22:1–23:49

What follows in chapters 22 and 23 is a comprehensive list of the sins and failings both of God's people and their enemies.

Jerusalem's sin 22:1–31

As we have seen many times in Ezekiel so far, the city is

accused of bloodshed, detestable practices, and idolatry (22:2–4). Her priests have violated God's laws (22:26), and her prophets have glossed over a myriad of evil deeds (22:28). In God's own city he cannot find a single man who could 'stand in the breach' before God so that his wrath should be averted (22:30).

The adulterous sisters 23:1–49

We are not left to wonder who Ezekiel is referring to when he uses the analogy of two sisters in chapter 23. Oholah is Samaria and Oholibah is Jerusalem (23:4). Samaria's sin is set out in 23:1–10, and Jerusalem's in 23:11–49. They are both accused of gross adultery. Adultery is more generally accepted today than in the past, even to the point of websites having been set up specifically for married people to engage in an illicit relationship with a stranger. According to a recent survey of one such website, 12% of those using its services claimed to be Christian.[2] But in the eyes of God adultery remains an evil and not merely a minor failing. It is a destructive act, tearing apart families, breaking hearts, decimating homes, and offending God. The marriage covenant is the only context that God recognises for the right enjoyment of sexual activity. We have seen all too often how infidelity within the marriage bond brings out the wrath of the offended person against

Adultery is more generally accepted today than in the past ... but in the eyes of God adultery remains an evil and not merely a minor failing.

their offending partner. This is the imagery that God uses to express the spiritual adultery of Jerusalem and Samaria. Such infidelity against God is self-destructive and brings upon one the wrath of God.[3]

Such spiritual infidelity is a constant danger to the church where worship is focussed more on meeting the desires and perceived needs of people than on declaring the unchanging character of God. But sexual promiscuity itself is also a constant danger to the church. Standards on sexual behaviour have certainly changed in society, and sadly this is too often reflected in the sexual activity of those who profess the name of Christ. We can turn a blind eye to sexual promiscuity. Our legitimate love of the sinner has eclipsed our hatred for the sin. But God challenges both sin and sinner. All Christians need to be serious about remaining in a close, life-transforming relationship with God, and turning their backs on the sinful ideologies and practices of those who deny the very existence of God. Calvin comments:

> The Lord sufficiently provided for us in this matter when he established marriage, the fellowship of which, begun on his authority, he also sanctified by his blessing. From this it is clear that any other union apart from marriage is accursed in his sight.[4]

The grace of God is sufficient to help us overcome all temptation—so it is paramount to maintain with vigour our relationship with the Lord. Furthermore, as Gill says, It is the duty of church-members to watch over one another; that they do not indulge to sinful lusts and pleasures, and make provision for the flesh, to fulfil the lust thereof; and so bring a reproach on the good ways of God, and the doctrines of Christ.[5]

The painful side of Christian leadership

As mentioned in the preamble to this chapter, Christian leadership is not all about pastors gently shepherding the flock of God. Much of the heartbreak that pastors face in going about their calling has to do with people who say they are Christians simply refusing to obey God's word. Not in everything of course. But too many Christians are picking and choosing the bits of God's word they want to obey. This means that Christian leaders are often called upon to confront those of God's children whose lives are simply incompatible with God's word. The problem is exacerbated if leaders themselves fail to live by God's standards.

We see this reflected in Ezekiel's latest message. The priests have not instructed the people of God as they should have done (22:26). As John Gill points out in his commentary on this verse, the priests have given a wrong explanation of God's word; they have twisted it to mean something it does not mean, and in so doing have taught and practised things that are actually contrary to it.[6] Those who should have been an example to others were among the worst offenders. Tragically some Christian leaders over the years have succumbed to the adulterous ways of our society and ripped apart families, damaged churches, and brought dishonour on the Lord's name in the process.

Ezekiel goes further: the prophets simply glossed over the false teaching of the priests and the extortion of the princes, with false proclamations (22:26–28). Instead of challenging the priests and princes about their behaviour, they became implicated in the sin. It is a sad day when church leaders turn their backs on God's truth. More than ever we need discerning leaders in the church who can recognise when an elder or pastor has misrepresented the word of God or is failing to live in accordance with it. The church also needs theologically literate church members. Unfortunately for Jerusalem not a single man could be found to stand up for God against the perversion of worship and the moral failings that were taking place there (22:30).

It was in addressing this sorry state of affairs that Ezekiel would experience the painful side leadership. When no one else seemed to care, Ezekiel is told to 'groan before them with broken heart and bitter grief' (21:6). He is to cry out aloud and wail for the judgement that the people are about to face (21:12). This was no mere display of acting skills. Ezekiel is to pronounce judgement on the city of Jerusalem (22:1); he is to confront the people with their sin (23:36). No preacher enjoys being the bearer of difficult messages. It is so much easier to encourage with kind words mixed with an acceptable level of humour. But some messages simply cannot be delivered in a light-hearted manner. Some messages involve the preacher digging deep into God-given resources and, in pain and anguish, delivering messages hard to bear.

Some messages involve the preacher digging deep into God-given resources and, in pain and anguish, delivering messages hard to bear.

In pointing out the authority delegated to a Christian leader John Owen states: 'His conversation is to be observed and diligently followed, so far as he walks in the steps of Jesus Christ.'[7] It is not the role of Christian leaders simply to encourage the people to change their ways, but rather point them to the God of all grace who alone can help them overcome sinful practices. Nothing short of God's servant speaking God's word to God's people in God's strength will suffice. God's people needed men of that calibre in Ezekiel's day, and the church needs pastors of that calibre today. Who will stand in the moral breach of our day? We need preachers who are faithful to the word of God, including the difficult parts, but who deliver that message with all tenderness and sympathy as those who have themselves experienced the tenderness and sympathy of the Saviour.

FOR FURTHER STUDY

1. Read Isa. 54:5; 62:5; Jer. 2:2; 3:14. What light do these passages shed on the strength of Ezekiel's message in this chapter?
2. The New Testament never explicitly says that the church is the bride of Christ. However, in Matt. 9:15; Mark 2:19–20; John 3:29; 2 Cor. 11:2; Rev. 19:7–9; Christ is referred to as the bridegroom. How do these passages show us the continuity between Old and New testaments and therefore how Ezekiel's message on spiritual adultery is as relevant today as it was in his day?
3. Read 2 Tim. 4:2. What does this verse teach us about the painful side of Christian leadership?
4. Read 1 Cor. 4:16; Heb. 13:7; 2 Thess. 3:7; Phil. 3:17; 1 Tim. 4:12; and 1 Pet. 5:3. What do these passages teach us about the nature and role of Christian leaders?

TO THINK ABOUT AND DISCUSS

1. God speaks of himself as a husband and a bridegroom of his people. What can we learn from this in terms of (i) our covenant obligations to God; and (ii) the covenant obligations within marriage?
2. Research found in *Christians Are Hate-Filled Hypocrites … and Other Lies You've Been Told*, shows that couples who are active in their faith are much less likely to divorce.[8] What do you think it means to be 'active' in your faith? What part does the word of God play in this and to what extent should it affect your lifestyle?
3. Sometimes pastors have difficult messages to preach. How can you encourage them in this task?
4. In Heb. 13:17 Christians are told to 'Obey your leaders and submit to them, for they are keeping watch over your souls, as those who will have to give an account. Let them do this with joy and not with groaning, for that would be of no advantage to you.' How might you apply this message in your church or your life personally? Why do you think some people resist this teaching? What if anything can leaders do to encourage such

obedience?

5. If you have access to *The Works of John Owen*, I encourage you to pick up Vol. 13 and read the relatively short chapter 'Eshcol, A Cluster of the Fruit of Canaan', and use it as the basis for discussion on the reciprocal duties and responsibilities of church members and their leaders.

13 The dangers of presumption

Ezekiel Chapter 24

God uses the message of the gospel to change lives. The power of the gospel does not depend on the messenger, yet the significance of the way in which the preacher himself engages with that message must not be underestimated. The people have been presuming on deliverance based on their history and the importance of the temple in Jerusalem, but the day has finally arrived when the King of Babylon lays siege the holy city. Ezekiel's personal life is to be an example of how the exiles should respond to the news. This is without doubt the toughest assignment the prophet is given.

In Bunyan's *Pilgrim's Progress*, immediately after having his burden removed at the cross, Christian comes upon three rather foolish pilgrims. He attempts to awaken them to the danger of their laid-back approach to their spiritual needs but is met with only more lethargy.[1] Although only one of the characters is called Presumption, all three are guilty of presuming on God's grace to see them through dangers without any effort on their part. In *Pilgrim's Progress: The Second Part* we read of Christiana (Pilgrim's wife) making her journey to the Celestial City:

> Now I saw still in my dream, That they [Christiana and company] went on until they were come to the place, that Simple, and Sloth, and Presumption, lay and slept in, when Christian went by on Pilgrimage: And behold they were hanged up in irons a little way off on the other side.
>
> Mercy. Then said Mercy to him that was their Guide and conductor, What are those three men? And for what are they hanged there?
>
> Great-heart. These three men were men of very bad qualities; they had no mind to be Pilgrims themselves, and whosoever they could they hinder'd; they were for sloth and folly themselves, and whosoever they could persuade with, they made so too; and taught them to presume that they should do well at last. They were asleep when Christian went by, and now you go by, they are hanged.[2]

True Christians are those who look to the cross and persevere in the faith.

Bunyan is making the point that their folly led to their eternal destruction, even though they were so close to the cross of Christ and the gospel. It is a warning for others not to make the same mistake. True Christians are those who look to the cross and persevere in the faith. These three individuals made the mistake of thinking that their nature after hearing the gospel could be just the same as before. It was enough for them to know of God's grace without acting upon that knowledge. Ezekiel's contemporaries were guilty of the same presumption.

In this chapter we are met with another very specific date (24:1). We are told that on this very day the final siege on Jerusalem begins (24:2). This is about four years and five months from Ezekiel's first prophecy.[3] Much has happened in the intervening years, and the exiles must have doubted this rather eccentric young prophet—who is still only about thirty-four years old. Despite all that Ezekiel has told them, they continued to presume that the God of their forefathers would not allow his people to be completely overrun by the Babylonians, that somehow they would be restored to Jerusalem and their precious temple. But the city and the temple, both symbolic of God's special presence among his people, have taken on an importance God never intended. The symbol had become more important than the reality, and 'formality had replaced authentic faith.'[4] So God speaks through his prophet once more, now with a finality that they cannot mistake. They can no longer continue in their unfounded presumptions.

Ezekiel chapter 24 divides clearly into two parts. Firstly the parable of the cooking pot; and secondly the record of the death of Ezekiel's young wife. Both sections highlight certain presumptions that God's people in Ezekiel's day were making, and God's response to them.

Presumptions about social position highlighted and condemned 24:1–14

In the parable of the cooking pot the presumption is that, as the last remaining inhabitants of Jerusalem, they were the privileged few whom God would never allow to fall to the Babylonians. Ezekiel again acts out the parable. He is told to put the cooking pot on the fire and pour water and pieces of meat into it. Indeed, it is to be the choice pieces and the best of the bones that are to go into the pot (24:3–5).

At first glance it seems a very positive and encouraging parable. It is making use of a well-known expression in Jewish culture at the time. The cooking pot represents Jerusalem, and the meat the people of God living there. The fact that Ezekiel is told to 'take the choicest one of the flock' (24:5a) seems to be a reference to the elite of Jerusalem society, the cream of the crop. You may remember that this same phrase was on the lips of the Jews themselves in Ezek. 11:3—'This city is the cauldron, and we are the meat'. Although strange to our ears, to the Israelites this was actually a proverb of encouragement. In effect it was saying that Jerusalem was a safe place to be. The fact of a solid cooking pot reflects the idea of Jerusalem's strength as a city, with the people, the new elite and hope of the nation, protected by its strong walls and fortifications. God, however, turns the parable on its head. God makes use of this common idea to highlight the mistaken ideas of the Jews, and to challenge their presumption. The cooking pot, the city, is not a safe place to be. In fact, this very day the siege ramps are being erected by the Babylonians which will lead to its downfall. It is now becoming a hot and dangerous place to be. Ezekiel is to represent this in his drama by taking the pot and placing it on the fire, placing the choice meat in it and stoking the fire to make it as hot as possible (24:5b). There even seems to be a deliberate increase in intensity in Ezekiel's drama as it unfolds. He is to heap the logs under it and bring it to the boil. The meaning is becoming more apparent. The 'bloody city … the pot …' is a clear reference to Jerusalem (24:6) and the 'corrosion' in it a reference to the pot's contents, that is, the meat or the residents. What a turnaround! They are no longer considered the choice meat, the cream of the crop. Yahweh says they are corrosive, destructive, and fit only to be cast out on the ground just as they have shed blood in their city (24:7).

Ezekiel is to take some of contents and throw it out. The direction given is very specific. He is not to pour it out on the ground where it could be swallowed up by the dust and dirt and quickly disappear. Rather, it is to be poured out on a rock where it will remain visible (24:7–8). This is to indicate the exposure of their sin. God wants what happens to them to be a perpetual reminder of how they have violated their sacred privileges. The King James Version renders 'corrosion' as 'scum' which is a helpful insight to what is happening here. The fire is to be stoked up again and now the pot, with presumably any remaining bits of meat and bone still in it, is to be heated to such an intensity that even the bones are consumed (24:9–10). But the heat of God's wrath against this people does not end there. The pot is again to be set on the coals with a view to burning off all the residue and corrosion, the scum that clings to the walls, as a final act of purification (24:11–14).

> God wants what happens to his people to be a perpetual reminder of how they have violated their sacred privileges.

God's holy city has been defiled by the sinful practices of its inhabitants and will therefore face the fires of purification. Indeed, they have already started. Nebuchadnezzar has that very day (24:1) laid siege to Jerusalem and the siege fires will soon be set against the city walls and gates. God had desired to cleanse his people. He desired their sincere repentance, but they would not be cleansed and turn from their sinful ways. Now God will punish them until he satisfies his anger. He will judge them in keeping with their own conduct and actions (24:14). They have been guilty of brazenly presuming upon their privileged social position and setting themselves above the holy, good, and pure law that God had given for their prosperity and spiritual health. In many quarters today God's law is again being dismissed as irrelevant. Those remaining in the city putting their hope in the great walls rather than in God did not stand a chance. The same is true of all who put their trust in the bricks and mortar of the church or in the institution itself. God will not be replaced even by such dedicated things. Our trust must be in God alone—and on his terms.

Our trust must be in God alone—and on his terms.

Presumptions about religious practice highlighted and condemned 24:15–27

This is surely amongst the saddest portions of the Bible. It tells us of the death of Ezekiel's wife. It is only from this passage that we even know that Ezekiel was married. She is described in the most beautiful terms—'the delight of his eyes' (24:16). With all the difficulties that Ezekiel has faced over the last four and a half years, one thing delighted him—his young wife. By now Ezekiel was about 34 years old, and his wife was probably even younger. Even though we know so little about her, what we do know paints a picture of a devoted and godly young wife. No doubt she was bewildered by the dramas of her husband's calling and yet she continued to support Ezekiel through it all, bringing delight to him during his traumatic ministry. She was the delight of his eyes and yet she is about to be taken by a sudden death made all the more difficult for Ezekiel because he knows it is coming but must not tell her (24:17–18). He is to continue with business as usual, and so we find that he spends time the next morning talking to the people, all the time knowing that every minute spent with them was a minute less to spend with the delight of his eyes whose time was all too painfully short.[5] Even after her death Ezekiel is to carry on as normal. He is not allowed to mourn her. This behaviour was clearly designed to make the people curious, to make them realise that it is a sign, and it worked. Eventually they come to Ezekiel (24:19) and ask what this sign means to them.

In keeping with Ezekiel's style throughout, we are not left to second-guess what this traumatic incident means. The delight of Ezekiel's eyes is taken as a sign to the people of Israel (24:24). The temple was everything to the Jews. It was the place of sacrifice, worship, and of God's special presence (although as we saw in chapter four God has already departed from the temple and Jerusalem). The temple in Jerusalem was the delight of their eyes and their heart's desire (24:21 and 25). God should have been the delight of their eyes and their heart's desire. Religion itself had become an idol to them and God was going to put an end to such idolatry. The death of Ezekiel's wife highlights the presumption that the temple and their unique relationship to it made them the privileged few whom God would never allow to fall to the Babylonians. Such presumption cannot go unchecked. God will take away the pride of their eyes and it will be confirmed in due course by a fugitive, one who escapes to bring the news to Ezekiel and the exiles. As Block says,

> To be sure, news of the loss of temple and city will shock the exiles and challenge all their theological presuppositions. But Ezekiel's relentless pronouncement of judgement had emphasized the need for the old order to be totally dismantled before the nation could be reconstituted.[6]

The purging has to come before God will dwell again among his people.

The presumption of generality

There is great comfort in the knowledge that we serve a loving and forgiving God. However, we should not presume upon the grace of God. This is the message that the Apostle Paul conveys in Romans 6:1ff. We should not assume that we can live as we please. It is presumption on God's grace to pick and choose what parts of God's Word to obey. It is dangerous to presume that God will always forgive us no matter how sinfully we live. This was the great mistake of the Israelites in Ezekiel's day. They presumed on God's grace on the basis that they had the right place of worship and the right religious system.

Another parallel in our day can be seen when formality or generality takes the place of an authentic faith. William Wilberforce recounts the same danger in his day noting that:

> There are many who satisfy themselves with what may be termed 'general Christianity.' They feel a general penitence and humiliation from a general sense of sinfulness and have general desires for holiness. Yet they neglect this vigilant and zealous care with which they should labour to destroy every particular form of corruption.[7]

Today there is widespread danger of people presuming they are automatically right with God because they are born into and live in a religious or even Christian environment. They attend or serve in a religious institution, whether mosque or church or temple and assume that they have built up enough credits with God to secure a safe passage into heaven, or paradise, or their religion's equivalent of paradise. This is the very mistake the people of God were making in Ezekiel's day. Living in a country that is rich in religious history is not enough. A mere profession of faith is not enough. True repentance leads to a holy and changed life because this is the work that God the Holy Spirit does in those that are his. Jesus himself taught us that not everyone who claimed to know him was actually saved. In Matt. 7:21 he says very clearly, 'Not everyone who says to me, "Lord, Lord," will enter the kingdom of heaven, but the one who does the will of my Father who is in heaven.' John Owen puts it like this,

> Today there is widespread danger of people presuming they are automatically right with God because they are born into and live in a religious or even Christian environment.

> Many, I say, the most of men who live under the dispensation [preaching] of the gospel, do woefully deceive their own souls in this matter. They do not believe what they profess themselves to believe, and what they think they believe.[8]

In other words, people make presumptions regarding their standing with God based on the general teaching of God's forgiveness. What they tend to ignore is personal application and how such forgiveness is made real to them. Mere attendance at a religious institution is not evidence of genuine salvation. These Jews had more religion than true faith. Indeed, their religious practices were probably the most disgusting thing in God's eyes. But there is hope with the Lord for all who truly put their trust in him. Therefore, as the psalmist says: 'Put your hope in the LORD! For with the LORD there is steadfast love, and with him is plentiful redemption.'[9]

Ezekiel on the other hand is the personification of godliness even under extreme personal pain. Thomas Murphy states that the pastor or preacher is appointed to be a living example of the gospel which he preaches.[10] If the people doubted Ezekiel because of his youth, then the example he sets his contemporaries by the Chebar canal in carrying out his ministerial duties in the face of such personal adversity must surely have made them take him more seriously. The same remains true for today. The significance of the preacher engaging personally with the message of the gospel of grace must not be underestimated. The godly life of the preacher is a visible sermon: he cannot be too diligent in cultivating his walk with God.[11]

FOR FURTHER STUDY

1. Read Psalm 5:5 and Romans 2:5. What bearing do these passages have on Ezekiel's message? What does this mean for us today?
2. Often Christians cite extenuating circumstances for living in a way that they know is not in keeping with God's word. What light does 1 Corinthians 10:6–13 shed on this line of reasoning?
3. Consider Romans 6:1–2. What connection does the Apostle Paul's teaching have with Ezekiel's?
4. Read John 3:16. What experiences does God share with his faithful servant Ezekiel?

TO THINK ABOUT AND DISCUSS

1. The Bible teaches that not all who profess the Christian faith are sure of heaven. Discuss the implications of this in the light of Matthew 7:21.
2. Many who profess faith fall away after a time. Why do you think this is the case? Is there anything we can be doing better to help such people?
3. Discuss the lesson John Bunyan is attempting to convey with his characters Simple, Sloth, and Presumption.

Judgement against the nations

14 Schadenfreude

Ezekiel Chapters 25–32

Chapters 25–32 bring a welcome change for the exiles as the spotlight of God's judgement is redirected from them to the nations around them. Indeed, the message of judgement against Israel's enemies is not just a welcome change but a sign of hope for the people of God.

'The name's Bond, James Bond.' So runs the now infamous punch-line from the films based on Ian Fleming's 007 series. Bond is renowned for getting himself into a bit of a pickle and then, almost miraculously, finding a way of escape. One of the hallmarks of Bond films is the obligatory Bond villain laughing with sinister glee at 007's latest dilemma. Who can forget the boyish grin of Jaws as he takes delight in Bond's discomfort and distress? There is just something about seeing our intrepid hero in a seemingly inescapable death-trap that evokes a maniacal laugh from his enemy, and the films just would not be the same if the villains did not get so much enjoyment out of their roguish endeavours.

Schadenfreude is one of those words adopted into the

English language because of its precision. The word literally means 'harm-joy' and in practice it refers to the pleasure derived by someone from another person's misfortune. But why is it that we secretly smile at the misfortunes of others? Well, according to Live Science,[1] researchers suggest that it is a way of making you feel better about yourself. 'If somebody enjoys the misfortune of others, then there is something in that misfortune that is good for the person.'[2] This sums up the attitude of Israel's enemies, watching on from the sidelines as Jerusalem faces its fall from grandeur. Twice in this section Ezekiel is told to prophesy against a nation because they said 'Aha!' in a scoffing tone. Once is when the temple in Jerusalem was profaned (25:3), and the other was in delight when the gate of the city was broken down (26:2). As we will see there are more incidents of taking pleasure over Israel's demise as the various enemies see an opportunity for themselves in her misfortune.

The sins of the nations 25–32

There is a very definite shift in focus in these chapters, from the fall of Jerusalem to God's judgement against her neighbours. However, 'The reasons for judgement are similar (social sins, hubris, etc.), the divine punishment is the same (the curses against Judah are turned against Judah's enemies), the vocabulary and tone are similar, and the forms are the same.'[3] Because of these similarities I will not deal with the judgements against the nations to the same extent that I have dealt with those against Israel. Rather I will attempt to give a general overview of these chapters, and try to bring some practical observations. The fugitive re-emerges right at the end of this section, in 33:21, eight chapters after his first mention in 24:26.[4] Notice that we have to wait eight chapters before we read again of one who escaped the siege of Jerusalem to bring news of the city's fall. In the meantime the focus is on Israel's neighbours.

As we shall consider later, these prophecies about the destruction of the nations were by implication positive messages for Israel, in that they indicated hope of eventual deliverance. But why are the nations to be judged?

> Prophecies about the destruction of the nations were by implication positive messages for Israel, in that they indicated hope of eventual deliverance.

These prophecies against the nations come around the time of Jerusalem's final collapse. They take issue with the tendency of Jerusalem's neighbours to gloat at her difficulties. The nations addressed are Moab and Ammon to the east, Edom and Philistia to the south, Tyre and Sidon to the north on the coast, and finally Egypt to the far south. Ezekiel predicts their downfall with a glimmer of hope for Egypt (29:13). Egypt will enjoy some recovery, but never to its former glory. Ezekiel does not prophesy against Babylon. Instead Babylon is portrayed as the instrument of divine wrath 'doing God's work and punishing his foes'.[5]

Ammon 25:1–7

Ammon is guilty of scoffing at Israel and rejoicing at her misfortunes (25:3, 6). The Ammonites were descended from Lot, the nephew of Abraham, and so were related to the Israelites but the relationship was stormy to say the least. In fact, the Ammonites were part of the army of Nebuchadnezzar that went up against the puppet king Jehoiakim when he rebelled against Nebuchadnezzar and sought an alliance with Egypt (2 Ki. 24:1–2). It is not difficult to imagine the Ammonites clapping their hands and stamping their feet in joy at the demise of their old rival (25:4). But God will not allow such gloating. In response we are told that God will stretch forth his hand against them and hand them over as plunder to other nations (25:7).

Moab and Seir 25:8–11

Moab and Seir are charged with 'denying Judah's special status among the nations'.[6] The Moabites too were descended from Lot. They resisted the arrival of the Israelites when they were entering the Promised Land (Num. 22–25), and so they too had a stormy relationship with Israel. Moab had been subdued by Saul (1 Sam. 14:47), but it was under King David that it was completely subjugated (2 Sam. 8:2)—ironic when you consider that the Moabite king had protected David during the time he was persecuted by Saul (1 Sam. 2:3). The chief deity of Moab was Chemosh, but they also worshipped Baal like the nations around them. Occasionally they offered their deities human sacrifices (2 Ki. 3:27). Bearing in mind Israel's condemnation for practicing idolatry and human sacrifice (16:15–34), and that it has come under the rule of Babylon, it seems that in saying 'the house of Judah is like all the other nations' (24:8) the Moabites were making two points about Israel: firstly their religious practice, and secondly their sovereign status. As we have already seen throughout Ezekiel, God's people were compromising their religion by their involvement in the idolatrous practices which they had adopted from neighbouring religions. The twin themes of religious practice and sovereign status converge in the implication that Yahweh was unable to deliver his people from their enemies. You can almost imagine the Moabites scoffing. If Yahweh is so great why do the Israelites need their idols? And why did not he protect his people? In scoffing at Judah the Moabites are scoffing God himself.

Many churches are becoming increasingly like the social contexts in which they witness. This often reflects the emergent church movement which looks for new ways of 'doing church'. The emphasis of such churches on exploring new ways to reach our generation is commendable and is something we can learn from. But when it comes to new interpretations of the gospel and the denial of biblical truth in favour of an individual's opinion then we must draw the line. The emergent church idea of mission is often not to tell people that salvation is found in Jesus alone, but to emphasise good works with a view to improving life for all in society. The problem with this is that it does not lead to what the Bible sets out as salvation. Such groups reject the idea of God's judgement in favour of a view that God will save everyone anyway. Experience is considered more important than doctrine. Biblical truth is no longer the touchstone for what they believe. In fact, truth and meaning are experienced rather than known. The result is that people can pretty much live as they please—even if that means living contrary to God's Word—and still be active in the church programme. Church is in danger of becoming indistinguishable from any

The church should never so embrace the culture in which it operates that the truth about how we are to live to please God is simply ignored.

other social group. Of course the church should welcome everyone and endeavour to understand the people it is trying to reach. At the same time, the church should never so embrace the culture in which it operates that the truth about how we are to live to please God is simply ignored. In Ezekiel's day the ungodly could say 'Look, Judah has become like all the other nations' (25:8), and today much of the church could come under the same scoffing tone from society at large.

Edom and Philistia 25:12–14 and 25:15–17

Vengefulness is the sin of both Edom and Philistia. A sibling rivalry that began between Jacob and Esau had continued down through the generations to their descendants Israel and Edom. Edom continued to look for opportunities to benefit from Judah's misfortune. According to Obadiah the Edomites helped the armies of Nebuchadnezzar by ambushing those citizens of Jerusalem who managed to flee the besieged city. Their exploitation of the oppressed Judeans is referred to in Psalm 137. According to 2 Chronicles 28:17, the Edomites also took advantage of Jerusalem's preoccupation with Nebuchadnezzar's siege on the city by raiding southern parts of Judah. They exploited Jerusalem's time of crisis by reclaiming the land and carrying off the spoil. It is entirely possible that in return for helping Nebuchadnezzar they were permitted to settle in parts of southern Israel. All of this is described by Ezekiel as acts of revenge or vengefulness. He tells us that the lands they have taken will be retaken by Israel, and that Edom would know that this was God's vengeance upon them for taking advantage of his people in their moment of weakness (25:14).

Originally from the islands of the Aegean Sea, the Philistines settled along the coastal area west of Israel, modern day Palestine. Time and again they appear in the Bible as Israel's main enemy. They too are accused of acting vengefully against Judah at a time of their weakness and, just like Edom, God will execute great vengeance upon them in return (25:17). As Derek Thomas points out, 'Vengeance, while proper in God as the reflex of his holy nature towards sin, is forbidden in man' (Rom. 12:9).[7]

Both Edom and Philistia are guilty of taking advantage of the misfortunes of another. We see this today in so many walks of life. Exploitation of the poor in sweatshops or grossly underpaid jobs so that we can fill our shops with cheap goods which in most cases we do not even need. At the time of writing it is estimated that there are more than 200 million children employed as child labourers, 73 million of whom are below 10 years old. They are thus deprived of a decent education and any hope of a better future.[8] Young men and women from deprived parts of the world are lured into a life of modern slavery. Refugees are exploited for financial gain as they flee war-torn homelands. Whilst it is God's prerogative to take vengeance on those who perpetrate such crimes, it is the duty of us all to do what we can and to support governments to eradicate such exploitation of the poor.

Tyre and Sidon 26:1–28:23[9]

Tyre is guilty of economic greed in taking advantage of Judah's downfall. Tyre was built with one part on the Mediterranean coast and another part on an offshore island. It is described as a fortified city in Joshua 19:29, defended by a 150-foot high wall on the coast side. An ancient city, Tyre was an established seaport and one of the foremost traders of the ancient Near East. It was renowned for its prosperity and trading with other nations going by sea as far as Britain to the west and Asia to the east. They no doubt had as much as any city or people really needed for a very comfortable lifestyle. But they obviously wanted more. 'Aha!' Tyre cheered, when they got the news of Jerusalem, exclaiming, 'Good! The gateway city is smashed! Now all her business comes my way. She's in ruins and I am in clover'(26:2).[10] Yet again we see the exploitation of Israel's difficulties, but in this instance for trading and economic gain. Such glee will be short-lived. But Tyre's sin goes beyond greed and glee. The prince of Tyre is accused of pride and blasphemy (28:2). It is easy to imagine the prince of Tyre sitting on his island-city amidst all the beauty and splendour of his palace, in the middle of the sun-kissed blue waters of the Mediterranean, and seeing it as a picture of heaven. But to claim 'I am a god, I sit in the seat of the gods' is to dethrone Yahweh the God of all creation. Therefore, Yahweh says that he will bring 'the most ruthless of nations' against her (28:2). God will bring many nations against Tyre and she will be reduced to a bare rock (26:4). That is quite a comedown for a city that was established on a coastal island! Tyre subsequently came under thirteen years of siege by the Babylonians after which some sort of agreement was reached. But Tyre was finally and totally subjugated by Alexander the Great after a six-month siege in 332 BC.[11]

Some people's appetite for wealth and personal gain is insatiable. And whilst some wealthy people use their wealth for the good of others, yet sadly too many others exploit the poor and weak. Avarice, the love of money, is one of the seven deadly sins (Proverbs 6:16–19) and comes under the judgement of God. Tyre is an example to all who would exploit the poor for personal gain. Whether Mafia extortion or corporate bullying, everyone who takes advantage of the misfortune of others will one day face the Judge of all the earth. History has shown that the fall from prominence can come suddenly.

> Avarice, the love of money, is one of the seven deadly sins and comes under the judgement of God.

We are not told what Sidon's crime against Judah was. However, as another major trading city in the region and closely associated with Tyre, it may be that they too were guilty of the same sinful opportunism in the event of Jerusalem's demise.[12] This may be borne out by the fact that Ezekiel moves from his attack on Tyre straight into his attack on Sidon.[13] Whatever the sin, they too will face God's righteous judgement and God's glory and holiness will be made known to and through her.

Whoever mocks the poor insults his Maker

All of the nations mentioned thus far were guilty of

schadenfreude, looking on gleefully as Judah suffered its final humiliating and traumatic defeat at the hands of the Babylonians. But God will remove these thorns in the flesh; and they will be left in no doubt that it is Yahweh meting out his punishment against them (28:24). God will not allow such heartless contempt to go unpunished. In Proverbs 17:5 we read, 'Whoever mocks the poor insults his Maker; he who is glad at calamity will not go unpunished.' God is punishing Israel, but he will not stand idly by and watch as others mock them in their distress. Instead of scoffing, the other nations should have reflected on their own behaviour. In God's economy the one who takes delight in the misfortune of another is actually insulting God! Such mockers will find their mockery turned back on themselves. As Block points out, 'For those who rejoice over the demise of God's people and mock them, there is no mercy.'[14]

God's correction is always an act of fatherly love with the aim that his children will realise the harm they are doing to themselves and potentially others in leading them astray.

God disciplines and chastises those whom he loves (Heb. 12:6). Such discipline is not so that others can make fun of the one afflicted but rather so that we learn from the example, that we might strive for peace with everyone and for the holiness without which no one will see the Lord (Heb. 12:14). In seeing the heavy hand of God's discipline upon Jerusalem, the nations should have sought their well-being and restoration and examined themselves. They did not do this and so suffered the same punishment. God's correction is always an act of fatherly love with the aim that his children will realise the harm they are doing to themselves and potentially others in leading them astray. It is designed to encourage them to turn back to the loving embrace of their heavenly father. As Eric Lane points out,

> Someone of a contemptuous spirit is likely to take a 'serve you right' attitude to misfortune. But as Jesus warned and Paul after him, we are judged by the criteria with which we judge others (Matt. 7:1f., Rom. 2:1–4). In the Old Testament nations which gloated over Israel's downfall were warned of their own impending overthrow (Ezek. 25, Obad. v.12). The New Testament is if anything more severe, saying that if material want does not arouse our pity and practical help then we ourselves are outside the love of God (1 John 3:17).[15]

Egypt 29:1–32:32

Ezekiel now turns his attention to Egypt, accusing her of taking and ascribing to herself what belongs to God. The date suggests that the siege of Jerusalem had been going on now for almost a year (29:1).[16] Egypt's blasphemy takes the form of claiming credit for the creation of the longest river in the world! Pharaoh King of Egypt boasts, 'My Nile is my own; I made it for myself', (29:3). The background to this arrogance is the Egyptian canal system. The Nile had been spread out across the plains of Egypt by an elaborate system of canals which meant that the plains were well watered. This meant that Egypt could manage its agriculture on very little rain. It was a great achievement of industry and ingenuity. But Pharaoh oversteps the mark by claiming to be the creator of the Nile itself. The Nile was a part of God's good creation and in claiming to have made it the Egyptians were claiming for themselves what belonged to God—that is, the glory of creation. Such blasphemy will not go unchallenged. We are told just over sixteen years later (29:17) that God is going to give the land of Egypt to Nebuchadnezzar. This is in part because Tyre never fully capitulated to the Babylonian king. The siege of Tyre was so long and exhausting, we are told, that the head and shoulder of every soldier was rubbed bare by the effort (29:18–19). And so in effect Egypt is given to Nebuchadnezzar in remuneration for his expenses on such a long and costly undertaking on God's behalf (29:20).[17] If the inhabitants of Jerusalem were holding out the hope that the strong arm of Egypt might still come to their rescue (remember Zedekiah's failed alliance with Egypt), then they are in for a final heart-rending disappointment. The arms that Jerusalem hopes will save them will be broken and the arms of their assailant strengthened to do God's work (30:21–26). Proud Egypt will be scattered among the nations and Pharaoh slain. God is sovereign over the nations and can, when he chooses, use even an ungodly nation such as Babylon to serve his purposes.

> In a day when Christians are apt to confine God to purely personal issues, we need to regain the cosmic perspective of the prophets as they speak of the Lord of the Universe intimately involved in the international issues of the day. There is not an item of news that the Lord is not involved in.[18]

Every event in the course of history is under God's sovereign control. Power in itself is not sinful. It is the abuse of power that God takes issue with. Whether on the international stage, or in the sweatshops of modern slavery, God will judge both injustice and schadenfreude.

The golden nugget of hope 28:24–26

In the midst of these eight chapters of judgement against the nations, God has Ezekiel insert a little nugget of hope just three verses long. Commenting on 28:24–26 Chris Wright gives this concise summary: 'They [these verses] make clear that the purpose of the surrounding oracles against the nations is indeed to provide "a backhanded message of hope" for Israel. Yahweh's action against their enemies will ultimately mean that their own fate will be secure, in spite of the catastrophe happening at the very time the oracles were delivered.'[19] Given their circumstances, all hope must now surely be fading for the exiles. As they sat there by the Chebar canal and listened to Ezekiel's words, and as news eventually filtered through to them about the destruction of their sacred city, it must have been hard to believe that any good could come from such disaster.

> Often it is when people finally give up all hope in human agents to rescue them that they realise God is there for them—and always has been.

Often it is when people finally give up all hope in human agents to rescue them that they realise God is there for them—and always has been. The apostle Paul talks of a near death experience that affected him deeply in his second letter to the Corinthian church (2 Cor. 1:8–11). He saw this as necessary to make him rely more on God. It would seem that Paul was in such grave danger that he was sure he would die and that any hope in human deliverance was vain. All he could do was cast himself upon God who alone had the power to save him. The effect of Paul's near-death experience was that he put total confidence in God for this life and the next.

It may seem a little morbid perhaps, but we all need to contemplate the idea of impending death as a way of focussing our minds on what is truly essential in life. If you knew that your time was up tomorrow, how would that affect your relationship with God? We do not have to look far to see broken people floundering with a desperate sense of hopelessness. Sometimes we need to be brought to an end of ourselves, running out of hope, sapped of every ounce of energy and strength, to realise that all along God has been there for us. God alone gives us true hope and dignity. All human power is transient. Nations rise and fall. Military strength can and does fail. Economic dependence will let us down. If we put our trust for the future in any of these things, we are in for disappointment and even despair. The only hope for humanity, whether at an international or personal level, whether for the children of God or the unsaved, lies in cultivating a deep and daily relationship with the crucified Saviour.

There is a hope that burns within my heart,
That gives me strength for every passing day;
A glimpse of glory now revealed in meagre part,
Yet drives all doubt away:
I stand in Christ, with sins forgiven;
And Christ in me, the hope of heaven!

My highest calling and my deepest joy,
To make His will my home.
There is a hope that lifts my weary head,
A consolation strong against despair,
That when the world has plunged me in its deepest pit,
I find the Saviour there!
Through present sufferings, future's fear,
He whispers 'courage' in my ear.
For I am safe in everlasting arms,
And they will lead me home.
There is a hope that stands the test of time,
That lifts my eyes beyond the beckoning grave,
To see the matchless beauty of a day divine
When I behold His face!
When sufferings cease and sorrows die,
And every longing satisfied.
Then joy unspeakable will flood my soul,
For I am truly home.[20]
(© 2007 Thankyou Music)

For further study ▶

FOR FURTHER STUDY

1. Read Proverbs 17:5 and 1 John 3:17. What do these verses teach us about schadenfreude? How are we to respond to the poor both at home and abroad? How does this verse impact upon the refugee crises that all too often arise out of war-torn nations?
2. According to Matthew 7:1–5 and Romans 2:1–4 on what basis can we point out sinful practice in another, if at all?
3. In 2 Corinthians 1:8–11 the Apostle Paul recounts a near death experience. In what ways did Paul's theology bring him hope in such a difficult situation? How important is theology to you?

TO THINK ABOUT AND DISCUSS

1. It is the abuse of power that God takes issue with. Discuss this phrase in the light of the history of the church. How can we avoid the mistakes of the past?
2. 'Vengeance is mine' says the Lord. This expression implies that it is improper for people to interfere in something that belongs to God. How does this apply when we become angry at something or someone who hurts us personally; or when we become indignant at the atrocities we see happening in our world? How can we properly respond to such events?
3. We are not to judge others according to Jesus in Matt. 7:1–5. Yet, when God's standards are being rejected he clearly expects us to do something about it. How can we keep these two things in balance? What Scripture can you use to support your conclusions?
4. How can we make the church a more welcoming place for the un-churched without becoming just another social group?

Hope and restoration

15 The watchman

Ezekiel Chapter 33

God wants people to live! This is a foundational message of Ezekiel to his contemporaries and the greatest hope for any generation. But people tend to hear only what they want to hear. For the past seven years the people have been in Ezekiel's presence and heard what he has to say. But still they are not listening. The watchman's responsibilities only extend as far as being faithful to what God tells him to say. Everyone will be held accountable for what they do with that message.

Chapter 33 is a turning point in Ezekiel's ministry. Prior to this God had chosen Ezekiel as a watchman to show Israel her sin, to proclaim judgement against their idolatry. He has time and again told the people about the impending destruction of Jerusalem and the dispersion of the people who still lived there. You may recall that in 3:27 Ezekiel is 'commanded to be silent except when Yahweh gave him something explicit to say.'[1] Perhaps the idea behind this intermittent dumbness is to give the exiles time for the message to sink in? As we have seen in the last chapter, the exiles have also had a break from Ezekiel pronouncing judgement on Judah. Instead his time had been taken up declaring God's judgement against the nations around them. Now, his attention is turned once again to the fate of Jerusalem. In this chapter we will see that once Jerusalem has finally fallen Ezekiel is allowed to break the rule on temporary silence (33:21–22). He still has to remind the people to abandon all false hopes (e.g. 33:23–29), yet from this point forward his prophetic ministry is predominantly one of hope—the true hope which can come only after false hopes have been exposed and cast aside. This is the renewed ministry to which Ezekiel is called.

Ezekiel's faithfulness as God's watchman 33:1–9

In ancient times, watchmen stood guard on a city's walls to see to the welfare of its citizens and to warn of coming trouble. Their role was to watch out for any approaching danger and warn the people in good time so that they could all enter the city and close the gates against the enemy. It was a simple enough job but one that carried great responsibility. If the watchman is diligent and warns the people in good time, he will have fulfilled his responsibility (33:1–5). If he fails to warn the people, he will be held accountable for their deaths (33:6). This is applied to Ezekiel in spiritual terms. As the watchman of Israel appointed by God he has a duty to warn the people of the approaching judgement (33:7–9). Just like the city watchman, if Ezekiel fails to warn the people he will be held accountable for their deaths. But if he fulfils his duty and warns the people of the dangers of ignoring God's judgement, then he is free of all guilt and the people are held responsible for their own action or inaction. We already know of course that Ezekiel has been faithful for the past seven years in warning the people. This has been the focus of the book to date. You may recall that the language of the watchman was used in Ezekiel's earlier call to ministry where the wording is almost identical (3:17–19). This reminder of Ezekiel's pastoral role comes at the time when news of Jerusalem's collapse reaches the exiles in Babylon (33:21). With this news false hopes are dashed but true hope is once again held out to the people.

Yahweh's way to life clearly explained 33:10–16

At some point the people have come to Ezekiel with what seems like a heartfelt lament. They may be referring to something Ezekiel had said previously, '… but you shall rot away in your iniquities and groan to one another …' (24:23). Having had some time to consider the prophet's words the people now come back to him with their concerns. 'Surely our transgressions and our sins are upon us, and we rot away because of them. How then can we live?' (33:10). Ezekiel has recognised the sin of the people for a long time and now it appears that the people are finally seeing it for themselves. But is this evidence of genuine repentance? Or is it nothing more than a manipulative cry of pain?[2] The answer to that can be seen in what the people do with God's offer of life. Before we come to that, we see God's impassioned response to their cry of despair. He reaches out with an unequivocal message of hope. He tells them clearly how they can live! 'As I live, declares the LORD God, I have no pleasure in the death of the wicked, but that the wicked turn from his way and live; turn back, turn back from your evil ways, for why will you die O house of Israel?' (33:11).

Repentance is the key 33:11

God wants people to live! All they have to do is repent. That is, turn from their sins, and turn to God for forgiveness. The God of all grace is reaching out to the exiles through his chosen watchman with a message of hope and reconciliation. As Peter Jeffery comments,

> The sinner's only hope of forgiveness and salvation rests exclusively in the grace of God. Prayer, faith and repentance would be of no use to us if God were not merciful. It was this mercy and grace that was responsible for Ezekiel's presence in Babylon. The God of the Old Testament is as full of grace as the God of the New Testament, and that is because he is the same God. Grace runs throughout all of God's dealings with mankind.[3]

Despite the fact that sin leads to death, death is needless and certainly not inevitable! '

The exiles despair that because of their sin they are without hope, rotting away and dying. God's response is a heartening appeal—repent! Despite the fact that sin leads to death (see also Rom. 6:16), death is needless and certainly not inevitable! 'Why will you die?' God implores the people, as he goes on to set out clearly his gospel of grace.

Personal works of righteousness do not save us 33:12–13

The first thing the people need to understand about this grace of God is that it cannot be earned by their own righteousness. 'The righteousness of the righteous shall not deliver him when he transgresses' (33:12). Notice it is not a matter of if he transgresses but when. The Apostle Paul emphasises this in his letter to the Romans. 'For all have sinned and fall short of the glory of God', (Rom. 3:23). Again, writing to Titus, the Apostle makes it clear that God does not save us because of 'works done by us in righteousness, but according to his own mercy, by the washing of regeneration and renewal of the Holy Spirit' (Titus 3:5). God's plan of salvation in both the Old and New Testaments was never based on our good works. If people could have been saved under their own steam then we would have no need of a Saviour. But the Bible is clear. It is a fundamental principle of the gospel that our good works contribute nothing to our salvation. God accepts us when we repent of our sin and accept by faith the merits of Christ's righteousness and atoning death on the cross (1 Cor. 1:30).

If people could have been saved under their own steam then we would have no need of a Saviour.

A lifetime of sin does not exclude us from salvation 33:14–16

Having removed the crutch of personal righteousness, God now addresses those who think that they are without hope because of their many sins.

> Again, though I say to the wicked, 'You shall surely die,' yet if he turns from his sin and does what is just and right ... and walks in the statutes of life, not doing injustice, he shall surely live; he shall not die (33:14–15).

Block notes that 'Speaking for Yahweh ... Ezekiel affirms that one's end is not determined by how one begins the race, by how one ends it'.[4] The thief on the cross is perhaps the most poignant example of someone who fits into this category. A W Pink writes, 'The dying thief had no good works either before or after conversion. Hence we are shut up to the conclusion that if saved at all he was certainly saved by sovereign grace'.[5] Good works then, before or after conversion, are ruled out as contributing anything to our salvation. And yet God states clearly that the repentant sinner should walk in 'the statutes of life' (33:15): not a contribution to their salvation but a mark of it. As the Apostle Paul argues so clearly, we are not saved by good works, but we are saved to perform good works (Eph. 2:8–10).

The wonderful news is that no one is excluded from God's life-giving grace. Repentance is a realization of our lost condition and our hopelessness to do anything about it. Only when we are brought to see our total inability to do anything for ourselves will we run to the one who alone can save us. But when we do that, the staggering news is that years of sin can be washed away in an instant! False hopes must be killed off so that true hope can take root and flourish. Salvation comes from God, but the people are personally accountable to respond to God's gracious offer and accept it. Douglas Stuart writes, 'A conversion even after a long life of evil in this world can produce eternal life with the Lord. What a promise to a people long debilitated by their sin! What a hope, indeed, guaranteed to everyone who hears the words of God and responds to them!'[6]

The people's superficiality exposed 33:17–33

Evasive discussions are common 33:17

Despite God's gracious appeal to save the people, they prefer to cling to their sin and excuses! 'Yet your people say, "The way of the LORD is not just"' (33:17, 20). This highlights the shallowness of their concern. Death can be averted by the simple act of repentance. But instead of listening to God's offer of life, they continue to make excuses and change the subject. How many conversations with the unsaved have taken a similar turn? There is a very important lesson here for the church. The gospel message is very simple. It is an act of repentance and faith. It is believing that what God says is true. God offers life to all who will simply turn away from sin and devote themselves to his way. But still people find excuses to cling to their sin. People will discuss all aspects of theology but ignore the offer of life!

Personal accountability is avoided 33:18–20

The people claim God's way is not just (33:17, 20), but God responds by pointing out that he judges men according to the way they choose to live (33:18–20). Many in our day live as they please without any thought for God. Yet, like the exiles in Ezekiel's day, they still want to pin the blame on God for the condition of the world and their own spiritual bankruptcy. 'You made me the way I am! Why did you allow this to happen? If God can do something about this, and does not, then he is unfair!' God's reply to these claims is to say that he has done something about the situation. He has provided a very simple solution to your sinful condition. All you have to do is repent and turn from your wicked ways and you can have life. 'I will judge each of you according to his ways' (33:20). How can it be unjust to treat each person in the way they deserve? The onus is upon the individual to accept God's offer. God makes no secret of the way that a person can be saved. There is no secret to how society can be transformed for the better, one person at a time. But each one is personally responsible to take up God's gracious offer. It is a simple case of taking God at his word, yet many prefer to remain just as they are (John 3:16–19). The one who depends for salvation on God alone no longer seeks to promote his own selfish interests but becomes wrapped up in promoting the glory of God in his day to day life. Where this has happened on a large scale in the past, society has been transformed for the better.[7]

The one who depends for salvation on God alone no longer seeks to promote his own selfish interests but becomes wrapped up in promoting the glory of God in his day to day life.

Self-interest is pervasive 33:23–29

Unfortunately some, despite their apparent interest in theology, are not quite ready to give up on their own selfish interests and hopes of returning to Jerusalem. The prevailing mindset of those who remained in the waste places (parts of Judah devastated by the Babylonian army) is very similar to what we have come across previously. It comes in the form of yet another popular expression, 'Abraham was only one man, yet he got possession of the land; but we are many; the land is surely given to us to possess' (33:24). Despite everything, these individuals see opportunity for personal gain rather than accepting personal responsibility. They are the new self-proclaimed cream of the crop! They consider themselves more deserving than Abraham, to whom the land was originally promised. God challenges their territorial claims and dashes their false hopes. Rather than inherit the land they too will fall by the sword. The very mountains of Israel shall be made desolate because of their sinful practices (33:27–29).

Superficial interest in the things of God is exposed 33:30–33

Throughout his years of ministry Ezekiel was certainly stirring up interest among the people. Whether leaning up against a wall or standing in their doorways, people were talking about Ezekiel. They were even going so far as to encourage one another to trundle along to hear what he had to say next (33:30). There is a picture here of a people eager to learn from a great teacher. As they sat before Ezekiel they had all the outward appearances of

> The perennial problem for any preacher is that people seem to listen well but do not put the message into practice.

those who were genuinely interested in hearing the word of God. But there is a problem. 'Their heart is set on their gain ... they hear what you say, but they will not do it' (33:31–32). The perennial problem for any preacher is that people seem to listen well but do not put the message into practice. Or, they speak well of the things of God, but their hearts remain unchanged. The people are showing an interest in hearing the word of God but all the while they refuse to take seriously its claims upon their lives.

How many are there sitting in our churches today, eyes fixed on the preacher, ears attuned to what he has to say, but walk out of the meeting totally unchanged? James tells us that it is not simply a matter of hearing the word but of putting it into practice (James 1:22–27). It is not enough to be punctual in attending church and to listen respectfully to the preacher. There are those who imagine that this is all that is required of them. Sincere and true faith is known not by keenly listening, but by firm resolve to put into practice what is learned.

God's servants are not called to success but to faithfulness

Ezekiel is proven as a true prophet of God as his prophecies against Jerusalem finally come to pass. The fugitive of chapter 24 has at last brought the news that the city has fallen to the Babylonian army. The last seven years of his ministry are now vindicated. All the scorn that was no doubt heaped upon him for his seemingly eccentric ways should now abate as the people recognise the seriousness of their plight. Or so one would hope. But even if the people still are not listening, he will not give up. He will continue to minister to the deep needs of his people, not in spite of but because of their unremitting failures. He knows that despite their superficiality God takes no pleasure in the death of the wicked. God persists in extending his grace to them and shows them in simple terms the way of salvation.

Ezekiel has faithfully served as Israel's watchman despite the great cost to himself. For years he faced ridicule, and even now the people are showing at best a superficial interest in his preaching. But he remains steadfast in telling the people what they need to hear, as opposed what they want to hear. There is a very clear and simple lesson in this for the church today. Robert Reymond states it in this way:

> Not only should we preach to the lost world; we should also take seriously, as did Paul, the 'watchman' principle of Ezekiel 33:7–9. Apply it to our mission labours today, and faithfully declare the whole counsel of God to Christ's church (Acts 20:27), rebuking her for her sin and warning her against apostasy, and doing so regardless of the cost to our physical safety, our reputations, and our earthly fortunes.[8]

FOR FURTHER STUDY

1. Read 2 Kings 9:17–18. What do these verses teach us about the role of a watchman in the Old Testament?

2. What light does Psalm 127 shed on the role of a watchman?

3. What can we learn from Nehemiah 4:9 in relation to watching out for the safety of others?

4. If we are saved by grace (Eph. 2:8), what does James 1:22–27 teach us about the nature of our salvation?

5. The Apostle Paul, in 2 Corinthians 5:20, teaches us that all Christians are ambassadors for Christ. What parallels can you see between the role of ambassador and watchman? What differences can you see?

TO THINK ABOUT AND DISCUSS

1. What is the nature of God's gospel of grace? What light do the following verses shed upon God's plan of salvation? Romans 3:23, 1 Corinthians 1:3, Titus 3:5.

2. The obligation that Ezekiel had to warn the people to repent and believe is an obligation that every Christian has. Discuss this statement.

3. 'I will judge each of you according to his ways' (Ezek. 33:20). How are we to understand this statement in the light of Ephesians 2:8–10?

4. How should we measure success in the church? What tangible evidence can we look for? What passages of Scripture can you point to in support of your views?

16 The King of love my Shepherd is

Ezekiel Chapter 34

People take advantage of others in every generation. But God is about to shine the spotlight on such behaviour and demonstrate his great love for his people by being their Shepherd. In time God will provide his people with a leader who will unite them as never before, and establish a covenant of peace that embraces the welfare of the whole of his creation. It will ensure a peace and harmony that has not been known since the Garden of Eden.

In every generation, and at every level, leaders have all too often failed in their duty of care to those under their authority. There have been self-seeking, greedy, power-hungry individuals who have taken advantage of those they were supposed to care for and protect. History is strewn with examples. Self-serving leaders crave power and position. They abuse that power and position to build themselves up and tear others down. They are driven to win over others and use them for their own ends. Their sense of self-worth is tied to being in charge and acquiring more power, money, and material things. Little thought is given to caring for those under them. Ezekiel now moves from Israel's faithful watchman in chapter 33 to the other end of the spectrum, and then on to the glorious truth of the Good Shepherd.

God's indignation of the abuse of power 34:1–10

In the opening verses of this chapter our faithful watchman is to pronounce God's displeasure against the shepherds of Israel (34:2, 10). Although the term shepherds relates to the kings of Israel who have failed miserably to protect the people under their charge[1] there is no doubt that besides rejecting the monarchy, God is not well pleased with others who abuse their leadership roles. The kings have certainly failed to rule with integrity, but the religious leaders have failed morally and spiritually, and the magistrates, civil servants, and almost all in positions of authority in Israel have served their own greed rather than the people's needs. So whilst the monarchy comes specifically under the spotlight here, God's displeasure with these shepherds can be seen as a rejection of self-serving leadership in general. The old despotic monarchy has to go, and all failed leadership challenged.

These shepherds are guilty of selfishness and greed. They feed themselves but do not feed the sheep (34:2). They feed off the sheep, consuming the milk products,[2] literally fleecing their flock, and feasting on the fattest of the flock. They do not tend and care for the sheep (34:3). The case for the prosecution continues. The shepherds have failed to help the weak, heal or attend to the sick, go out in search of the lost, bring back those driven out and isolated by the threat of predators. In other words, the shepherds are guilty of neglect, wilful abuse, and failing to provide their sheep with even the most basic care (34:3–4). The sheep are scattered for lack of a shepherd and have become victims of other natural predators (34:5–6): 'They became food for all the wild animals'. In other words, they are the prey of the nations around them. You may recall God's pronouncements against these nations in chapters 25–32 precisely because many of them were taking advantage of Israel's plight with the Babylonians. But it is the shepherds that are under examination here. Because they have failed in their duty of care on all the above points, God is against them and he will rescue his sheep from these devouring shepherds (ch. 7–10). The abuse of power is coming to an end. Notice how many times God uses the phrase my sheep in this passage—fourteen times in all if we include the reference to my flock in v. 22. These are God's sheep. The kings were mere hirelings who were entrusted with the welfare of God's flock, but they have not done a very good job. God's people are like sheep that have been grossly neglected by their hireling shepherds. Gill notes that, 'Instead of being shepherds to feed the flock, [they] were no other than wolves in sheep's clothing, and ravenous lions and bears, which devoured the flock; but this they should do no longer.'[3] God's response is to say, 'No longer shall the shepherds feed themselves. I will rescue my sheep from their mouths, that they may not be food for them' (34:10).

From false shepherds to the Good Shepherd 34:11–16a

Because of the failure of Israel's shepherds God will intervene.

In verse 10 we saw how God has said he will remove the false shepherds. Now he takes his providential care for his flock to the next level. He will personally become their shepherd. He will search out the sheep that are prone to wander from the safety of the fold, deliver or rescue them from the places where they have been scattered, gather them from the nations, feed them, give them rest, and bind up the wounds of the injured (34:11–16). The loving shepherd of the flock will put in place a wide-ranging care package. The old monarchy will be removed and the King of all creation will take personal care of his children. This is what we see in the course of Israel's history following the destruction of Jerusalem.

The loving shepherd of the flock will put in place a wide-ranging care package.

In captivity

We see God's providential care of his people during their years of captivity—initially under the Babylonians and then under the Persians (538 BC onwards). The Israelites remained in captivity for seventy years. Yet in all that time God remained with them, kept his promises to them, and shepherded them through Ezekiel, Jeremiah, Daniel and even Queen Esther.

In restoration to the land

God states clearly, 'I will bring them out from the peoples and gather them from the countries, and will bring them into their own land. And I will feed them on the mountains of Israel' (34:13). Yahweh has promised to bring his sheep back from the places where they have been scattered and this is exactly what he did. The monarchy was never reinstated but the people were. We read in Nehemiah's time of great blessing and protection for the people of God. They returned to Jerusalem, rebuilt he walls and the temple. There were many social and religious reforms as God shepherded his people through leaders like Ezra and Nehemiah.

Although the picture seems bleak for the exiles by the Chebar canal, God has promised to bring his people back to their homeland where he will personally take care of them, feeding them in the ravines and with good pasture land on the mountains of Israel (34:13–14). There is a clear echo of Psalm 23 here. 'I myself will make them lie down, declares the LORD' (34:15). The Psalmist puts it like this: 'The LORD is my shepherd; I shall not want. He makes me lie down in green pastures'. Peter Jeffery captures the beauty of this when he says, 'This is not some theoretical proposition and neither is it wishful thinking; it is far more even than just a theological statement. This is the experience of all God's people! This is what we are saved to, and the reality of what we are saved to is known as we submit to the care of the Shepherd. There is no use saying, "The Lord is my shepherd" and then worrying yourself sick about where you are going to find green pastures. If the green pastures and quiet waters are found as a result only of your efforts, you

There is no use saying, 'The Lord is my shepherd' and then worrying yourself sick about where you are going to find green pastures.

do not need a shepherd.'[4] There is no need to worry when the Lord is our shepherd. He will feed his people as he has promised and meet our every need.

In the 400 years between the Old and New Testaments.

Although this was a period when God remained silent, he was still with his people. The ground was being prepared for something even more dramatic in God's eternal plan for his people. But we will come back to this under the Davidic shepherd below.

Fat sheep and thin sheep 34:16b–22

It was not only the kings that were exploiting the people. There are fat sheep as well as fat shepherds! 'I will strengthen the weak, and the fat and the strong I will destroy … I will judge between sheep and sheep, between rams and male goats' (34:16b–17, 20, 22). There were other bullies among the flock taking advantage of the weak. They will not get away unscathed. These fat sheep are characterised as bullies who take what they want and spoil the rest of the food and water so that others cannot even enjoy the basics (34:18–19). They drink what they want then muddy the water and render it undrinkable; they feed on the lush pastures but trample down the rest, spoiling it for others. God is indignant with them: 'And must my sheep eat what you have trodden with your feet, and drink what you have muddied with your feet?' (34:19). God will demonstrate his loving care for the weak, protecting them from those who bulldoze their way to the top at the expense of others (34: 21). The picture relates to the strong and powerful people in the land, who use their power against the small man. Any form of bullying comes under this condemnation, whether in the school playground, the abuse of military power, or the abuse of the law courts by large international companies to get the next lucrative deal at the expense of the powerless. God cautions them that he will destroy them, that he will 'feed them in justice' (34:16b). They will get their just deserts at the hand of righteous judge of all the earth. The destruction of these oppressors shows God's concern for the oppressed. It should spur us on to confront all forms of bullying and oppression, corporate scandals and social injustice in our day.

The Davidic shepherd 34:23–24

We have seen in verses 11–22 how God has promised to look after his sheep and to care for them. Now this promise is taken a step further. We are told that God intends to establish one shepherd over the people. But who is this one shepherd?

One Shepherd

First of all, to state the obvious, but he will be one shepherd! This idea of a single shepherd seems to be pointing to a future of unity amongst the people of God. This is rather important in light of Israel's history up to the time of Ezekiel. It is a history of a divided kingdom and a divided people with divided loyalties. To all of this division God intends to bring unity, establishing one shepherd to rule over them and care for them.

My servant David

The shepherd is given a number of designations. He is called my servant David who shall be a prince among them. This one shepherd, prince, servant, will rule the people with authority but also compassion. We have the example of David who as a young boy sat amongst his sheep and protected them from the wild animals, fighting off the bears and lions, searching out sheep that wandered from the fold and bringing them back safely. The shepherd God is a going to establish over his people will, like David, be one who is prepared to risk his life for his sheep. This is not a reference to yet another human kingdom. Rather, God is going to rule in the midst of his people. How this worked out in the history of Israel following the fall of Jerusalem, the Babylonian captivity, and restoration to the land was touched on above. However, the ultimate fulfilment of this promise of the one shepherd to the one people of God is to be seen in the coming of Jesus the promised Messiah.[5]

It is in the person of Jesus that we can hold together all that Ezekiel has just said about God being shepherd to his people, and his promise to install a shepherd in the line of David. Wright says: 'At the time of Jesus' birth Luke records the expectation of the event in a series of encounters which are saturated in language of the restoration of the Davidic kingdom forever'.[6] Jesus the Messiah is the Prince of Peace of Isaiah 9:6. He is our Immanuel, God in our midst, according to Isaiah 7:14 and Matthew 1:23. He is called the Son of David in Matthew 1:1; 12:23; Luke 1:32; and Romans 1:3. And of course

> Divine love is not an empty, sentimental pity, but it demonstrates itself in an act of propitiation.

he is the Good Shepherd of John 10:1–21. As Jeffery comments, 'In Jesus, God came to seek and save the lost. It was not that we loved him but that he loved us. And what a love! Divine love is not an empty, sentimental pity, but it demonstrates itself in an act of propitiation. Propitiation ... means that on the cross, bearing our sin and guilt, Jesus endured the wrath of God instead of us, and paid fully on our behalf the debt we owed to God for breaking his holy law.'[7] As the Good Shepherd, Jesus will establish a covenant of peace.

God, through the Good Shepherd, is going to establish a covenant of peace with his whole creation, bringing in previously unknown harmony.

The covenant of peace 34:25–31

When God establishes his Good Shepherd he will also inaugurate a covenant of peace. Peace in Hebrew thought is much more comprehensive than in English. It is not simply the absence of war. It also encompasses the welfare of all God's creation. It covers relationships between humans and the natural world (34: 25, 27, 29), as well as the relationships between all of creation and God. God, through the Good Shepherd, is going to establish a covenant of peace with his whole creation, bringing in previously unknown harmony. The scope of the covenant of peace includes safety and security (34:25). There will be showers of blessing brought about by the rain in its season replenishing the earth and promoting fruitfulness in the trees (34:26–27). God's people shall no longer be prey to the nations but shall dwell in safety and without fear of hurt or hunger or reproach (34:28–29).

What hope for a world that has wars raging in many parts, and terrorist threats on our very streets! What hope for the children of God who face persecution in many parts of the world even in our day.[8] This promise of a covenant of peace was issued to God's people in Ezekiel's war-ravaged days, and it remains true for the people of God throughout the centuries. If one asks, 'Where is this peace?' we must remember that it has not yet reached its full expression. There is what theologians call the tension between the already and the not yet of eschatology. This simply means that in Christ we can now experience this peace, a peace that passes all human understanding. Yet, it is evident that this world has not yet been fully and finally reconciled to God. This will only happen at the second coming of Christ and the inauguration of the new heavens and new earth (Isa. 65:17; 66:22; 2 Pet. 3:13). It is then that we will experience the true and ultimate shalom of God.

The King of Love my shepherd is

There are always those who are prepared to exploit their position for private gain. They will brazenly 'feed off' the very people they are supposed to feed and protect. Even the church is not without its ravenous wolves. Pastors of bling, who preach money, money, money; who drive brand new top of the range cars; wearing clothes, watches and jewellery worth thousands of pounds, while appealing to the poor in their congregation to dig deeper into their pockets! There are so called shepherds who never preach a clear message of hope—a message of salvation by grace through faith (Eph. 2:8–10); who never challenge poor lost and estranged people as to how they can be reconciled to God through the simple act of faith and repentance. But, just as in Ezekiel's day, God will not allow such conduct to go unchallenged. As we saw in the depiction of the watchman, such men will be held accountable for failing to warn the lost of the danger they are in. How different are such leaders to the Shepherd King, who rules with compassion and rather than taking from his sheep he gives his all, even his life.

> The excellent character of this shepherd is shown especially in this, The good shepherd lays down his life for his sheep [John 10:11]. In the sense in which this is meant it cannot apply to an ordinary sheep-herder, no matter how good he may be. Such a shepherd may, indeed, risk his life in the defence of his sheep (1 Sam. 17:34–36), but he does not really lay down his life; he does not yield his life as a voluntary sacrifice. Also, in ordinary life the death of the herder means loss and possible death for the herd. In this case the death of the shepherd means life for the sheep.[9]

The Shepherd King is also the Prince of Peace (Isa. 9:6). We can experience God's perfect peace in our hearts even today. But when the Shepherd King returns in all his glory we will experience it in ways currently unimaginable.

> The King of love my Shepherd is,
> Whose goodness faileth never;
> I nothing lack if I am His,
> And He is mine forever.
>
> Where streams of living water flow
> My ransomed soul He leadeth,
> And, where the verdant pastures grow,
> With food celestial feedeth.

Perverse and foolish oft I strayed,
But yet in love He sought me,
And on His shoulder gently laid,
And home rejoicing brought me.

And so through all the length of days
Thy goodness faileth never;
Good Shepherd, may I sing Thy praise
Within Thy house forever.

For further study ▶

FOR FURTHER STUDY

1. In the Bible kings and rulers are often called 'shepherds.' Check out the following passages: Isa. 44:28; Jer. 2:8; 10:21; 23:1–6; 25:34–38. Especially Isa. 63:11, and Psalm 78:70–72.
2. Read John 10:1–18. Make a list of the qualities of the Good Shepherd. Compare your findings against the shepherds of Ezekiel 34.
3. What do the following passages teach us about the Davidic Shepherd? Matt 1:1; 12:23; Luke 1:32; and Rom. 1:3.

TO THINK ABOUT AND DISCUSS

1. As Christ's ambassadors (2 Cor. 5:20), what lessons can we learn from Ezekiel chapter 34 that will help us serve God and others?
2. Are you involved in Christian leadership at any level? How might you take the principles of the shepherd and apply them to your ministry?
3. The prosperity gospel, also often referred to as the health and wealth gospel or Gospel of greed, is prominent in the contemporary church. How do such claims—that financial prosperity is a measure of spiritual prosperity—compare to the words of Jesus in Luke 6:24; Matthew 6:24; and Luke 12:15?
4. The biblical picture of wealth is that it is not inherently sinful. How do we bring real biblical hope to people who live in poverty, whilst avoiding the dangers of the prosperity gospel?

17 God heals the broken-hearted

Ezekiel Chapter 35:1–36:15

In a message that came to the exiles soon after the final fall of Jerusalem God denounces Edom for blatantly exploiting the misfortunes of Israel for personal gain. Israel, on the other hand, is encouraged with the news that they will once again inhabit their beloved land. Despite their current downturn and brokenness, the future is looking good. God will heal the broken-hearted.

At the time of writing the conflict in Syria is bringing devastation and displacement to many Syrian families. Heartrending images of displaced people haunt our television screens as thousands of refugees make the arduous life-threatening journey across land and sea in search of a better future in Europe. But not everyone is touched by the pain and loss of these families. There are many who eagerly await an opportunity to exploit the displaced people. What little money they have left is quickly snatched up by those who see the refugees as a commodity, and who charge exorbitant prices to send them on the perilous journey across the Mediterranean Sea on craft simply not designed for that purpose. Having escaped the bombs and bullets back home, men, women, and children have lost their lives at sea attempting to make that crossing, while the exploiters go home content having made their profit. No doubt when this conflict and all its harsh images fade in our memories there will be another to take its place.

The tension in Jerusalem during the final siege is recounted by Jeremiah in chapters 37–38. The Judean king Zedekiah had been torn between the counsel of some who advised rebellion and others such as Jeremiah who counselled submission to Babylon. In the end Zedekiah chose to rebel against Nebuchadnezzar who promptly laid siege to Jerusalem. The city enjoyed a short time of respite when the army of Pharaoh came up from Egypt in support of Jerusalem causing the Babylonians to withdraw for a while (Jer. 37:5). But the Egyptians left, the Babylonian resumed their siege, and despite the city's strong defences Jerusalem finally fell in 587–86 BC. The punishment was harsh. Zedekiah's sons were killed before his eyes, and we are told that he was then blinded and taken to Babylon in chains (2 Kings 25:7; Jer. 52:10–11).

In this latest episode of Ezekiel's ministry, Jerusalem has succumbed to its final assault. In the aftermath many of the Israelites fled the city hoping to find safety in the hills. But having escaped the sword of the Babylonians many find themselves cut down by the sword of the Edomites who jump on the bandwagon to assist the King of Babylon and exploit the Israelites' misfortune. In two evenly balanced parts

God first chastises triumphant Edom (35:1–15) and then encourages the down-beaten Israel (36:1–15). Mount Seir is told that God is against her (35:3), whereas the Mountains of Israel are encouraged with the knowledge that God is for her (36:9). The aim is simple. On the one hand it is a warning against those who would exploit the misfortunes of another. On the other hand it is encouragement for the people of God at a time when they were feeling at their lowest.

The prophecy of chastisement against the Mountains of Seir 35:1–15

It is interesting to find yet another prophecy of judgement in Ezekiel, especially since we determined that the end of chapter 32 was a major turning point from judgement to hope in Ezekiel's ministry. But it will all make sense when taken in context as we shall see a little later in this chapter. At the outset God declares himself against Mount Seir or Edom (35:1–4).[1] The reasons for this declaration of war are quickly made clear. Edom had harboured an ancient grudge against Israel and had killed many Israelites by the sword as they fled the Babylonians (35:5). The history of Edom's grudge against Israel was a long one going back to the conflict between Jacob (Israel) and Esau (Edom) (Gen. 25:22–34; 27; 36:1). They were also guilty of coveting Israel's land and took advantage of Israel's misfortune by expanding their territory

> Edom was also guilty of blasphemy; of boasting against God; and for gloating at Israel's demise.

into south eastern Judah at a time when God's punishment on Israel was at its climax (35:10). Edom was also guilty of blasphemy; of boasting against God (35:13); and for gloating at Israel's demise (35:15).

God's reaction to Edom's sinful behaviour is to punish the Edomites like for like. Because they were quick to shed more Israelite blood in the aftermath of the sacking of Jerusalem, God will ensure that their blood will also flow (35:6). He will make Edom a desolate waste (35:7–9), just as the Edomites preyed on Israel when it was weak and desolate. God will treat them as they treated the Israelites (35:11). And finally, God will ensure that others will rejoice at their misfortune just as they rejoiced at Israel's misfortune (35:14–15; Psalm 137:7). In other words, Edom will get in return what it has been dishing out to Israel.

God's reaction to Edom's sinful behaviour is to punish the Edomites like for like.

Other prophets also foretold God's judgement on Edom for her bitter treatment of Jerusalem (Jer. 49:7–22; Joel 3:19; Amos 9:12; and Obad. 10ff.). But as a point of historical interest Edom was not the only country to exploit the situation. God's judgement against Edom and the other nations (36:5) took place just a short time later. The permanent expulsion of the Edomites from their land happened around 500 BC when they were routed by the Nabateans approximately 80 years later, and many of the surrounding nations were also overrun by the Babylonians.[2] The desolation inflicted on Edom would result in them knowing that the one who had brought this discipline upon them was Yahweh the God of Israel (35:4, 9, 15).

What are we to learn from this that is practical and relevant to us today? What abiding principles can we draw out of this passage that will help us understand the world we live in today? Let us look briefly again at the points of God's rebuke against the Edomites.

Grudge bearing

We have seen in verse 5 that God chastises the Edomites for holding an ancient grudge against the Israelites. Furthermore, this grudge seems to have manifested itself in outbursts of anger and jealousy (35:11). Like a lion lying in wait and watching its prey, the Edomites seize the most appropriate moment to inflict the most possible harm on their old adversary. People from all walks of life today who harbour grudges wait for a moment of weakness to take advantage. Although not all behave in this way, yet we must acknowledge that this is at least in part the philosophy of the world. This is the very essence of Darwinism, the survival of the fittest. This is the way of the world, but it is a mindset is all too prevalent in Christian circles, indeed even amongst those who serve the Lord as missionaries and pastors. It manifests itself in so many ways, both overtly and in more subtle ways. Something happens, someone is hurt, and a grudge-seed is sown which often surpasses the mustard seed in its exponential growth. How should we as Christians deal with it? In a fallen world the victim will often wait their chance for payback. However, for Christians and for Christian work, we must never accept the ways of a fallen world as the norm. We must not take our lead from a world affected by sin. Indeed we must actively resist such behaviour in both ourselves and those who are our brothers and sisters in the Lord. Harbouring grudges is the destroyer of harmony in many homes and churches. I have known people who hold a grudge against a brother or sister in the Lord, or even against a pastor for some failing on his part, perhaps a momentary lack of judgement, or a surly word. This is not to say that we accept such shortcomings, but there is a biblical way of dealing with such things that will bring glory to God. Bearing a grudge and pouncing at a moment when someone is weak is not what God has in mind. Consider this excerpt from Dennis Maynard:

> Do you love your parish [church]? Are you fond of your pastor? Would you believe that in just a matter of a few weeks your pastor and his family could be abused, humiliated, and unemployed? In just a matter of days your parish could be split down the middle. A couple of months from now close to forty percent of the people you currently see at worship could no longer be there. Close to half of those will never again attend worship or participate in any church. Friends that you see talking and laughing this Sunday may never speak again.[3]

Maynard's little book goes on to highlight the frightening reality of just how far some people in the church will go to have things their way, with the authoritative word of God set aside in favour of personal opinion. The truth of biblical reconciliation is overruled by gut instinct. So-called unity and peace are sought by getting rid of the objectionable individual. But as Francis Schaeffer points out, 'Any unity, any peace, that is not rooted in [Divine] truth is nothing!'[4] Not every disagreement in the church ends quite so badly of course. Nevertheless, many pastors and their families have been deeply hurt by those they were called to feed and nurture. Without getting into the whole issue of biblical reconciliation, are we not told quite simply that rather than harbour a grudge, disagreements ought to be resolved if possible before we lay our heads on our pillows to sleep that very night? The Apostle Paul in his letter to the church at Ephesus says, 'Be angry and do not sin; do not let the sun go down on your anger' (Eph. 4:6).

Bloodshed

As we have seen in the case of the Edomites, bearing a grudge can lead to outbursts of jealousy and anger. Worse than that, it led to the shedding of innocent blood. We saw how the Edomites were guilty of slaughtering the Israelites as they fled from the Babylonians (Ezek. 35:5). In our fallen world there is much bloodshed in many places today, and God will hold the guilty accountable. But what about Christians? I think it is fair to say that by and large our grudge moments, even if they are not dealt with biblically, do not lead to the shedding of blood. Or do they? I find it immensely challenging how Jesus redefined bloodshed or murder.

Bearing a grudge can lead to outbursts of jealousy and anger. Worse than that, it led to the shedding of innocent blood.

> You have heard that it was said to those of old, 'You shall not murder; and whoever murders will be liable to judgement.' But I say to you that everyone who is angry with his brother

> will be liable to judgement; whoever insults his brother will be liable to the council; and whoever says, 'You fool!' will be liable to the hell of fire (Matt. 5:21–22).

Jesus takes the teaching to an altogether different level: when we speak badly of someone, he says, it is the same as if we are guilty of murder![5]

I believe it is in keeping with our Lord's intended meaning when I take it a step further by saying that those who use the sweetest words in conversation yet harbour hate in their hearts are equally guilty. Some people are adept at damning another by their sweet and soft-spoken words. I find this incredibly challenging. When someone mistreats me or hurts me, my instinctive reaction is to defend myself and even get angry with them for the pain I am experiencing. Anger, or that feeling which we get when we are hurt, and which leads to an instinctive reaction when in danger, is a natural feeling, given to us as a means whereby we can defend our ourselves when attacked. The problem arises when the danger is past and we fail to seek reconciliation with those that hurt us. It is harbouring the grudge that leads to a breach of the sixth commandment, as the Apostle John reminds us when he says, 'Everyone who hates his brother is a murderer,' (1 John 3:15).

It is harbouring the grudge that leads to a breach of the sixth commandment, as the Apostle John reminds us when he says, 'Everyone who hates his brother is a murderer,' (1 John 3:15).

Albert Barnes points out in his commentary on this verse, 'He has a feeling which would lead him to commit murder, if it were fully acted out'.

So what is the answer to our failings in this very practical challenge in our relationships? The essential starting point is recognizing this behaviour for what it is—sin. Jesus goes on in his teaching on the Sermon on the Mount to tell us that recognising any grudge as a barrier to our relationship with God, we should go find the other person and be reconciled.[6] The Apostle Paul in his letter to the church in Rome, reflecting the teaching of the Sermon on the Mount, tells us that rather than repay hurt with hurt we should try as far as is in our means to live at peace with all people. He goes on to suggest that if we really think that someone is deserving of vengeance then we should leave it with God, and rather than seeking to avenge ourselves we should do good to those that have hurt us.[7] Is there a grudge that you are harbouring that you need deal with? Is there someone with whom you need to be reconciled?

Coveting and exploitation

Getting back to Ezekiel's latest announcement, we saw how the Edomites took advantage of Israel's defeat by the Babylonians, to move in and take Israelite territory in the southeast of the country (35:10). They had coveted the land for a long time and now they would exploit the situation to grab what they could. We do not have to look far back in history to see similar situations. The spread of communism into warn-torn Eastern Europe after WWII; or the violent clashes in former Yugoslavia as the various ethnic groupings slaughtered each other to gain more territory after the collapse of communism; and even more recently Russia's annexing of the Crimea.

But coveting can take different guises other than one nation encroaching into another's territory (and in the process leaving death, destruction, and bloodshed in their wake). I have known of local land disputes where, not unlike the film *The Field* starring Richard Harris, people have lost their lives over a patch of dirt. I served God for many years in Albania and every now and again I would hear of someone dying at the end of an AK47 assault rifle over where the boundary of a piece of land lay. The story of David and Bathsheba serves as a reminder of how desire and lack of self-control can lead to devastating consequences including actual murder. This is a further example of how coveting is often the precursor to exploitation. People want what belongs to someone else, and so the strong exploit the weak, taking what little they have.

The popularity of television programmes such as *The Apprentice* are built upon these very principles of wanting what someone else has got. In it we see young men and women fighting and arguing and stepping on one another in their attempt to get to the top. Ambition is by no means wrong. The problem is what the human heart is prepared to do to achieve that ambition. The key is to realise our ambitions without falling into the traps of coveting and exploitation, and avoid the sin of worshipping what one politician has termed, 'the idol of the free market.'[8] Unfortunately there are Christian leaders who are guilty of exactly the same worldly principles as they trample underfoot those who would obstruct their quest for riches, prestige, and position.

Coveting also manifests itself in the form of economic exploitation. According to the International Labour Organisation (ILO) young women and girls make up the majority of those who are economically exploited in sweatshops, and as domestic servants. More alarmingly millions of people are tricked or forced into leaving their homes to be exploited or abused. Human trafficking is found in almost every country. Many of the victims are pawns in an illegal sex trade. No doubt William Wilberforce and his friends, who fought for the abolition of the slave trade in their day, would be shocked by the staggering statistics of slavery today.[9] There is an urgent need for Christians to raise their voices against this modern slave trade. As John Stott has written, 'The weak and vulnerable were carefully protected by the Mosaic Law. Far from exploiting them, God's people were to be the voice of the voiceless and the champion of the powerless, including their enemies'.[10]

No doubt William Wilberforce and his friends, who fought for the abolition of the slave trade in their day, would be shocked by the staggering statistics of slavery today.

May God bless you with anger at injustice,
oppression and exploitation of people,
so that you will work for justice, equity and peace.[11]

Blasphemy

The Edomites have been guilty of boasting against Israel,

especially in their latest defeat. But God takes their taunts personally: 'You have magnified yourselves against me ...,' God says to them. 'You have multiplied your words against me' (35:13). Block captures the mood perfectly when he puts it like this: 'To deride the land of Israel is to taunt the true owner of the land. His tenants may have been expelled, but Yahweh remains the divine landLORD, and he will not tolerate such belittling of the mountains of Israel ... Yahweh interprets Seir's claim to the mountains of Israel as a blasphemous and presumptuous challenge against himself'.[12] God's good name is at stake here and he will not sit idly by and allow it to be further tarnished, either by Israel's behaviour, or by her enemies' taunts. God will do what is necessary to protect his name—as we shall see in the next chapter.

Gloating

The Edomites have '... rejoiced over the inheritance of the house of Israel, because it was desolate' (35:15). In other words, they have not only taken advantage of the situation but have added insult to injury by gloating over Israel's demise. Rather than show sympathy they have shown great delight in the misfortune of their neighbour. As far as the Edomites are concerned, Israel has got her comeuppance. Obadiah picks up on Edom's gloating and gives a stark warning

> It is hard sometimes, even for Christians, not to feel a sense of satisfaction when someone who has hurt us gets their comeuppance.

to them when he says, 'Do not gloat over the day of your brother in the day of his misfortune; do not rejoice over the people of Judah in the day of their ruin; do not boast in the day of distress ... For the day of the LORD is near upon all the nations. As you have done, it shall be done to you; your deeds shall return on your own head' (Obad. 1:12 and 15).

It is hard sometimes, even for Christians, not to feel a sense of satisfaction when someone who has hurt us gets their comeuppance. We must resist it however, or we too face the prospect of God's discipline. Surely it is a hard heart that rejoices in the misfortunes of those who have acted unkindly towards us. For us to behave in this way is the same in God's eyes as if we were the one who acted spitefully against us in the first place. Christ's answer is to love our enemy and pray for those who hurt us (Matt. 5:44). But who can rise to such a challenge? It is not natural for a man to help the one who is his antagonist. But as Christians we are not dependent on the natural man but on the Spirit of Christ that makes us new creatures. It is for Christians to rise above the ways of the world and exhibit the love and compassion of the Saviour who bore much worse in reaching out to us while we were yet in our sin, and prayed for the forgiveness of those who crucified him.

Summary

We are living in days of great advances in many fields of knowledge and technology, but there is perhaps more exploitation of the weak now than at any other period in history. We read of child labour in places like China and India, so that we can have our shops filled with the latest fashions and buy our jeans and sportswear at the best possible prices. Children and young women are exploited in the sex trade, and this is taking place even in so-called developed countries like the UK. We might well ask: where is God in all of this? I am sure that the Israelites were asking the very same question. They must have wondered when or if God was ever going to intervene. For many it was a lifetime's waiting for that change; for others it was their lot to die in those circumstances. But in the end God punished the exploiters and restored his people. Of course, we will experience the ultimate fulfilment of this in the resurrection, when we enjoy new life in the new heavens and new earth. The day is coming when there will be no more exploitation of the weak, and God will be exalted as never before. In the meantime we are called to be responsible citizens both of the country we live in now, and of the one we will inherit with God in time to come. We must be prepared to speak out against exploitation when we have opportunity and make wise and careful use of our votes when it comes to local and parliamentary elections and use all available means to help the helpless.

The prophecy of encouragement for the mountains of Israel 36:1–15

The passage can be divided into two distinctive parts: assurance that Israel's enemies will be punished (v. 1–7) and assurance that the mountains of Israel will be inhabited again (v. 8–15). Both are messages of hope for the exiles in Babylon. If they have been wondering whether Yahweh will abandon them and their land forever, then here is the answer. Far from abandoning them forever, God has great plans for them, to restore them to a bountiful and fruitful land.

Rebuke for the nations

The first seven verses repeat many of the themes of 35:1–15. For example, the glee with which the enemy looked upon Israel's demise and their plans to exploit the situation by land-grabbing (36:2). We see again how Israel's enemies made their desolation worse by crushing them from all sides and making them the object of evil gossip (36:3). Therefore, because Israel has suffered the reproach of the nations, God declares that he will pour out his hot jealousy against Edom in particular, and the nations will themselves become objects of reproach (36:4–7).

Because Israel has suffered the reproach of the nations, God declares that he will pour out his hot jealousy against Edom in particular.

Restoration for the mountains of Israel

This judgement against the nations is a message of hope for Israel. Things may be dark now, but God has plans to pour out his blessings upon the mountains of Israel. As Block comments, 'What follows is an exciting and excited announcement of the reversal of the land's humiliation'.[13] The mountains are described as a tree shooting out its fruit-laden branches with the express purpose of feeding 'my people Israel' because they are soon to return home (36:8).

To quote Block again, 'What a welcome sound it should have been for Ezekiel's audience to hear Yahweh referring to Israel endearingly as 'ammî' 'my people,' once again'.[14] It must have warmed their hearts as they sat by the Chebar canal downhearted and defeated. Their pride in self had been crushed. No longer could they hold on to the arrogance of the past or dependence on Egypt to help them keep their precious city. They have been brought to an end of themselves, and it is exactly at that point that God says to them that he will ensure that they return their homeland and prosper. It is he who will make provision for them in ways that they never could themselves. Sometimes God's children need to be brought to an end of their own efforts so that they find true comfort and solace and provision in the arms of our all-powerful heavenly Father, our Yahweh Yireh—the Lord who provides.[15]

Sometimes God's children need to be brought to an end of their own efforts so that they find true comfort and solace and provision in the arms of our all-powerful heavenly Father.

God will heal the broken-hearted

Written around the time of Nehemiah, when the walls of Jerusalem had been successfully rebuilt and God's people were once again experiencing prosperity and security, Psalm 147 sounds out the national sense of joy: 'The LORD builds up Jerusalem; he gathers the outcasts of Israel. He heals the broken-hearted and binds up their wounds' (Psalm 147:2–3). As Leupold states,

> The healing of the 'brokenhearted' is to be taken in the broadest sense by including those who grieve over their sins as well as those who are afflicted by life's manifold adversities. Similar is the thought of binding up of wounds. In either case the gentle pity of the Lord is beautifully depicted as He stands by to comfort or to act the part of the kindly physician.[16]

God is at work in history. The dispossessed exiles will return home to a land that abundantly meets their needs. But there can be no doubt as to who their patron is. It is Yahweh their Lord who will restore them, gathering them from their enforced exile, healing their broken hearts, and giving them a sure foundation (36:15). We shall see more of what this means in the chapters that follow.

For further study ▶

FOR FURTHER STUDY

1. What light does Genesis 32:3 shed on this chapter?
2. Read 2 Peter 2:1–3. Continuing Ezekiel's theme of blasphemy, in what other ways according to Peter can the church be affected by blasphemy?
3. What does Psalm 137 teach us about this period in the lives of this displaced people? How can we reconcile the images of verses 7–9 with the teaching of Jesus to love our enemies in Matthew 5:44?
4. Read Joel 3:19–21 (and if you have time Obadiah). How do these passages reinforce the twin concept of judgement and hope found in this chapter?

TO THINK ABOUT AND DISCUSS

1. Read again Dennis Maynard's comments cited in the chapter above. How can we address concerns in the church without it getting to this frightening impasse?
2. Albert Barnes in his commentary on 2 Peter 2:1–3 says that false teachers treat God's people as a 'bale of goods ... that is, they would endeavour to make money out of them, and regard them as only fitted to promote that object'. Discuss.
3. How should Christians deal with 'grudge moments'?
4. How can we as Christians respond to the modern slave trade?
5. In what ways have you witnessed the biblical truth that God heals the broken hearted? How might this be applied to situations you are personally facing or are aware of in the church?

18 A change of heart

Ezekiel Chapter 36:16–38

Sometimes it seems that you just cannot win! God's reputation had suffered through the sinful behaviour of his people when they had lived in their own land. But even as they sit in exile under God's judgement his people are still the root cause of God's name being treated with contempt. The implication is that Yahweh cannot be much of a God if he cannot protect his people. But Yahweh is about to restore his good name by restoring his people. Their restoration will not be some outward change for the sake of appearances. Rather than simply change their circumstances God is about to change their very hearts.

One of Chris Browne's cartoons of *Hagar the Horrible* depicts Hagar having a rather sullen moment with his wife during which he says, 'I am tired of your sarcastic remarks about my weight problems.' To which his wife smugly retorts, 'Lighten up!' It seems that sometimes you just cannot win. In the passage under consideration another word comes to Ezekiel (36:16) reminding him that when the Israelites lived in their own land their sinful ways and doings defiled the holy land that God had given them. Using the metaphor of the uncleanness of a woman's menstrual cycle (36:17) God implies that the whole land was defiled and the people were in a state of ceremonial uncleanness.[1] Their behaviour had been disgusting, dragging God's name through the mud. Therefore God judged the Israelites and punished them pouring out his wrath upon them and removing them from the land (36:18–19).

However, even among the nations where they have been exiled, God's holy name continues to be treated with contempt. It seems that God cannot win. The people among whom they have been dispersed are essentially pointing the finger of blame at Yahweh for the predicament the Israelites find themselves in. 'What sort of a God is this Yahweh?' they seem to be saying. 'These are his people and yet they had to go out of his land!' (36:20). The implication is that this God cannot even protect his own people in his own land. God's name which has been tarnished by the sinful behaviour of the Israelites when in their own land is now being tarnished precisely as a result of him reproving them. The people among whom the Israelites have been dispersed are guilty of blasphemy. They are profaning God's name by suggesting that he is so weak that he cannot provide for his people or protect them from Marduk the god of Babylon (36:20). For people who do not actually believe in this Yahweh, they seem to enjoy ridiculing him. I wonder do we see something similar in today's essentially humanist culture. Modern culture asserts 'There is no God'; yet it is precisely God who gets the blame for just about every natural disaster in our fallen world. Tragedies are euphemistically called 'Acts of God.' There is no God—but it is still his fault when things go wrong!

God's concern for his name 36:16–22

Understandably God is concerned for his holy name (36:21). But what's in a name? In the case of God, everything! All the names by which God is known reflect different aspects of his nature. The Israelites were living in exile among nations who believed in various gods known by many different names. These gods were made in the image of the peoples who created them, with all their vices and virtues. The true God of all creation, however, was not created but is the Creator. It is for the people to reflect the nature of Yahweh and not the other way around. The problem throughout Ezekiel's prophecy has been that God's people were not reflecting his virtue but the vices of the gods and peoples around them. But God will not suffer reproach for much longer. He is going to gather his exiled people from all the nations and bring them back into their own land (36:24). It is for the sake of his holy name (36:32). It is because they are children of the promise he made

> The problem throughout Ezekiel's prophecy has been that God's people were not reflecting his virtue but the vices of the gods and peoples around them.

to their forefather Abraham (36:28). It is an act of grace. There is to be no doubt about God's motives. He is bringing them back to the land at this time to vindicate his holy name (36:21, 22, 23, 32).

Christians too are children of the promise (Gal. 4:28) and the favours we enjoy from God are undeserved (Eph. 2:8–10). Our right standing with God is all of grace. The good news of the gospel is intricately connected with God's glory, God's reputation. Indeed, as Wright comments, 'Only for God's own sake is it good news at all. For only that which brings honour and glory to God himself can be good news for anybody else'.[2] God is about to vindicate his holy name, restoring his honour—not only among his own people but also among the nations (36:23, 36). The honour of God's name should be at the heart of all our evangelistic endeavours. In this passage we find nine ways in which God will restore the honour of his name. We will consider them under three general headings.

The honour of God's name should be at the heart of all our evangelistic endeavours.

God restores the honour of his holy name by establishing his justice 36:16–19

By showing that his punishment of Israel was deserved 36:16–19

We have seen that Israel's wayward behaviour was such that God could no longer let it go unpunished. If the honour of his name was to be upheld, then his people needed to be punished for their sin. This is what we have seen so often throughout

Ezekiel. But now his reputation is being attacked precisely because he had disciplined his people by sending them into slavery. The peoples of the nations into which the Israelites had been dispersed were taunting the Israelites and, in doing so, taunting God (v. 20). The implication is that he was not much of a God who could not protect his people from their enemies. This was a common mindset in ancient cultures. The strongest army had the strongest god. It simply did not make sense for a strong god to allow his people to suffer the humiliation of defeat. God now makes clear that the Israelites are in slavery because he is punishing them, not because he is too weak to protect them. Furthermore, he makes clear that his punishment of Israel was just: 'I poured out my wrath upon them for the blood they had shed in the land, for the idols with which they had defiled it. I scattered them among the nations …' (36:18–19).

God's just punishment of sin is a fundamental starting point in understanding the wonder of his grace, and nothing makes any sense apart from this plain teaching of Scripture. If we fail to understand God's justice then we fail to properly understand his forgiveness. It is only when we appreciate God's just anger at sin and rebellion that we can then appreciate his mercy in restoring us to himself.[3] Likewise we only really come to understand our own sin when we have experienced God's saving and restoring mercy. Both are sides of the same coin. If God is to restore Israel, it is not because they now deserve better. Rather it is an expression of his undeserved mercy and undiminished commitment to his promise to Abraham.

God restores the honour of his holy name by the external and tangible restoration of his people Israel 36:24

By bringing the people back to the land 36:24 and 8–15

God's restorative measures begin with gathering them out of all the countries to which they have been scattered. Block refers to this as a new exodus.[4] Ezekiel's prophecy goes back to the promises of Deut. 30:1–10. Although we may fail to understand God's ways, he is faithful to his promises. This should instil in God's people of every generation a deep-seated confidence in the Bible as God's written word. The words of that wonderful Getty and Townend song comes to mind:

> From the breaking of the dawn to the setting of the sun,
> I will stand on every promise of Your word.
> Words of power, strong to save, that will never pass away,
> I will stand on every promise of Your word.
> For your covenant is sure, and on this I am secure,
> I can stand on every promise of Your word.

God's covenant with his people in every age is secure. Nothing can thwart the gracious promises that he has made. Directly addressing the mocking taunts of Israel's foes, God will show that he is more than capable of keeping his children, his land, and especially his promises.

By making the people and the land fruitful 36:29–30 and 37–38

In essence God is here upholding his promise to Abraham that his seed would be as numerous as the sand on the seashore or as the stars in the sky (Gen. 12:2–3 and 22:17). This promise will not be fulfilled in the lands to which the people have been scattered but in the land that God promised to Abraham all those years earlier. This alone will silence the taunts of the enemy (36:13–23). The fulfilment of Ezekiel's word did not come immediately but some fifty years later. Ezra and Nehemiah recount the story of Israel's return from exile. We are told that King Cyrus of Persia at that time decreed that the Israelites could return to Jerusalem and rebuild the walls and temple.

The question arises as to when the restoration promised here will be fulfilled in its entirety. It is clear from history that it was certainly fulfilled in part when the Jews returned to the land under Cyrus, but it also has further fulfilment in the church. There are many New Testament passages that understand the church as the new Israel and the new people of God. For example, Paul can say in Rom. 9:6–8 that '… not all who are descended from Israel belong to Israel, and not all are children of Abraham because they are his offspring … This means that it is not the children of the flesh who are the children of God, but the children of the promise are counted as offspring'. It is not that God has abandoned the Jewish people (Rom. 11:1) but simply that Christians are also included in the family of Israel. There is a natural sense in which those physically descended from Abraham are rightly called Jews, but the New Testament teaches that there is also

It is not that God has abandoned the Jewish people but simply that Christians are also included in the family of Israel.

a deeper spiritual sense in which the true Jew is one who is inwardly a believer and whose heart has been cleansed by God.[5] This is what we shall see emphasised shortly in this very passage. If we do not see the complete fulfilment of these promises of restoration in the history of Israel, it is because that is a first-stage fulfilment with the more complete fulfilment through the church in the New Testament age.

All of these promises were partially fulfilled in the people returning to the land of Israel; are being fulfilled now as many from all nations are being drawn to Christ; and will be completely fulfilled when Christ returns and inaugurates the new heavens and new earth. This idea of 'past, present and future' fulfilment develops further in the remaining promises within this passage. Both for the exiles in Ezekiel's day and for us today, it is only when we are in a restored relationship with God that we can experience what it means to be truly fruitful, bearing fruit in keeping with the Spirit of God that dwells in our hearts (Gal. 5:16–26).

It is only when we are in a restored relationship with God that we can experience what it means to be truly fruitful.

God restores the honour of his holy name by the internal and personal renewal of his people 36:25–38

By making a new covenant with his people 36:28

Here we find the standard Old Testament formula for a covenant with God, 'You shall be my people and I will be your God'. This becomes more apparent in the next chapter (esp. 37: 26–27) so I will only touch on it here by opening up the following ideas associated with that new covenant.

By cleansing Israel 36:25

As part of this new covenant God's people are told that he will 'sprinkle clean water' on them and that they will be clean. This is probably based on the Israelite understanding of ritual cleansing and washing that was so much a part of their sacrificial system outlined in the book of Leviticus. The ritual washings were indicative of the need for cleansed hearts. All Israelites would have understood their religious duty to cleanse themselves. Even Isaiah says, 'Wash yourselves; make yourselves clean; remove the evil of your deeds from before my eyes; cease to do evil, learn to do good' (Isa. 1:16–17). Likewise Jeremiah commands the people, 'O Jerusalem, wash your heart from evil, that you may be saved. How long shall your wicked thoughts lodge within you?' (Jer 4:14). The Israelites would have understood the need for personal attention to root out the sin in their lives.[6] But that is not the emphasis here in Ezekiel. That we are to be active in cleansing ourselves from all impurities is clear, yet ultimately only God can cleanse us from our sin.

The Psalmist David when faced with his sin regarding Bathsheba and Uriah cries out to God: 'Create in me a clean heart, O God, and renew a right spirit within me' (Ps. 51:10). John similarly teaches us that 'If we confess our sins, he is faithful and just to forgive us our sins and to cleanse us from all unrighteousness' (1 John 1:9). Sin seems to be soft-peddled in some evangelical circles today. I want to suggest that we soft-peddle the reality, extent, and ramifications of sin to the peril of our generation. We need to understand the extent to which sin pollutes. Sin is not an abstract idea but a fundamental problem in every man woman and child. The Bible makes clear that the pollution of sin separates us from God (Isa. 59:2; Eph. 2:12, 4:18), and the bottom line is that God alone has the ability to cleanse us from that sin and restore our relationship with him. This rules out the possibility of boasting, or salvation through some form of self-help (Eph. 2:8–10). The gospel of God's redeeming grace is not about us cleansing ourselves, but about God graciously cleansing us and so doing for us what we cannot do for ourselves.

By giving them a new heart and new Spirit 36:26

One of my favourite songs—because of the simplicity of its message—is, 'I am a new creation, no more in condemnation, here in the grace of God I stand.' Ezekiel tells us that God is going to give his children a new heart and a new spirit. From this we can see that the problem of the Israelites, and indeed the problem of every individual who ever lived, is not simply their behaviour but the source of their behaviour—their hearts. The Lord highlights our predicament when he says, 'For out of the heart come evil thoughts, murder, adultery, sexual immorality, theft, false witness, slander' (Matt 15:19). Sin is always conceived in the heart before it ever reaches our tongues or hands, before it is spoken or acted upon. The only hope that we have of conquering sin is by having the source purified. Our putrid hearts need to be oxygenated. And the only hope of achieving that is if God does it for us. God alone can oxygenate our hearts by an infusion of his Holy Spirit. According to Ezekiel God intends to fully address this fundamental problem in his children. He is not leaving anything to chance. He is going to give every true Israelite, every true child of his, a new heart and a new spirit. In a similar vein the Apostle Paul reminds us that 'If anyone is in Christ, he is a new creation' (2 Cor. 5:17). A person may well reform his behaviour but only God can reform a person's heart and make him a whole new person. And that is what he has promised as part of his new covenant. What an encouragement for his children! We shall see more of what this entails in the next chapter.

A person may well reform his behaviour but only God can reform a person's heart and make him a whole new person.

By making them obedient 36:27

A mark of true conversion is obedience to God's word. Look again at what Ezekiel says: 'I will put my Spirit within you, and cause you to walk in my statutes and be careful to obey my rules'. It is possible for a preacher so to emphasise God's love that the only application is that we should love God and love our neighbour. Of course this is a biblical truth. But our love for God and each other is expressed in obedience. This is not simply an Old Testament teaching. It is true also for New Testament children of God.

The Apostle John puts it like this: 'And by this we know that we have come to know him, if we keep his commandments' (1 John 2:3). He goes on to say, 'By this we know that we love the children of God, when we love God and obey his commandments' (1 John 5:2). The Apostle John sees absolutely no contradiction between being saved or justified by faith alone and, at the same time, expressing our new freedom in Christ by obeying God's commandments. Neither does he see any contradiction between loving God—our first and greatest commandment—and keeping God's commandments. John clearly sees keeping God's law as an expression of our love for God and our neighbour. Obeying God is not a burden. Obeying God is not some slavish obedience to an imposed set of laws or rules but rather a heartfelt desire to know more of the holy character of God as revealed in his law, and to reflect more of that holy character in our lives. Our communion with God begins with his love for us and ends in our love for him, and our love for God is seen in our obedience to God. Our love is not expressed in a vacuum. It is not some sentimental froth that has no substance, but rather it is rooted in the law of God which is an expression of the character of God.

Our obedience is not some sentimental froth that has no substance, but rather it is rooted in the law of God which is an expression of the character of God.

John Owen anticipates opposition to this teaching by raising the question, 'If the righteousness and obedience of Christ to the law is accredited to us when we trust him as our Saviour ... then why do we still need to obey the law?'[7]

Owen's response is to suggest that we need to place our obedience on a right footing. Firstly, our obedience to God's commandments must not be 'exalted to a position or use or end or purpose that God has not given it'. In other words, we cannot be saved by, nor enhance our standing with God through, obedience to the law. On the other hand we should not dilute any use or end or purpose that God has given the law. It still has a part to play in the lives of believers. The Psalmist delighted in the law of God (Psalm 1:1–3). Similarly the Apostle Paul sees the law of God as 'holy, righteous and good' (Rom. 7:12). To quote Bridges again: 'God's law is not onerous or burdensome, but is given to help us please God and live lives that are productive and satisfying (see Psalm 1:3). One who delights in the law of God sees the Bible not just as a book of rules that are difficult to live by, but as the Word of his or her heavenly Father who is the God of all grace and deals with him or her in grace'.[8]

By causing them to be ashamed of their sin 36:31

This is not something that many Christians like to hear. Many much prefer to emphasise that if God chooses never to remember our sins (Isa. 43:25), then why should we still carry this burden about with us? Surely this is the very burden that John Bunyan so graphically describes as falling from Christian's back when he met the saviour on the cross? Indeed it is. Yet I have to confess that my ability to 'not remember' is not as good as God's. In fact, on the basis of what Ezekiel is teaching us here, I would say that the ability of all believers 'not to remember' sin will not be as good as God's ability. Of course we ought not to allow our sin to be a burden that so weighs us down that we become crippled, ineffective Christians, unable to forgive ourselves. We must not carry a burden that God would not have us carry. And when memories of those sins that have been dealt with on the cross begin to creep in, and would rob us of our joy in the Lord, we must, like God, actively choose to remember them no more. And yet shame for sin is a mark of the truly saved person, the one who has bowed the knee in humble confession and sought God's forgiveness. Chris Wright goes as far as to say that although God no longer remembers our sin, yet '... they are still to be remembered by the sinner, as a cause for shame and yet simultaneously as a cause for rejoicing in the grace of God'.[9]

This teaching is not designed to make the one whose conscience is already tender even more pained by memories of their sin, but to help them cast aside the burden of those memories and rejoice in the goodness of God's redeeming and cleansing love. Jerry Bridges puts it like this:

> If you have trusted Christ as your Saviour, then all the expressions of God's forgiveness are true of you. He has removed your sins as far as the east is from the west. He has put them behind His back and hurled them into the depths of the sea. He has blotted them out of His record book and promised never to bring them up again. You are free from accusation, not because of anything whatsoever in you, but because of His grace alone through Jesus Christ.[10]

Shame for sin is healthy in that it is the catalyst that makes us rejoice again in God's condemnation-slaying grace (Rom. 8:1–2).

These two things, shame for sin and obedience, are the

essence of practical holiness (sanctification) as distinct from essential holiness (justification). God makes us holy, and yet God also calls us to be holy—that is, obedient to his commands and his claim upon our lives. According to Ezekiel shame for sin and obedience will be distinguishing marks of the true child of God. But God does not leave us to work it all out for ourselves. He provides his children with everything necessary to live holy lives by giving us new hearts and a new spirit.

By responding to the prayers of his people 36:37–38

God had previously said that because of their sin he would not listen to their prayers (14:3; 20:3). A direct line to our heavenly Father in prayer is one of the greatest blessings the child of God enjoys, and to have that severed must surely result in floundering. But God is once again going to open his ear to the cries of his people. In prayer we see a wonderful example of the relationship between God's sovereign power over all his creation and the responsibility of his children to ask him to fulfil his promises. God does not need our prayer, yet it is his desire that his plans and purposes are worked out in partnership with the prayers of his people. The Israelites are going to be restored to their land and their numbers replenished following the devastating wars and famine. But still God requires his children to ask him to do this. That this comes in the context of God giving his people

God does not need our prayer, yet it is his desire that his plans and purposes are worked out in partnership with the prayers of his people.

a new heart and new spirit is no coincidence. Without the special work of the Holy Spirit we cannot be convinced or our need to pray. As John Owen puts it, 'He [the Holy Spirit] alone is able to give us such an understanding of our wants as that we may be able to make our thoughts about them known unto God in prayer'.[11] God uses means, and he has ordained prayer to accomplish what he has promised.

Name above all names Philippians 2:9–12

Sometimes it seems as though you just cannot win. God's name was being discredited whether he disciplined his people or not. Whilst his chastisement was just, it was not enough to restore his relationship with his people. Something more radical was needed—grace. Often our response to a crisis is to address the externals; to change the situation, get away from those who are causing us grief, or throw money at the problem to see what happens. These measures may indeed help—yet they will only partly alleviate the problems. God gets right to the root of the problem. If he is to maintain the honour of his name then it will only be through a people whose hearts have been graciously and completely renewed and infused with his Holy Spirit.

> Often our response to a crisis is to address the externals ... God gets right to the root of the problem.

If God's name was important in Ezekiel, then it is equally important in the present day. The Apostle Paul tells us that God so exalted Christ that he bestowed on him the name that is above every name, so that at the name of Jesus every knee should bow and every tongue confess him Lord to the glory of the Father (Phil. 2:9–12; see also Isa. 45:23). As Luter says, 'The exalted Christ shares the universal Lordship known to Yahweh, and is thus given the name "LORD".'[12] The name by which Jesus became known in the early church was Lord, the word by which Yahweh was translated in the Greek version of the Hebrew Old Testament. It implies that he is the divine, pre-existent, sovereign creator of the universe and owner of all life. He is Lord over all the affairs of man.

We need to recognise that failure or sin on the part of God's people is a bad reflection on the Lord and Saviour we confess. When we fail or fall into sin people do not simply scoff at us; they take great delight in scoffing at God. So let us be diligent in maintaining our relationship with God, recognising in thankfulness what he has done for us. He has cleansed us from our sin. He makes us ashamed of our sin. He has given us the power we need to be obedient citizens. Let us also recognise what God continues to do for us, responding to our prayers and ever attentive to our deepest needs. May our obedience to God not be that of duty, but rather the obedience of thankful hearts.

In reaching out to our community, social programmes play an important part. But in a world where God's name is seen as a joke and uttered daily in blasphemous tones, what fallen humanity needs is a fundamental cleansing, a divine heart transplant, and an infusion of the divine Spirit. Our future—the future of the true Israel of God—rests on God's eternal promises to us as his covenant people. We can rejoice knowing that his covenant is sure, and we can therefore stand on every promise of his word.

For further study ▶

FOR FURTHER STUDY

1. When God revealed himself to Moses as 'I AM WHO I AM' in Exodus 3:14–15 he was essentially instructing Moses that he is to be known in the context of his everlasting covenant. What bearing does this have on God's concern for his name in Ezekiel 36?
2. Jesus is designated 'Lord' in the New Testament. What are the implications of this for humanity, especially in the light of Philippians 2:8–12?
3. Read Jeremiah 29:10–14. What overlap do we find here with Ezekiel's prophecy that God will restore his people?
4. Read Deuteronomy 30:1–10 and compare it with Ezekiel 36:16–38.
5. Compare the following passages—Ezekiel 11:19, 18:31, 36:26; Jeremiah 32:39. What do these passages teach us about the significance of receiving this new heart in relation to keeping God's commandments and statutes?
6. Many in the church today suggest that since we are no longer under the law (e.g. Galatians 3:10–14), the commandments of God have no relevance to the church. Yet in 1 John 2:3–6, 5:1–5 we are explicitly challenged to obey God's commandments. How can we reconcile the two biblical truths that on the one hand we are no longer under the law, yet on the other hand God has given us new hearts so that we can actually obey his commandments and statutes? See especially Paul's teaching in Romans 7 that we are released from the law, and yet he delights in the law of God (Romans 7:22). What can Ezekiel 36:22–27 bring to the discussion?

TO THINK ABOUT AND DISCUSS

1. From this passage, in what ways is God's grace radical?
2. 'It is for the people to reflect the nature of Yahweh and not the other way around. The problem throughout Ezekiel's prophecy has been that God's people were not reflecting his virtue but the vices of the gods and peoples of the nations around them.' Discuss potential implications of this statement for the church today.
3. John Calvin commenting on 1 John 2:3–6 says: 'But there is no one who in everything

keeps them [God's commandments]; there would thus be no knowledge of God in the world. To this I answer, that the Apostle is in no means inconsistent with himself; since he has before shewed that all are guilty before God, he does not understand that those who keep his commandments wholly satisfy the law (no such example can be found in the world;) but that they are such as strive, according to the capacity of human infirmity, to form their life in conformity to the will of God'. What light do these words shed on Ezekiel's message in this chapter? What do you think it means to strive according to the capacity of human infirmity?

19 Can these bones live?

Ezekiel Chapter 37

People need a doctor because they are ill. They need God because they are dead! Nothing but the grace of God can breathe new life into someone who is dead in sin.[1] This is the central message of hope for all who accept the grace of God, and a powerful declaration of hope for life after death.

Car SOS is a popular television programme in which the two presenters—Fuzz Townshend and Tim Shaw, backed up by a team of car specialists—restore classic cars for owners who have been unable to carry out the work themselves due to life-debilitating illnesses or circumstances. It is fascinating to watch as they take a car that to all intents and purposes is dead. Rusting wrecks with engines that have seized solid through years of disuse and decay are stripped back to the frame and rebuilt and painted to a standard reminiscent of how they would have rolled off the production line when new. But a body and paint job is not all that is required to make these old machines roadworthy again. To breathe new life into these amazing classics, it is often necessary to replace or rebuild their aging engines to near-new specification.

In this chapter Ezekiel witnesses the power of God as he takes a valley full of decaying dry bones and restores to them all that is necessary to make them complete perfect bodies once more. But more than that, Ezekiel watches as God breathes into those dead bodies and restores them to new life. It is a message of great hope in the direst of circumstances and most hopeless of situations. These bones have nothing within themselves to change their desperate condition. Nothing but the grace of God could breathe new life into the death and decay that Ezekiel found on that valley floor. It is a picture of the natural condition of all who remain dead in their sin (Eph. 2:1; Col. 2:13). As Christians we are not called to preach a message of healing from sickness,[2] but a message of life from the dead. People are not simply sick with sin but dead in sin and trespasses, and nothing short of a spiritual resurrection from the dead, a new birth, can alter their dead condition. This is from first to last a work of God; yet he calls us to speak his life-giving message.

Ezekiel's day trip 37:1–10

Yet again we find Ezekiel being spirited away for another lesson-filled vision. On this occasion he is carried by the Spirit of God to a valley which is strewn with bones. It is possibly the scene of an old battle where there was extensive loss of life. The remains scattered there have been exposed to the elements for so long that they do not even constitute skeletons but rather disconnected bones that are well advanced in the

What Ezekiel witnesses is a scene of death and decay, condemnation and utter hopelessness.

process of decay. As Ezekiel is led around the valley he becomes acutely aware of two things about these bones: they were there in abundance and they were very dry (37:1–2). That these bones were unburied was evidence not just of death, but of death under a curse.[3] What Ezekiel witnesses is a scene of death and decay, condemnation and utter hopelessness. As Jeffery comments,

> The prophet must have been shocked at what he saw. He had seen nothing like this before, and revulsion must have filled his heart. But the vision was meant by God to do just this; it was meant to hit him hard.[4]

The bewildering question 37:3

Having walked Ezekiel through this staggering sight, God then puts a rather bewildering question to him: 'Can these bones live?' The question is not designed to catch Ezekiel out, but rather to focus his thoughts. As someone who has been schooled on the stories of Elijah raising the widow of Zarephath's son from the dead (1 Kings 17:17–24), and of Elisha raising the Shunammite's son (2 Kings 4:18–37), Ezekiel understood that with God nothing is impossible. Yet looking at this desolate scene must have given him a sense of despair and hopelessness.

Having been trained up for the priesthood and, especially over these last few years, having experienced God's power first-hand, Ezekiel knows only too well that if God made Adam from the dust of the earth and breathed life into him, raising up these bones was not impossible for him. Yet standing in the middle of that desperate scene he cannot bring himself to answer in the affirmative. Ezekiel knew only too well that neither he nor any other earthly agent could revive these bones, so he wisely refers the question back to an all knowing, all powerful God.[5] Ezekiel tentatively responds by stating that God alone knows the answer. He is not trying to avoid the question, but rather '... casts himself entirely upon the will and the power of God'.[6] And of course his response was true: God did know, and was about to make that point very clear.

Talking to the dead 37:4–8

> Then he said to me, 'Prophesy over these bones, and say to them, "O dry bones, hear the word of the LORD"' (37:4).

What a command! There he is, in the middle of this valley of 'very dry' bones, a hopeless situation indeed, and God tells him to preach to the bones. It is a seemingly absurd request. A contemporary equivalent would be to send a young preacher out to the nearest cemetery and tell him to preach to its inhabitants. From a human vantage point it is a pointless exercise, yet Ezekiel obeyed. To his credit he simply did as he was told. Ezekiel's sermon begins with the words, 'Hear the word of the LORD'. As he is preaching to the bones they actually begin to come together: sinews and veins, and then muscle and flesh, appear over the bones, and finally even the skin returns, just as God had declared through his prophet. But there is still something missing—life!

Talking to the breath of life 37:9–10

By this stage Ezekiel must have been utterly amazed at what

he had just witnessed. But God is about to give a further demonstration of his power. Looking down on those now complete but lifeless bodies, God tells Ezekiel to prophesy to the breath (or 'Spirit', or 'wind').[7] He is to summon the breath from the four winds or four corners of the earth to breathe into the bodies so that they might be restored to new life. Again Ezekiel obeys the command of God and the corpses receive their breath, their life, and they stand up on their feet—a vast army. What an incredible sight! A valley full of bones—no life, no hope—and yet God brings them back to life. Not just one or two of them but a whole army. It is as if he wants to make his point absolutely clear: nothing is too difficult for God.

But what does all this mean to Ezekiel's audience by the Chebar canal? What is God's point in all of this at a time when he has just allowed the nation to be overrun by the Babylonians? Typically Ezekiel does not leave us to second-guess the purpose of the vision.

The meaning and purpose of the vision 37:11–14

The bones represent the whole house of Israel. The people have been lamenting their situation with the words of yet another popular saying: 'Our bones have dried up, and our hope is lost; we are indeed cut off' (37:11). God has once again taken the words of the people, turned them on their head, and expressed his intention of a positive future for them. The exiles are understandably dejected following the final sacking of Jerusalem. It seems all hope is gone. They talk in terms of their bones having dried up; they are without hope, cut off from their cherished home and temple. God now takes their expression and reassures them through the prophet that he is not finished with them. He will open their graves, raise up their dry dead bones, and restore them to their precious land once more (37:11–12). The reference to graves is simply another picture like the vision of the valley of bones. It represents life out of death and hope out of hopelessness. It is a promise of returning to the land of Israel out of the despair of exile. It is God's intention to take his people and raise them up again. Putting his Spirit within his people he will resuscitate them, breathing into them new and abundant life with the express purpose that '… you shall know that I am LORD' (37:13–14).

> It is God's intention to take his people and raise them up again.

Essentially what we see here is God's promise to reverse the death or exile of his people and restore them to their own land. You may recall that Ezekiel 36:16–38 was about the restoration of Israel for the sake of God's holy name. Now in 37:1–14 we see the revival and restoration of Israel by the preaching of God's holy word (prophecy) and in the power of his Holy Spirit (breath). In 36:16–38 we see the importance of God's name. In 37:1–14 we see a demonstration of God's Word and Spirit. To summarise another way: in 36:16–38 we see Israel restored, as they are given back the land to demonstrate the glory of God's name. In 37:1–14 we see Israel revived, given new life out of death and exile to demonstrate God's power.

But there is a deeper level of meaning to Ezekiel's latest vision. As Block points out,

> [It] affirms that there is life after death, and there is hope

> beyond the grave ... this vision of the resuscitation of dry bones is not only for the nation of Israel. The valley represents the whole world, and the bones the entire human race under the curse of death for its rebellion against God. Accordingly, this text holds out hope for all who accept the grace of God in Christ (Eph. 2:1–10).[8]

Never give up

The similarities between this incident and God's creation of Adam cannot go unnoticed. The spirit of life is from God. It was so for Adam who, having been formed from the dust of the earth, had the breath of life breathed into him by God. It was true of this vast army in Ezekiel's valley, and it is true of every person who will listen to God's voice and accept his wonderful offer of salvation. This vision represents the power and the grace of God in restoring lost and helpless sinners. The Apostle Paul says to the Ephesian church that those without Christ are dead in their trespasses and sins. Only the life-giving Spirit of God can change that. We are destitute and helpless in and of ourselves. We are dead! We can do nothing to effect our own salvation. Salvation is necessarily a work of God the Holy Spirit who infuses us with new life.

We can do nothing to effect our own salvation. Salvation is necessarily a work of God the Holy Spirit who infuses us with new life.

The Word and the Spirit

Note the twin tasks of sharing God's Word and utter

dependence on the Holy Spirit for this life-giving assignment. John Stott, reflecting on 1 Corinthians 2:6–16, speaks of the dual role of the Word of God and the Spirit of God. He gives a superb four point summary showing how the Holy Spirit (i) searches the heart and thoughts of God, (ii) revealed his findings to the apostles and other biblical writers, (iii) inspired the biblical authors to share the message through words chosen by him, and (iv) enlightens the minds of those who read the Bible to understand the message of the biblical authors. Stott concludes by saying, 'So we need to humble ourselves before both the Word and the Spirit. We still have to study the Word, to ponder its meaning and application, but we also need to cry to the Holy Spirit for enlightenment. Humble prayer and diligent study need to be combined'.[9] This principle extends to evangelism. The Apostle Paul sums it up in his letter to the church at Thessalonica: 'Our gospel came to you not only in word, but also in power and in the Holy Spirit and with full conviction' (I Thes. 1:5).

Preaching the gospel, or simply sharing it with our family or friends or work colleagues, may sometimes seem like a pointless exercise. Some of us have been praying for years for the salvation of our loved ones. It is a burden that weighs heavily on our hearts to think of them not accepting Christ's most gracious offer of salvation. We may begin to doubt if some will ever come to faith in Christ and experience that wonderful new life that is found only in a right relationship with him. We may even wonder if we are praying in accordance with God's will. But the message of Ezekiel's vision of the valley of dry bones is one of immense encouragement not to give up, no matter how hopeless a situation may seem. Writing to the church in Rome, Paul tells us that faith comes from hearing and hearing from the word of Christ (Rom. 10:13–17). People lost, indeed people dead in their sin can only know of the life-giving power of God if we tell them. But knowledge is not enough. There is no substitute for earnest and urgent prayer: prayer that summons the breath of God from the four winds to breathe spiritual life into our loved ones, and neighbours, and friends. As Jeffery puts it,

> The spiritual condition of our land is frightening, but is it past hope? Can these bones live today? Can our unbelieving relatives be saved? Can that foul-mouthed, blaspheming man at work come to Christ? Can those pleasant but spiritually lost neighbours who have no time for God be converted? Is God telling us to witness to dry bones such as these, to tell them the gospel? ...It may be that we feel totally inadequate to meet the needs of today, but we could not be more inadequate than Ezekiel in the valley of dry bones ... What really matters is this: do we trust God to work?[10]

The word of God is powerful

Through the prophet Isaiah[11] the Lord tells us that his word is like snow and rain that fall on the earth, watering it and causing it to produce crops. So his word when it is shared with others will produce the fruit for which it is designed. In the case of the valley of dry bones it brought about miraculous restoration. That word has not lost its power. People still need to hear the message of God's powerful life-changing word as he has revealed it to us in the Bible. In a world of no absolutes the gospel message remains the power of God for salvation

(Rom. 1:16–17). Life can seem meaningless, but the word of God makes known to us the reason for our very existence. As Christians we are certainly to live authentic lives before our unsaved neighbours. But lifestyle alone does not have the power to pour life into one who is spiritually dead. There is no substitute for the word of God and prayer. It is the gospel that is the power of God for salvation. It exposes our shortcomings and provides all that we need to be transformed from death to life. Furthermore, there can be no doubt as to who breathes new life into people: 'I will put my Spirit within you, and you shall live' says Yahweh (37:14). Salvation belongs to the Lord. Revival in our day will not come from church programmes or by dumbing down the gospel. Revival will come when, through the earnest sharing of God's word and utter dependence on the Holy Spirit, God breathes his life-giving breath on those who are dead in sin.

Lifestyle alone does not have the power to pour life into one who is spiritually dead. There is no substitute for the word of God and prayer.

Furthermore, our spiritual resuscitation is but a precursor to the eschatological promise of life after death. God will one day raise up from the grave all who have been born again of the Spirit of God, with the promise that we will live with him for all eternity. Surely this is the greatest hope of all for those suffering bereavement. The apostle Paul encourages us with the teaching that all believers in Christ share in his resurrection (1 Thessalonians 4:13–18). The resurrection of Christ brings hope. Just as God would extend hope to the exiles by the Chebar canal in Ezekiel's day, so he extends hope to all in our day: that our sin can be forgiven, and that there is a life without pain or tears with our heavenly Father for all eternity.

Breathe on me, Breath of God,
fill me with life anew,
that I may love the way you love,
and do what you would do.
Breathe on me, Breath of God,
until my heart is pure,
until my will is one with yours,
to do and to endure.
Breathe on me, Breath of God,
so shall I never die,
but live with you the perfect life
for all eternity.
(Edwin Hatch 1835–1889)

God's everlasting covenant with Israel

37:15–28

God is about to demonstrate his covenant faithfulness by not only restoring the exiles to the land of their birth but also reuniting the split kingdom.

Following his traumatic day trip, the word of God comes to Ezekiel another time. This latest oracle contains the promise that the divided kingdom of Israel is to be reunited. As the exiles sit by the Chebar canal watching Ezekiel take to the stage once again to perform his latest skit, they are a divided and broken people. Ever since the time of Rehoboam, the son of Solomon, Israel has been a divided kingdom. But God is about to demonstrate his covenant faithfulness by not only restoring the exiles to the land of their birth but also reuniting the split kingdom. This is to be a demonstration of God's faithfulness to the covenant he made with Abraham when he promised to make from him a great nation (Gen. 12:2).

Ezekiel's latest drama 37:15–17

This time Ezekiel is to take two sticks and write on them (37:16). On the first he is to write 'For Judah, and the people of Israel associated with him'. This is a reference to the two southern tribes of Israel. On the second he is to write 'For Joseph (the stick of Ephraim) and all the house of Israel associated with him'. The reference this time is to the ten northern tribes of Israel. Ephraim is the name given to the ten northern tribes of Israel because Jeroboam, the first king of the separated northern kingdom, was from the tribe of Ephraim.[12] Ezekiel is now instructed to join the two sticks together so that they become one in his hand (37:17).

True to Ezekiel's form we are not left to guess what all of this means. Notice that on both sticks Ezekiel was to write, 'and the house of Israel associated with him.' Both the southern and the northern kingdoms were called Israel. The point being made is that the two sticks represent the divided kingdom, the divided people, the divided nation of Israel.

Ezekiel's explanation of the two sticks drama 37:18–28

Joining the two sticks represents joining together the two separate kingdoms, the reunification of Israel as one political and religious entity. This becomes clear in this portion of Ezekiel's prophecy. When his countrymen ask what it all means, Ezekiel is to tell them that God intends to take both sticks, or nations, and make them one in his hand (37:18–19). The point is clarified further in the next few verses. God is going to take this divided people from the nations where they are currently dispersed, return them to the mountains of Israel, and make the two kingdoms one nation in his land (37:20–22). More than that, God will place one shepherd-king over them (37:22)—none other than David his servant (37:24). There is a hint here that this renewal will go beyond physical Israel returning from exile. The restoration is to take place in the context of an everlasting covenant of peace (37:26). God is going to reunite his scattered people, make them one nation, with one shepherd-king, under one covenant of peace. Note the repetition of one. It is used at least ten times in verses 16–24. This is to emphasise the unity of what God is going to bring about.

The kingdom of Jesus the Messiah

Has this reunification ever taken place? Although the exiles returned to Jerusalem in the days of Nehemiah, the unity spoken of in Ezekiel chapter 37 never happened in its fullest sense to the nation of Israel. As Wright notes, 'The dispersion of the northern tribes by the Assyrians after the destruction of Samaria in 721 was never really reversed in the same way that the exiles of Judah returned from Babylon after the edict of Cyrus in 538'.[13] Furthermore, as Derek Thomas points out, neither should we see the fulfilment of this in the establishment of the nation of Israel in 1948. Even that does not do justice to the unity that God promises here.

How then are we to understand this? The first indication of what this means in the long run can be found in verse 24. God will make his servant David king over them. Now of course we know that God has nowhere in the Bible promised to resurrect David for this purpose. Rather, David is a reference to the Messianic son of David, the Messiah, the Lord Jesus Christ. The restoration of the exiles to the land of Israel is but a step towards the coming of the promised King and Prince of Peace, the Lord Jesus Christ. It is Christ who will gather into his kingdom the true Israel of God. According to the apostle Paul in his letter to the church at Rome, true Israel consists of all those who by faith accept Christ as their King. The reign of the one shepherd-king, David, is the reign of Christ in his kingdom made known through the church.[14]

It is Christ who will gather into his kingdom the true Israel of God.

This is something we have already seen in Ezekiel 34. Jesus is variously known as the Prince of Peace, Immanuel—God in our midst, the Son of David, and the good shepherd.[15] Ezekiel's promise of unification is part and parcel of God's one covenant for his one people under his one Shepherd-King. This one Shepherd-King, according to John 10:16, has sheep from another sheep fold, a reference to the Gentiles being incorporated into the covenant. This is in keeping with Ezekiel 37:28 and the idea that '… the nations will know that I am Lord'. A key purpose of the vision of the valley of dry bones was so that Israel—'you my people'—would know that Yahweh was Lord (37:13). It now seems that a key purpose of the two sticks dramatization is so that the nations will know that Yahweh is Lord (37:28). God is showing us, even here in Ezekiel, that he intends to bring the Gentiles into his covenant of peace (37:26). The word of God never fails.

So although this prophecy did not see ultimate fulfilment in the return from exile, it is being fulfilled through the church. Paul tells us in Romans 9:6–12 that not all those from the nation of Israel or descended from Abraham are the true children of God. Rather, it is those who by faith in Christ are adopted into God's family. Paul's argument is that Abraham believed the Lord and it was counted to him as righteousness. In other words, God declared Abraham righteous because of his faith in just the same way that he declares us righteous when we exercise faith in Christ. Our adoption into God's family and the kingdom of his Son is by faith. It is not on account of our having the right DNA, ethnicity, or land of birth. Furthermore, it is not because of our religious affiliation. The true Israel comprises all those who have been circumcised in their hearts and have put their faith in the Messiah. This is both an Old Testament and New Testament teaching—Deuteronomy 10:16; 30:6; and Rom 2:29. Paul writing to the Galatians also makes it clear that if we belong to Christ then we are Abraham's children and therefore the Israel of God (Gal. 3:29; 6:16). This promise of

The true Israel comprises all those who have been circumcised in their hearts and have put their faith in the Messiah.

course does not exclude the nation of Israel. The apostle goes on in Romans chapter 9 to express the promise that although many branches, or individuals within the nation of Israel, are broken-off from the promise because of failing to believe in and trust the Messiah; yet there will be many saved from that nation. Israelites by natural birth can become members of true Israel in the same way as Gentile believers, by the circumcision of their hearts or new spiritual birth. In this way, the future looks bright for both Jew and Gentile.

The purpose of Ezekiel's vision of dry bones and latest drama is to restore hope to the disheartened and crushed nation of Israel. Both bring a message of hope for their restoration to the land promised to their forefathers. But the vision of the valley of dry bones also brings hope to this generation. It is the message of the hope of new life through faith in Christ. It is a message of hope of eternal life, life after death. Ezekiel's excursion through the valley of dry bones with all its death and destruction was intended to hit him hard and make an impact, but it was a prerequisite to the wonderful expression of God's power over death that followed. Likewise, until people see themselves as God sees them—dead in trespasses and sin—they will not understand their need, nor God's wonderful provision of life through faith in his Son. The greatest hope for a despairing generation is that God would breathe his breath upon us and raise us up to life in its fullest sense. This is the message of hope to all who accept the grace of God in Christ.

For further study ▶

FOR FURTHER STUDY

1. Consider Ezekiel 37 in the light of Genesis 2:1–7. What bearing does the Genesis passage have on Ezekiel's message about the valley of dry bones?
2. Read John 11:17–27 and compare it with Ezekiel 37. What are the similarities between the two passages? What do they both teach us about God's power over life and death?
3. What light do Eph. 2:1 and Col. 2:13 shed on Ezekiel's vision of the valley of dry bones?
4. The Bible's teaching on our inability to bring about our own salvation is not popular today. Search the following passages for a brief insight into this teaching: Psalm 51:5; 58:3; Isiah 64:6; Jeremiah 17:9; John 6:44; Romans 3:10–11; Ephesians 2:1–5.
5. What comfort can we draw from Paul's teaching in 1 Thessalonians 4:13–18? How does this relate to Ezekiel chapter 37?
6. What light does Galatians 3:28 shed on the unity expressed in Ezekiel 37?
7. What do the following passages teach about the importance of preaching or sharing the Bible's message and how that is connected to people coming to faith in Christ? Romans 10:13–17; James 1:18; 1 Peter 1:23–25.

TO THINK ABOUT AND DISCUSS

1. Read the stories of Elijah raising the widow of Zarephath's son from the dead (1 Kings 17:17–24); and of Elisha raising the Shunammite's son (2 Kings 4:18–37). Discuss the similarities and differences between these and Ezekiel's vision of the dry bones. According to John 11:38–44 (the raising of Lazarus), what is the main purpose of such displays of power?
2. The English poet Edward Young (1683–1765) is renowned for his literary legacy. One of his better-known quotes from 'Night Thoughts' is: 'Our birth is nothing but our death begun'. In context—

> While man is growing, life is in decrease,
> And cradles rock us nearer to the tomb.

> Our birth is nothing but our death begun;
>
> As tapers [candles] waste that instant they take fire.

Turn this quote on its head—'Our death is nothing but our life begun.' Discuss the implications for those who are saved and for the unsaved.

3. In a postmodern world where the denial of absolute truth brings despair, how might we use the Word of God to restore real hope? How might the teaching of Ezekiel 37 influence the ministry of your church?

20 The enemies of God will not succeed

Ezekiel Chapters 38–39

The true church of Christ has been under attack in every generation since its inception. From Nero's barbaric treatment of Christians, to present day terrorist attacks on Christians gathered for worship on the Lord's Day; to pastors and street preachers being arrested in the UK for citing the Bible in response to moral questions,[1] the church is under attack. Ezekiel's latest vision of a vast army arising against God's people can be understood as symbolic of such assaults on the church. But even this is a further message of hope. The enemies of God will not succeed. Remembering that we too were once enemies of God, it is our duty to continue to bring the good news of his loving salvation to the nations. In fighting the good fight of the faith,[2] God's children must not become warmongers but the ultimate peacemakers.

Throughout history there have been coalitions between nations against a common foe. The aim of such alliances is to make victory all but inevitable. In a vision of the future, long after the Israelites have returned from their exile by the Chebar canal, Ezekiel sees a coalition of nations advancing against the people of God. However, God's enemies will be wiped out; his people will know his protection and blessing; and all will know that God alone is Lord over all creation.

If some of the details of these two chapters are complicated, the overall message is straightforward. God's name had been profaned by his people and so he acted against them in allowing them to be overrun by their enemies. This in turn led to the nations profaning God's name as he is considered unable to protect his people. Coming full circle, God will now obliterate his enemies and restore his people. He will vindicate his holiness in the sight of both Israel and the nations (38:16; 39:27). God's final victory over evil is seen through two lenses. Chapter 38 focuses on God's victory over evil from the perspective of Gog's plans and intentions. Chapter 39 focuses on God's victory over evil from the perspective of Gog's absolute and horrific defeat.

A great army gathers against the people of God 38:1–9

The coalition of nations alluded to above is headed up by an individual referred to as Gog of Magog[3] the chief prince of Meshech, and Tubal (38:2–3), and includes the nations of Persia, Cush, and Put. Two other leaders are also part of this alliance, Gomer and Beth-togarmah (38:5–6). We have come across Meshech and Tubal previously in Ezekiel 32:26

where they are condemned to Sheol together with Egypt. The families of Meshech, Tubal, Togmorah, and Gomer are all mentioned as the nations descended from Noah in Genesis 10:2–3.

Some commentators have suggested that Meshech is a reference to modern day Moscow, and Tubal represents modern Tobolsk, the historic capital of Siberia. However, T.C. Mitchell in his article in the *New Bible Dictionary*[4] gives an alternative historical insight into this ancient people. Douglas Stuart taking a similar line sums it up as follows: The people of Meshech are called the 'Muski' in Assyrian documents and the 'Moschoi' in Greek literature. We know quite a bit about their history: how they were an Indo-European people who migrated to what is now part of Armenia, southeast of the Black Sea, how they allied with the people of Tubal in the same region, fought often with the Assyrians, etc. We know then, that Meshech has nothing whatever to do with 'Moscow' or tubal with 'Tobolsk,' but are simply distant, fierce, warlike nations that are mentioned in the Bible to signify the forces opposed to the Lord's people.[5]

This war-hungry league of nations that is coming against God's people is so numerous that Ezekiel describes them as a cloud covering the land (38:6–9 and 16). But, with all their combined military power and sheer mass, they are no match for God. From the outset Ezekiel makes it clear that even this warring horde is under God's supreme control. Even today farmers control large animals like bulls by a chain attached to a ring through the animal's nose. With similar imagery God shows his control of the warring hordes: 'I will turn you about and put hooks in your jaws, and I will bring you out …' (38:3–6). God not only declares his opposition to them, but his control of their every move. He not only brings them out but steers them as those being led by hooks through their jaws.

The evil reasons for the gathering spelled out 38:10–13

As an army chaplain I have found myself on many occasions on training exercises with the troops, standing around a well-constructed model of the local area as those in charge relay their plan for taking an 'enemy' position. It is normal to have a plan when going into battle and Gog and his unholy coalition have theirs. The first thing we are told about the coalition's plan is that it is evil (38:10). They are scheming to attack a nation at peace and without even the most basic protection of walls around their towns and villages. The attackers are going for easy pickings (38:11–13).

> God is controlling Gog and his allies as an ancient king might have controlled his prisoners—with hooks through their jaws.

God's holy purpose is behind Gog's evil purpose 38:14–16

This impressive and threatening host of nations will come out of their place in the furthest parts of the north, an army so large it covers the land like a cloud. They are coming out, but it is God who is bringing them out according to verse 16. We have already seen in verse 4 that God is controlling Gog and his allies as an ancient king might have controlled his prisoners—with hooks through their jaws. God is clearly using Gog for his own purposes. 'I will bring you against my land, that the nations may know me, when through you, O Gog, I vindicate my holiness before their eyes' (38:16). As Block puts it, 'Yahweh's purpose in bringing on the hordes of Gog is to convince the nations of his presence and his person. He is not satisfied with his own people drawing this conclusion from their full restoration as his people; as the sovereign of all nations he desires that all know him, specifically his holiness'.[6] There will come a time at the end of history when everyone will recognise God. A time when every knee will bow before him, and even the tongues of his enemies shall confess his name (Romans 14:10; Philippians 2:10).

There will come a time at the end of history when everyone will recognise God.

God intervenes so that Gog and his allies are utterly defeated 38:17–23

Confirming the trustworthiness of his prophets and the truth of their messages over the years, God addresses Gog as the one who is to come against his people (38:17). 'Gog is totally oblivious to the fact that he is but a puppet on Yahweh's strings. He imagines he is campaigning against Israel of his own free will'.[7] God will intervene on behalf of his people and with passionate anger against Gog (38:17–19). God will use natural events to defeat his foe (38:19–20 and22), as well as causing such confusion that Gog's army will turn their swords on each other (38:21). Their defeat will be absolute. 'The many nations of the invading force (6) would find themselves many nations under the torrent of God's destructive judgement (22), which would prove the greatness and the holiness of God in the sight of the many nations (23)'.[8]

Gog attacks Israel but is destroyed without Israel lifting a weapon 39:1–16

In the first few verses of chapter 39 we find some repetition. Ezekiel is to repeat God's opposition to Gog. God is once again shown as the one in control as he brings Gog against his people but then disarms him (39:1–3). Gog and his armies will fall on the mountains and open fields of Israel and his own homeland will be devoured with fire (39:4–6). The purpose behind God's outpouring of wrath is once again spelled out; it is so that his holy name will be known by Israel and the nations. This day of which God speaks will certainly come: 'It is coming and it will be brought about, declares the LORD God' (39:7–8).

The number seven becomes significant over the next few verses. We are told that the scattered weapons of Gog and his hordes will provide seven years' worth of firewood; and it will take seven months to bury the dead (39:9–16). Grier suggests that '... taking this literally, on a moderate estimate, it would involve an aggregate of 360,000,000 corpses'.[9] However, it is unlikely that the numbers cited here are meant to be taken literally. As Grier goes on to point out, 'The numbers "seven years" and "seven months" are without doubt symbolical. Seven is the number of perfection and what is emphasised is the completeness of the overthrow of the multitude of His people's enemies.'[10] The enemies of God in any generation may think that they have the upper hand, but even their moves to humiliate or eradicate the people of God are within God's sovereign control. God will have the final victory.

The horrors of war—wild birds and animals feast on Gog's slain 39:17–20

Ezekiel's attention now turns from Gog to deliver what Chris Wright has described as 'invitation cards on behalf of God himself to every kind of bird and all the wild animals'.[11] Between the slaughter of Gog's army and the burial of it, the birds and wild animals are invited to feast on the corpses of the slain until their bellies are filled and they are drunk on the blood (39:17–20; see also v. 4). Although the invitation is made to the birds and beasts, it is not for the sake of those creatures but rather to emphasise to men the certainty of God's victory over his enemies.[12] A similar invitation is sent out by the angel following the Battle of Armageddon in Revelation 19:17. As Fowler White notes, 'The angel's message is virtually a verbatim quotation of the invitation issued for the Gog-Magog crisis in Ezekiel's prophecy (39:17–20)'.[13]

Furthermore, John refers to Ezekiel's reference to Gog in 20:1–10. In doing this the apostle '... based his description of both the Armageddon revolt (19:17–21) and the Gog-Magog revolt (20:7–10) on the same prophetic passage, Ezekiel 38–39'.[14] The reason for drawing attention to these parallels is to highlight the yet future element of Ezekiel's prophecy as understood by John in Revelation. This also has bearing on how we are to understand the remaining chapters of Ezekiel, as we shall see.

The restoration of Israel is the vindication of God's holiness 39:21–29

There can be no doubt that God's driving motive is the vindication of his holiness. The house of Israel will know that God has not forsaken them to their exile by the Chebar canal; and the nations will now understand that it was not due to weakness on God's part that his people were thus defeated, but rather it was at his command that they suffered on account of their own sinfulness (39:21–24).

> There can be no doubt that God's driving motive is the vindication of his holiness.

After they have borne their shame and disgrace among the nations, God states clearly that Israel will be restored to their land and experience no longer his anger but his mercy, as they dwell safely in their land. It is through this act of allowing his people to be sent into exile, followed by his most gracious restoration of them, that God's holiness will be vindicated, and his name exalted among the nations (39:25–28). The section closes with a promise that God will never again hide his face from his people when he pours out his Spirit upon them (39:29). History has shown that Israel was indeed restored to its land during the time of Nehemiah, but there is a hint that this promise also points to a time in the distant future. The beginning of the fulfilment can be seen in the outpouring of the Holy Spirit on the day of Pentecost (Acts 2:1–21); but this promise shall see its completion at a time yet in the future.

In order to better understand what this ferocious battle

against Gog of Magog refers to, it is important that we consider John's reference to Gog in Revelation 19:13–20:15.

The persecuted church

God's chastisement of his people in sending them into exile will be vindicated as he shows that his control over the affairs of men is absolute. God's people will experience God's protection while his enemies will be conclusively defeated.

From Ezekiel's perspective this is a future event, a time long after the Babylonian exiles have been restored to their home. The people are living in peace and the waste places have been re-inhabited (38:11–12). His reference to the latter years in 38:8 and latter days, 38:16, give a further clue that what God is teaching through his prophet is an end-times event, and the fact that Ezekiel's teaching is picked up by John in Revelation chapters 19–20 indicates that for the apostle it was also still in the future.

God's chastisement of his people in sending them into exile will be vindicated as he shows that his control over the affairs of men is absolute.

In the Bible the phrases latter years and latter days (38:8 and 16) are generally understood as the latter days of Christ's kingdom on earth. Last days can be seen as representing all the days from the crucifixion and ascension of Jesus until his second coming; but it would seem that there is to be a period just prior to the second advent when hostility to God's people will increase.

The Bible does make clear that there will be an upsurge in

hostility against the people of God in the last days. This theme and language of Ezekiel 38–39 is taken up in Revelation, showing that the church will undergo an unspecified period of persecution under the leadership of a certain Gog (Revelation 20:8). Bearing in mind that the armies of Gog mentioned in Ezekiel are very numerous, they 'could adequately symbolize world-wide opposition to the Church in the days just preceding Christ's second coming'.[15]

John's use of Ezekiel's imagery is set in the context of Satan's brief release from prison (Rev. 20:3 and 8). Satan will deceive the nations and stir up Gog for battle. But as the opposition to God's people is at its height and the church appears defeated, fire will descend from heaven and consume them. This is the immediate prelude to Christ coming down from heaven, when the devil is thrown into the lake of fire, and the new heavens and new earth are established in which righteousness dwells (2 Peter 3:13). The good news that flows out of all of this is that there is coming a day when all evil will be overthrown by God once and for all and God's kingdom will be established for all eternity.

2016–17 saw yet another increase in the number of Christians facing persecution worldwide, with Open Doors identifying 2016 as the '… worst year yet'. 'Persecution rose globally again for the third year in a row, indicating how volatile the situation has become', stated Open Doors. 'Countries in South and Southeast Asia rapidly rose to unprecedented levels and now rank among such violent areas as the Middle East and Sub-Saharan Africa.'[16] But even with this level of persecution, it would seem that there is yet further and potentially greater persecution to come.

So how near are we to this final overthrow of evil? God has deliberately not specified the time. The Bible authors sometimes speak as if it is very near and at other times as if it remains a long way off. But that is only from a human perspective. We must remember that '… with the Lord a day is like a thousand years, and a thousand years are like a day' (2 Peter 3:8). It has been about 2000 years since Peter penned these words, so perhaps this day is not so far away. After all, significant Bible events occur on the third day.

FOR FURTHER STUDY

1. Read 1 Timothy 6:12 and Matthew 5:43–48. How can we as Christians hold these two biblical truths in a way that pleases God?
2. Consider Isaiah 10:5–12. In what way does this passage support what we are learning from Ezekiel 38:17–23; and what parallels can you see between the two passages?
3. Read Romans 14:10–12 and Philippians 2:10. What is implied by the phrase bow the knee in these passages? How might these relate to Ezekiel chapters 38–39?
4. Check out the parallels between Ezekiel 38–39 and Revelation 19:17–21 and 20:7–10.

TO THINK ABOUT AND DISCUSS

1. Go to a website such as: www.christian.org.uk or www.opendoorsuk.org or www.barnabasfund.org to gain an impression of how the church is being persecuted in many places in the world today. In what ways can you and your church help alleviate such threats and suffering?

21 The final temple

Ezekiel Chapters 40:1–43:27

The privilege of every true believer is that God makes their heart his home. One of the great differences between pagan temples and the temple of God in Jerusalem was not so much the absence of idols in Israelite worship but the presence of the living God.[1] The Christian is a temple of the living God by virtue of God the Holy Spirit taking up residence in their heart.[2]

Much of my adult life has been lived far from the place where I grew up. I have very happy memories of my childhood growing up in the countryside, and it is lovely to visit the old haunts when time permits. But one of the things about any place that one revisits is that it is rarely the same. Change is inevitable. There is development; surroundings change; people change; relationships change. There remains a certain familiarity, yet it is simply not as it once was. God is about to revisit his temple. In his latest visionary excursion Ezekiel describes in detail the plan for the temple of God; and as one might expect from such a revisit, things are changing. God will return to his temple, but his plan is developing to another stage. This is crucial to our understanding of Ezekiel's vision of the temple.

Ezekiel meets an angelic surveyor 40:1–4

In the opening verses of this passage we are met once again with a very specific date. Although what follows over the next few chapters is another vision, Ezekiel's experience took place in historic space-time.[3] It is the 25th year of the exile and 14 years since the city of Jerusalem had been razed together with the temple. There is some indication here that what Ezekiel is about to witness is not meant to be taken literally. We are told in verse 2 that he is taken in visions to a very high mountain, to a structure like a city (40:1–2). Although very detailed, there seems to be deliberate ambiguity in what Ezekiel is about to witness. This is not Jerusalem as Ezekiel would have known it. Rather, it is a structure like a city on a mountain that from the description of its elevation does not fit with either the reality of Jerusalem or the possibility of having a river flowing from its southern side (47:1–12). This vision is designed to bring hope to the exiles, in language and imagery that they will understand; but it is also a vision that has significance beyond any physical restoration—as we shall see over the next few chapters.

Having been taken to this very high mountain from which he has a grandstand view of this visionary city, Ezekiel is now introduced to an angelic surveyor, who has in his hands two measuring instruments akin to a long builder's measuring tape and a ruler. The man speaks to Ezekiel and tells him to pay close attention to all that he is about to see, with the express purpose that he will be able to relay the message and details to his fellow exiles in Babylon (40:3–4).

The East Gate to the Outer Court 40:5–16

We are now introduced to what the surveyor is preparing to measure. It is a new temple. He starts by measuring the height and thickness of the outer wall, but his attention quickly turns to the eastern facing gate. For a gateway it is a rather grand edifice, large enough to have three rooms to either side, a vestibule or lobby, and windows all around with jambs decorated with palm trees (40:6–16).

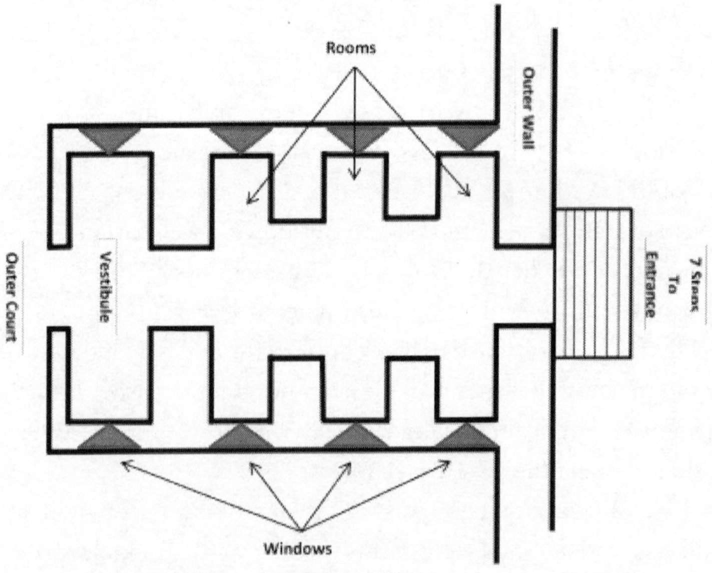

Figure 1 **Plan of East Gate**

The Outer Court 40:17–23

Having shown Ezekiel the detailed east gate the angelic surveyor now brings him in through the gate to the outer court. It is a large area of approximately 50,625 metres square, or 225 metres long by 225 metres wide.[4] Lining the walls of the courtyard were thirty chambers or rooms for worshippers, with a pavement running all the way around in front of those rooms.

The North and South Gates 40:20–27

Ezekiel is methodically shown around the temple complex. He is taken briefly to the north gate, then the south gate. He pauses just long enough at each of these two gates to see that they are the same in size and structure as the east gate. Furthermore, we are now introduced to the fact that directly opposite each of the outer gates there is a corresponding inner gate leading to the inner court.

The Inner Court 40:28–43

Ezekiel is now led across the outer courtyard from the south gate to the southernmost inner gate and led into the inner court. We are immediately told that the three gates to the inner court are essentially mirror images, the same in dimensions and layout to their corresponding outer gates (40:28–37). Just next to the north gate of the inner court Ezekiel is shown a small chamber where the burnt offerings were to be washed—possibly part of or adjoining the priests' chambers (40:38). He is also shown tables placed on either side of the

Figure 2 **Temple Courts Plan**

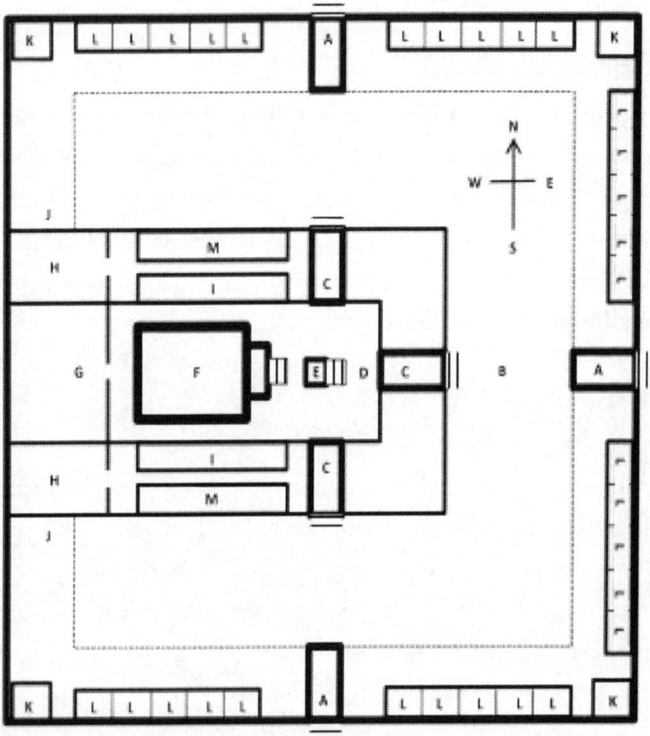

Key

A Outer Gates (40:5-16; 20-27)
B Outer Court (40:17-19)
C Inner Gates (40:28-37)
D Inner Court (40:44)
E Altar (40:47; 43:13-17)
F Temple (40:48-41:11, 15-16)
G West Building (41:12-14
H Priests' Kitchens (46:19-20)
I Priests' Chambers (40:44-46)
J Pavement (40:40:17; 41:8)
K Kitchens (46:19-24)
L The Thirty Chambers (40:17)
M Temple Chambers (42:1-14)

gate, and hooks that were to be used for the preparation of the various offerings (40:39–43). As Stuart points out,

> A main function of priests in Bible times was butchering meat for sacrifice. For this butchering they needed workrooms, storage rooms, meat tables, implement tables, etc., and these are seen in the inner court where the actual sacrificing took place (vv.38–43). The tables for the preparation of the meat may have been located in the vestibules, but that is not clear in the original and is a detail not terribly important to the vision as a whole.[5]

Chambers for the priests 40:44–47

Leading off the inner court were two chambers for the priests. The one next to the north gate was for the priests who looked after the temple; and the one next to the south gate for the priests who were in charge of the altar. We are told that the altar was in the middle of the inner court just in front of the temple steps.

The Temple 40:48–41:26

From the inner court Ezekiel had to climb ten steps to enter the temple, which was divided into three main areas—the vestibule, the nave or holy place, and the inner room or most holy place (40:48–41:4).

There are many other details of this magnificent building such as side chambers all around the outer walls built up three stories high, passageways that led to the temple yard, detailed measurements, and ornate carvings (41:5–20).

The following verses give the impression that having been shown the Most Holy Place Ezekiel (with his angelic guide) is now heading for the outer court again. However, before leaving the main temple building and en route to the door Ezekiel's attention is drawn to a number of other features. The first is something resembling an altar of wood, sitting just outside the doorway to the Most Holy Place in the nave. The angelic surveyor describes this as '... the table that is before the LORD' (41:21–22). His attention is then drawn to the detailed composition of the temple doors and finally the windows in the vestibule (41:23–26).

The Temple's chambers and overall dimensions 42:1–20

Making his way out of the temple now, back down the ten steps and to the outer court through the inner north gate, Ezekiel is taken to what the ESV describes as the temple's chambers. Again many details are given; not least that they

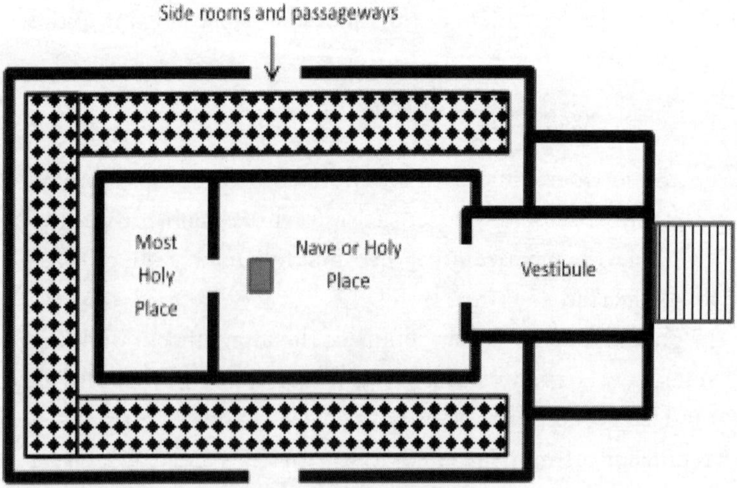

Figure 3 **Temple Building Layout**

are three storeys high (42:1–8). It seems that these chambers have passageways giving access from the outer court to the priest's kitchens and main temple building, without the priests having to go through the main entrance (42:10–12). We are told that these chambers are essentially dining rooms for the priests and a place where they can dress for their priestly role within the temple and to remove their priestly garments before leaving the temple and entering the outer courts where the regular worshippers gather (42:13–14). The overall dimensions are given as 500 cubits by 500 cubits, which equates to approximately 50,625 metres square. Furthermore, we are told that the reason the temple is surrounded by such an impressive wall is '… to make a separation between the holy and the common' (42:15–20). It is clearly a large area, able to hold a large number of worshippers. However, the overall size of the temple complex—impressive as it is—is not the main focus of Ezekiel's vision. It is to that grander purpose that Ezekiel now draws our attention.

The glory of the Lord fills the temple 43:1–12

Ezekiel is taken full circle in his tour of the temple complex as his angelic surveyor-guide takes him back across the outer court to the east gate. Here he will witness what he has longed to see for nineteen years: the glory of God returning to the temple he had abandoned because of Israel's sin. We must remember, however, that this is only a vision of the glory of God returning. From Ezekiel's perspective this is still a future event. He tells us that this vision of God's glory is just like the vision he had seen by the Chebar canal (1:28), and just as on that occasion, witnessing the glory of God is such an overwhelming experience that Ezekiel falls on his face in reverent fear (43:3). He was clearly affected when confronted with the holiness of the true and living God, and no doubt he was overcome by God's display of grace in returning to the temple he had previously forsaken. There is an indisputable connection between our sense of God's glory and true humility.[6]

But Ezekiel is not left prostrate for long. As God enters the temple he picks Ezekiel up and carries him to the inner court to witness the temple being filled once more with the glory of God (43:4–5). At this point God speaks directly to Ezekiel reminding him of the purpose of his temple. It is the place where he will dwell among his people forever (43:6–7a). But it comes with a caveat—God will no longer tolerate the sort of sinful behaviour that characterised his temple before his departure. The Lord will dwell in their midst forever, but first the sin that is such a barrier between God and his people must be dealt with once and for all (43:7b–9). To this end God tells Ezekiel to be careful to describe to the house of Israel all the details of this new temple—so that the emphasis on separation from the world, and the holiness of God so evident in those details will cause those who come to him to be ashamed of their sin (43:10–12).

An impossible task

God seems to be presenting the Israelites with an impossible task: to live up to the standards expected from the design of the temple and in keeping with all its statutes. They must have been only too aware of their past failings and wondered if they could possibly meet such standards of holiness.[7] Of course they cannot: God is holy beyond anything that man can imagine. The Lord uses the imagery of the temple to help them grasp something of this holiness. It is not something man can attain in and of himself. And yet in his boundless mercy God invites sinful man to enter into relationship with him. More than that; because man cannot meet the standards of holiness required for this relationship, God meets those standards on man's behalf! Only divine heart-surgery as detailed in Ezekiel chapter 36 can make anyone truly holy. Only the indwelling of the Holy Spirit in their hearts through the new birth can prepare a man or woman to meet with the true and living God. This is the reality that Ezekiel's vision of the temple is pointing forward to.

Because man cannot meet the standards of holiness required for this relationship, God meets those standards on man's behalf!

The special presence of God

As we have seen earlier in Ezekiel's prophecies, the temple without the presence of God is nothing more than bricks and mortar. He had witnessed the departure of God's glory from the temple as God made his way from the Most Holy Place to the threshold of the temple, on towards the east gate, and finally off to the mountain to the east of the city (11:22–23). Ezekiel now finds himself standing at the east gate once more, this time to witness the return of God's glory. As the Spirit of God comes through the east gate, he lifts Ezekiel and carries him to the inner court where he witnesses the glory of the Lord filling the temple (43:4–5). It is God's special presence that makes the temple a special place of worship. The same is true today of any church building. God is of course to be found in all places at all times. The Psalmist is very much aware that there is absolutely nowhere that we can go where we are not in the presence of the God of all creation (Psalm 139). And yet throughout the history of God's people there have been places associated with his special presence: Moses' encounter with God at the burning bush (Exod. 3:1–6); the tabernacle in the desert (Exod. 40:34–38); the temple in Jerusalem as explained by Ezekiel; and perhaps most clearly the special presence of God can be seen in the incarnation of the Son of God in the birth of the Lord Jesus Christ (John 1:14).

There is much emphasis put on styles of worship in our day. But the style of our worship is not as important as our purpose in worship. If we get our purpose for gathering together right, then the style will be right. Our purpose in gathering for worship is to come into the special presence of the true and living God. We need an instinctive understanding of this holy purpose, because when we get that right it will not matter if you worship in a more formal style or with music that is a bit more upbeat. What matters is a clear understanding that when we meet for worship we are coming into the special presence of God. It is a challenge to all Christians just how little we experience God in our day to day lives. When Christians meet on the Lord's Day they can talk about all kinds of

It is a challenge to all Christians just how little we experience God in our day to day lives.

things, from the weather to the Christian ministries they are involved in, but there may be little on how they have experienced God's presence throughout the week. We have God's special presence in our hearts, and when we gather together for worship that special presence is there in another way. In 1 Cor. 3:16–17 Paul speaks of the gathered body of believers as the temple of God, indwelt by the Holy Spirit. This passage is important to our understanding of the church as the body of believers and not the building. Paul draws a parallel between the temple of the Old Testament where, as we have been seeing in Ezekiel, God met his people in a special way; and the gathered body of believers as the temple of the New Testament. Are we drawing near to God so that he might draw near to us? (James 4:8). Are we coming to church on a Sunday morning with expectant hearts, ready to enter the special presence of God?

The altar 43:13–27

Its design

Our attention is drawn back to the altar that Ezekiel saw in the inner court. We are given very specific measurements and details. It is to be a square construction on a number of levels and to a height that requires steps leading up to the hearth so that the priests can burn the sacrifices there. The hearth is to have a horn at each corner pointing upwards and is approached by steps that face the east gate (43:13–17).[8] This is a large item, approximately 11 x 11 metres square, and from top to bottom just over 3 metres tall. Block estimates that the gutter that runs around the altar is large enough to hold up to 3,800 U.S. gallons of blood. He comments that, 'This was sufficient capacity for the blood of hundreds of animals, and would probably have enabled the uninterrupted slaughter of sacrificial victims from morning to night'.[9]

Its dedication

Ezekiel is now given directions for the dedication of the altar. On the first day of dedication the Levitical priests are to sacrifice a bull, place some of its blood on the four horns of the altar as a sign of cleansing and then burn the rest of the animal outside the sacred area (43:13–21). The second day the priests are to perform a similar ritual only this time with a male goat. Then a bull and a ram are presented as burnt offerings. This procedure is to be followed for seven days with the express purpose of dedicating the altar. Only from the eighth day onwards can the priests begin to offer burnt offerings and peace offerings on behalf of the people so that they may be found acceptable to God (43:22–27).

What does it all represent? What does the altar and its sacrifices point forward to? Ultimately God is demonstrating that not only does he want a meaningful relationship with his people, but he has provided the means of making that relationship possible. It is not a relationship based on human effort but on God graciously reaching out to sinners in need of his grace. Block writes,

> Interpreted in light of the sacrifice of Christ, Christians may rejoice because: (a) they have a mediator superior in quality and effectiveness to Moses and Ezekiel (Heb. 3); (b) they have a permanent high priest who has direct access to the heavenly throne of God and who offers perpetual intercession

on their behalf (Heb. 4:14–7:28); (c) the blood of a perfectly unblemished sacrifice has purchased favour with God, and eliminated the need for any further sacrifices (Heb. 9:1–10:31). God has provided a way![10]

The altar teaches that without the shedding of blood there is no remission of sins. It points to the cross of the Lord Jesus Christ, the Great Shepherd of the sheep who is also the Lamb who takes away the sins of the world.

The altar teaches that without the shedding of blood there is no remission of sins.

The final temple—Christ and his disciples[11]

There are differing views as to why Ezekiel has been given such a detailed overview of the future temple. There are several layers to prophecy in general and this is true of Ezekiel's vision of the temple. The first layer applies to the exiles by the Chebar canal. The message of the temple is designed to be one of hope and restoration for them. This was fulfilled in principle, if not in detail, on their restoration to Jerusalem under Cyrus. The next two layers relate to the use of the term temple in talking of Jesus and his disciples. This layer has application for the church today and for the people of God in the new heavens and new earth when Christ returns. We will consider this in some detail over the rest of this chapter.

The use of symbolism in the Old Testament

All theologians agree that much of the Old Testament is a symbolic representation of something greater. Perhaps the greatest example of this is the Jewish Passover. The Passover was a symbolic representation of Jesus who became our Passover Lamb. The temple too is symbolic of something greater that is yet to come. To understand the temple as it features in the Old Testament we need to ask what was God pointing forward to? What does the temple symbolise?

God's presence

The tabernacle in the wilderness during the forty years of wanderings was a place where Moses and the Israelites could meet with God. In Exod. 29:42–46 the tabernacle is called the tent of meeting. In other words, it was the place where God would meet with Moses and the Israelites. It was the place where God would dwell among them. It was the place of God's special presence. This was true of Solomon's temple also. There were many other temples in the world at that time, like the temples of pagan deities such as Dagon the god of the Philistines (Jdg. 16:23; 1 Sam. 5:2ff, 7; 1 Chr. 10:10). What made the Jewish temple so special? The key difference was not simply the absence of pagan idols or deities, but rather the presence of Yahweh. As Clowney puts it, 'At the temple Israel worshipped the God who was there!'[12] The presence of Yahweh was the important thing. The temple is the meeting place between God and his people.

What made the Jewish temple so special? The key difference was not simply the absence of pagan idols or deities, but rather the presence of Yahweh.

The gateway to God

Furthermore, the temple is not simply the dwelling place of God among his people, and the place where they can meet with him; it is the gateway to God.[13] At the temple the way is opened into God's holy presence. At that gateway sacrifice was made and blood was shed, so that the worshipper could come before God. As Clowney points out,

> The shedding of sacrificial blood is indispensable in the tabernacle-temple symbolism, for only through the shedding of blood can there be atonement: 'apart from the shedding of blood there is no remission' (Heb 9:22).[14]

But now there is a problem! In Ezekiel 11:22–23 we read about God leaving the temple. It is no longer the place of God's special presence. It is no longer the gateway to God. The sacrificial system has been halted by the Babylonian takeover and the Israelites are carried far away from their special divine meeting place to sing the Lord's song in a foreign land (Psalm 37:4). So what does God do? He himself became a sanctuary or a temple for them even in exile. 'Therefore say, "Thus says the Lord God: Though I removed them far off among the nations, and though I scattered them among the countries, yet I have been a sanctuary to them for a while in the countries where they have gone"' (Ezekiel 11:16).

This is very important symbolism. It is crucial to catch the importance of this action on the part of God. Clowney yet again summarises it beautifully, 'Proud Israel was left a sanctuary without the Glory, but humbled Israel found a sanctuary in the Glory'.[15] He goes on to state, 'Nothing in the further symbolism of Ezekiel's prophecy surpasses the implications of this revelation. The indestructible temple is the presence of God in Glory with his people'.[16] In other words, God was no longer to be found simply in the temple. God is now to be found wherever his true children gather to worship him. This is also the teaching we find in the New Testament.

Jesus the Messiah is the fulfilment of the temple

Jesus' encounter with the woman of Samaria gives us some insight into this development in what it means to worship God. We read of that encounter in the gospel of John. 'Our fathers worshiped on this mountain, but you say that in Jerusalem is the place where people ought to worship.' Jesus said to her, 'Woman, believe me, the hour is coming when neither on this mountain nor in Jerusalem will you worship the Father' (John 4:20–21). Here we find the same emphasis as Ezekiel. That is, God is no longer going to be associated with a particular place or race.

Jesus the Messiah is greater than the temple

Referring to himself, the Lord Jesus makes the point that one greater than the temple is here (Matt. 12:6). The Lord of the Sabbath, Jesus, is greater than the temple and all that it stood for. Spurgeon puts it like this: He is so manifestly because he is God, 'God over all, blessed forever.' He who dwells in the house is greater than the house in which he dwells, so that as God our Lord Jesus is greater than the temple. It needs no arguing that it must be so: the divine must be infinitely greater than anything which is of human workmanship; the self-existent must infinitely excel the noblest of created things.[17]

Jesus is the anti-type of which the temple was the type. He is the fulfilment of what the temple symbolised.[18] The temple in the Old Testament was symbolic of what God was going to do through Jesus.

Jesus the Messiah is the temple

> The temple in the Old Testament was symbolic of what God was going to do through Jesus.

When Jesus saw how the temple had been turned into a commercial centre he was so outraged that he took a whip and drove the money changers out of the temple. In the hostile exchange with the Jewish authorities Jesus was asked to give a good reason for his drastic actions. But rather than satisfy the curiosity of the authorities Jesus replied with these words: 'Destroy this temple, and in three days I will raise it up.' The passage recorded in the Gospel of John goes on to explain. 'The Jews then said, "It has taken forty-six years to build this temple, and will you raise it up in three days?" But he was speaking about the temple of his body' (John 2:19–21). Here we see Jesus clearly aligning himself with the physical temple in Jerusalem, referring to his body as the temple. The Jews only see a literal temple but had they understood their own Scriptures they would have known that the temple was only a type destined for destruction (Psalm 40:6–7; Jer. 3:16).[19] Regarding Christ's claim, 'Destroy this temple; and within three days I shall raise it up again,' the Apostle John explains that he was referring to the temple that was his body. As De Vaux comments, 'The old economy came to an end because it was superseded: the privileges of the material temple, seat of the divine presence and sign of election, were transferred to the body of the Word made flesh, who from that time onward becomes the 'place' where we encounter the Presence and the Salvation of God'.[20] But not all accepted this in his day. Jesus is referred to as the 'cornerstone that the builders rejected' (Psalm 118:22; Matt. 21:42; Mark 12:10; Luke 20:17; Acts 4:11; 1 Pet. 2:4, 7). Neither do all accept this today.

Jesus the Messiah builds his temple in his disciples

Each person who has been born again by the Spirit of God, redeemed by the precious blood of Jesus, has been united to him in such a way as to become the dwelling place or the temple of the Holy Spirit (1 Cor. 6:19). Furthermore, speaking of the gathered body of believers, Paul twice refers to them as the temple of God's special presence (1 Cor. 3:16–17; Eph. 2:19–22). Both individually and corporately, Christians are the temple of God. In the Old Testament the tabernacle or temple was said to be the place where the glory of God lived among his people. That was the place of God's special presence. Now the place of God's special presence is in every individual Christian; and when those believers are gathered together to worship him, that becomes the place of God's special presence. Jesus builds his temple in his followers.

> Both individually and corporately, Christians are the temple of God ... Jesus builds his temple in his followers.

Jesus the Messiah fulfils the function of the temple

If the temple in the Old Testament was the gateway to God, then that function has been taken over by Jesus. It is by him and him alone that we now have access to God (Eph. 2:18). In Ezekiel's incredible vision of a future temple, the picture that emerges is one of development. There is something familiar but there is also change. The temple was rebuilt after Cyrus decreed that the Jews could return home from exile, but it was only ever meant to be symbolic of the coming Messiah, the Lord Jesus Christ, and the temple that he was going to build, made up of (i) himself as the chief cornerstone, and (ii) his Apostles built upon his foundation. Christ also fulfils the function of the altar (Heb. 13:10) and is the final, all-atoning sacrifice. Scripture teaches us that the blood shed by Jesus on the cross brings cleansing so that we can enter into God's presence (Heb. 9:13–14). Christ is both altar and sacrifice. Furthermore, we are told that there will be no temple in the heavenly Jerusalem. There, as with the exiles by the Chebar canal, the Lord God Almighty and the Lamb is the temple (Rev. 21:22).

Ezekiel has had a vision of the temple being revisited. The glory of God is returning—but with a difference. This temple was explained to Ezekiel's hearers in terms that they would have understood; in terms that would have been an encouragement to them. This was partially fulfilled many years later when the exiles returned to their land and rebuilt the temple (Ezra 6:13–18). Whilst this temple may not have been as grand as Solomon's or as detailed as Ezekiel's vision, it nonetheless signified the renewal of Israelite life after the exile. What could have been more encouraging for the exiles than to know that the pride of their eyes was to be restored? Yet, although there is a certain familiarity there is also change. This change is carried on into the New Testament and beyond. The ultimate fulfilment of Ezekiel's temple is Christ. And through Christ, the temple is Christ's disciples. As Clowney comments, 'No man can lay another foundation: Jesus Christ is the true, the final, the real temple. He is the glory of Israel, and to him must the gathering of the nations be'.[21]

FOR FURTHER STUDY

1. In what way does Christ fulfil Ezekiel's vision of the temple? See Matt. 6:12; John 2:19–21.
2. What is the significance of the altar in Ezekiel's vision in relation to Christ? See Hebrews 9:13–14; and 13:10.
3. In what ways can Christians be understood to be the temple? See 1 Cor. 6:19; 1 Cor. 3:16–17, Eph. 2:19–22.

TO THINK ABOUT AND DISCUSS

1. In what way do you think such an elaborate description of the new temple would have been an encouragement to the exiles?
2. How should our understanding of the temple as a place of God's special presence affect our approach to (a) worship (b) our everyday lives?

22 Authenticity in the new temple

Ezekiel Chapter 44

If Christians are to have an impact on the millennial generation then they must be seen to be authentically different from the society they are trying to reach with the gospel.

Having set down detailed plans for the new temple in the previous chapters, Ezekiel is now given details relating to access, accountability, and authenticity in the temple. Once again Ezekiel is speaking in terms that are familiar to his audience by the Chebar canal. Although much of what he sets forth here will find expression in the post-exilic temple in Jerusalem, there are principles that carry through to the final temple which is Christ and his followers. There is much to be gleaned here, from entrance requirements to the temple, to regulations for the priests, to principles of giving. God is essentially calling the Israelites back to the standards they should have been living by all along. He is calling them back to an authentic Yahweh-centric life. In all of this there is an underlying message that God's kingdom of priests, that is to say Christians, are to live authentic lives in obedience to God's word.

Hope in the new temple 44:1–3

Ezekiel is brought back to the east gate and it is shut. God does not leave Ezekiel to ponder why the gate is closed but immediately spells out the reason. It was by this gate that the Lord had entered the temple therefore it is not for use by anyone else. There is one exception: the prince may eat his sacrificial meal here, but even he is not allowed to enter through the east gate's main entrance but must enter from the vestibule. God alone may enter from the outside, and since he has already done this the way is closed to all, from foreigners to the prince himself. There is great emphasis on the fact that this is the gate through which God has re-entered the temple. It is an emphasis on the holiness of the gate's use; and perhaps there is more than a hint of permanence to the Lord's stay in the temple. The Lord has returned to dwell among his people and he will not be leaving again.[1] Herein lies the greatest hope for the child of God. God will never leave us nor forsake us. There is nothing in all creation that can separate the true child of God from his love in Christ Jesus (Rom. 8:38–39; Heb. 13:5).

Access to the temple restricted to the true people of God 44:4–8

God here stipulates the basis upon which someone may enter his most holy temple. Ezekiel is firstly reminded that this temple is filled with the glory of the Lord; then he is told to pay close attention to the regulations God is about to reveal to him. The old ways of allowing all and sundry to enter the temple, and thereby profaning it, has come to an end. There is to be no going back to such liberal practices (44:4–7). Only the true people of God are to have access to the new temple. No one of uncircumcised heart or flesh is to be permitted to enter (44:8–9).

The Apostle John echoes these thoughts: '... but nothing unclean will ever enter it, nor anyone who does what is detestable or false, but only those who are written in the Lamb's book of life' (Rev. 21:27). John's reasoning is that only those who are truly Christ's, those who are one with him and the Father (John 17:21), have access into the new heavenly Jerusalem. Since the whole of Ezekiel's vision has application beyond the return from exile and applies to the church of Christ on earth in the latter days; there is a clear implication that no one with an uncircumcised heart can be a member of the true, universal, spiritual, church of Christ. That being the case it is reasonable to expect implications for the local church also. Access to church membership and the privileges of duty that this affords should be restricted to those who are born again by the Spirit of God. Of course God alone can see with absolute certainty those who are his and those who remain as yet unsaved. But as far as is humanly discernible, membership of the local church should be restricted to those who are circumcised in their hearts; that is, born again.

God has taken exception to the fact that in the former temple people who were not supposed to enter were encouraged to do so by the priests. The first thing that God emphasises to Ezekiel is the grounds upon which one may enter his new temple. God does not begin with secondary issues of how we are to conduct ourselves in the temple, as important as such issues are. Rather, he addresses the very fundamental issue of who is actually allowed to enter the temple in the first place. Bear in mind that in New Testament terms we are not talking about the physical temple building, but the true temple; that is, Christ's body, the church, the body of God's people represented here on earth. Therefore, exclusion from the temple does not mean exclusion from the physical building or place of worship, but rather, exclusion from membership of the true body of Christ. However, even with such restrictions there is hope for all in this new temple.

Hope comes in the form of meeting the basic entrance requirement—a circumcised heart (44:7–9). If God was grieved that the priests of the previous temple allowed those who were neither circumcised in the flesh nor the heart to enter the temple, he will want to address this in the new temple. The emphasis on circumcision in the flesh was a feature of the post-exilic Jewish temple, but it was always only an outward sign of the need for the inner circumcision of the heart (Deut. 10:16; 30:6; Jer. 4:4; 9:25–26; Acts 7:51; Rom. 2:28–29). Circumcision of the heart means regeneration. It refers to those who have been made alive in Christ, given a new heart. Only those who are born again have the right to enter the temple. The true temple is made up of living stones (1 Peter 2:5) and those who enter must be alive in the Spirit.

Hope comes in the form of meeting the basic entrance requirement—a circumcised heart.

Belonging before believing

In recent times there has been an upsurge in the concept of 'belonging before believing'. The idea is well-intentioned though fundamentally flawed. It is thought that opening up the community of believers to those who are as yet unbelievers will help the latter to see what Christianity is all about and encourage them to take part. It is thought that such non-Christians will become 'seekers' who will find Christ and then become believers. The idea is that we are all, Christians and non-Christians, simply fellow travellers on a shared journey, all at different points on that journey; either moving closer to or further away from Christ at the centre. In practice this involves encouraging unbelievers to join in all aspects of church life from making the tea, to greeting folk at the door, to being involved in the worship group. Everyone is included on this journey regardless of belief. The idea is that almost unwittingly the unbelievers, through being involved, will not only feel that they belong but believe that they belong. Belonging before believing is akin to saying you do not need to be a sheep to belong to the shepherd. This is not far removed from what was happening in the temple prior to the exile and, as we have seen, there are very real dangers with this sort of thinking. It redefines what the church actually is. The church is the gathered community of those who believe in Jesus. To put belonging

Belonging before believing is akin to saying you do not need to be a sheep to belong to the shepherd.

to that community before belief in Jesus not only redefines the church but destroys it. The church becomes something else altogether—yet another social group and nothing more. The church has already tried this and it has failed.[2] Liberal churches which downplay the need for repentance and faith are the very churches that are experiencing the worst decline in attendance.[3] Compromising God's standards simply does not work. The true church is the true community of believers for all time.[4] Even on the day of Pentecost, that began with heartfelt repentance and belief (Acts 2:37–42).

Real hope for those who want to belong

In Ezekiel's words, 'No foreigner, uncircumcised in heart and flesh, of all the foreigners who are among the people of Israel, shall enter my sanctuary' (44:9). This is a rule that is to be observed in the new temple which is Christ and his followers. No unregenerate person can be admitted as members of the New Testament church. However, for those that as yet do not believe and therefore do not belong to the church, the good news is that Christ invites you to both believe and belong! The church needs more people who are wholly committed to believing in the only Saviour, belonging to his community, and being salt and light in the world. The invitation to all is to come in, while there is still time (e.g. Matt. 11:28–30).

Accountability tempered by grace in the new temple 44:9–14

No foreigner or uncircumcised in heart may hold a position of responsibility in the new temple, but the wayward Levites may. Ezekiel's opening to this portion takes us back to the widespread problems of idolatry that we witnessed in Ezekiel chapters 8–11. Because of their part in that idolatry the Levites will bear the punishment of any foreigner or uncircumcised of heart that manages to enter the temple (44:9–10).[5] Gentiles or foreigners were permitted to enter the outer court but they were excluded from entering any of the inner courts, and it was the job of the Levites to ensure that this separation was upheld. Similarly, all church leaders today are responsible for ensuring that the criteria of a regenerate heart is upheld for membership of the church, whilst at the same time warmly welcoming all newcomers to the place where they too can experience God's special presence and the power of salvation.

As a result of the Levites' part in the idolatry of the past they are now barred from serving as priests in the new temple. They must not come near God's holy things or his offerings but will serve as assistants to the Zadokite priests (44:10–14). Part of the problem was that things had become lax in the temple prior to the exile. The Levites had taken on duties that belonged to the descendants of Aaron (1 Chron. 6:1–8). The Levites were in charge of the gates of the temple and assisting the people (44:11); whereas the Zadokite priests alone were allowed to enter the most holy place and offer sacrifices (44:15–16).[6] But the Levites were so focussed on doing someone else's ministry that they failed in their own. No doubt there is another salutary lesson here for the church today. The Levites had failed in their duties to maintain purity in temple worship, but God is returning to them the privilege of that responsibility. Their mistake, grievous though it was, did not bar them from further service in the courts of God. Although God holds the Levites accountable for their past actions, he extends his grace to them in allowing them to continue in what had always been their essential role (Num. 18:1–3). Despite their past sin the Levites are graciously and fully reinstated.[7] Thankfully with God there is grace in abundance and forgiveness (Psalm 130:1–8). In God's house accountability is tempered by grace.

Today God still expects higher standards of those who minister in the church.

Today God still expects higher standards of those who minister in the church. This should be seen as a higher standard but not a double standard, as God expects all of his children to maintain high standards of holiness (1 Pet. 1:14–16). Furthermore, it is important that each person is faithful to their own calling. It is God who administers gifts to the church and it is for us, with the help of godly leaders, to recognise those gifts in ourselves and exercise them. God had appointed the Levites to assist Aaron and his sons. The Levites were given duties in the outer temple area so that Aaron and his sons would be able to focus on their role of serving in the inner temple where they ministered before the Lord. It is entirely possible that the apostles had this fact in mind when they appointed the first deacons to minister at tables and other practical ministries while they devoted themselves to prayer and ministry of the word (Acts 6:1–7).

If you are serving in a supportive role within your church then you are fulfilling a vital role. God gives us gifts to serve the church; so whatever gift you have been given and whatever role you find yourself in, do it wholeheartedly for the Lord. We are, after all, one body with many parts and each part is necessary for the body to function with health and vitality (1 Cor. 12:12–17). It may well be that Peter also had this distinction of duties in mind when he reminds us that we are to use our gifts to serve not only God but one another, whether speaking the oracles of God or serving. 'As each of you has received a gift, use it to serve one another, as good stewards of God's varied grace' (1 Pet. 4:10–11). In Peter's words there is also more than a hint of Ezekiel's underlying message that all should be done so that God may be glorified.

> We are to use our gifts to serve not only God but one another, whether speaking the oracles of God or serving.

The people of God are to be visibly different in the new temple 44:15–31

The Zadokite priests must have failed at least in terms of not guarding their own role from infiltration by the Levites. Yet because of their relative faithfulness in the midst of the carnage of the past, they are commended once again to their priestly charge in the inner temple (44:15–16). Again God's mercy is evident. Over the following verses there are various regulations that typify the need for holiness when it comes to serving the Lord. For the priests who serve in the inner sanctuary there are clothing regulations (44:17–19). Garments made of wool were prohibited because they caused sweating, whereas the wearing of the priestly linen garments among the people '… would have violated the holiness of the temple by distributing its sanctity … There is no need for Ezekiel to elaborate on the contagion of holiness because the idea was commonly accepted'.[8] Hair was to be kept neatly trimmed, neither long nor shaven (44:20). The priest was not to drink wine when he entered the inner court (44:21). He was forbidden to marry a widow or a divorcee (44:22). Besides the regulations surrounding preparation for entering God's presence we also learn from Ezekiel that ministers are to teach God's people the difference between the holy and the common, to arbitrate in disputes, and be an example in keeping God holy days (44:23–24). Furthermore, there were special regulations for priests around the issue of death and mourning (44:25–27).

What can all these regulations mean? Are there any practical implications for the church today? These regulations will have made perfect sense in the rebuilt temple after the exile. And although we should not expect them to transpose to the church in every detail, yet these regulations evidently imply that God's standards differ from the world around us. We can learn the need for purity in coming into the presence of God. Since we cannot meet those standards ourselves, God has provided our holiness through the righteousness of Christ (Rom. 3:22). By virtue of this imputed and infused righteousness, the people of God should be visibly different from the unsaved around us. We live by different standards and must not allow the standards of society at large to shape our thinking. This will sometimes involve what Francis Schaeffer describes as loving confrontation with those practices in society that contradict the clear teaching of the Bible. He writes: 'We must indeed give a practical demonstration of love in the midst of differences [between the church and society]. But at the same time God's truth and the work of Christ's church both must insist that truth demands loving confrontation but confrontation'.[9] If the millennial generation are to take seriously the claims of the Christian gospel then they must see Christians living authentic Christ-centred lives with God's standards visible in our day-to-day engagement with others. Not that we can expect to be perfect in this life, nor that we should be 'holier than thou'. But it is to suggest that we should be authentic ambassadors for Christ; seeking, with joy in our hearts towards God and love in our hearts towards our neighbours, to show society a better way.

The role of giving in new temple worship 44:28–30

Priests are to have no inheritance except God himself. Put positively, priests have the greatest inheritance of all! God is their portion. In a world that emphasises setting ourselves —and our children—up for the future, it sounds foolish to suggest that material inheritance is not important. But here are the Levitical priests, and when it comes to dividing up the land amongst the twelve tribes of Israel they are not to receive any part of it (44:28). Rather, God is to be their inheritance and as such will meet their needs. Of course, they still need the means to eat and live, so God ensures they are provided for through the giving of the rest of God's people. To ensure that these needs are met God sets up a system. They are to eat from the various offerings that people bring to the temple (44:29–30). Far from eating the leftovers of the other tribes, the priests will enjoy the first fruits of all kinds and from every offering brought into the temple. There is even a prohibition against eating unclean food, such as carrion of any kind, in keeping with the regulations set out in Exod.

22:31 (Ezek. 44:31). In not having a physical inheritance the Levites are abundantly blessed by God's appointed system of meeting their needs. But they are not the only ones blessed by this system. There is equal blessing for those that give the required offerings: 'You shall also give to the priests ... that a blessing may rest on your house' (44:30).

God has made us a kingdom of priests and a royal priesthood (Exod. 19:6; Rev. 1:6, 5:10; 1 Pet. 2:9). The greatest inheritance we have is God himself as our everlasting possession (Heb. 9:15; 1 Pet. 1:4). Within that kingdom God has established similar principles for meeting the needs of those called by him to serve and teach his people. Just as the Levitical priests were not to be impoverished by their lack of a land inheritance, so too in the New Testament church ministers and their families should be fully provided for by God's people. The priests were dependent on the obedience of God's people to provide. On this point I want to quote Chris Wright at length.

The priests were dependent on the obedience of God's people to provide.

> The principle that those who serve God and teach God's people should be fully provided for by God's people is emphatically re-applied in the NT. Galatians 6:6 applies it to Christian teachers (cf. 1 Tim. 5:17f.). Paul actually makes reference to OT priestly dues, along with many other supporting arguments (including another Deuteronomic law, 25:4, and a command of Christ) in establishing the responsibility of Christian churches to provide for the material need of those who work for the cause of the Gospel (1 Cor. 9:13). Paul had

> freely chosen to waive this right in his own personal case, but he explicitly makes himself an exception to the principle he insists on for others. Unfortunately, some Christian organizations have turned Paul's exception, rather than his rule, into a policy imposed on their workers. But in view of the teaching of both OT and NT, churches or other Christian groups that fail to pay their workers adequate living wages are not 'living by faith,' but are simply living in disobedience.[10]

If we are to reach this millennial generation then we must be people living in an authentic relationship with God. Whatever your role within the church, it will involve serving with joyful obedience to his word. If ministers are to be an example of living by faith, then God's people are to be an example of faithful living.

FOR FURTHER STUDY

1. What are the wonderful promises for the children of God in Romans 8:38–39 and Hebrews 13:5?
2. What do the following passages teach us about who is truly a member of the church? Romans 2:28–29; Revelation 21:27; Ezekiel 44:7–9. See also Deut. 10:16; 30:6; Jer. 4:4; 9:25–26; Acts 7:51.
3. Compare Ezekiel 44:9–14 with Acts 6:1–7. Draw out the parallels in the teaching from these two passages.

TO THINK ABOUT AND DISCUSS

1. In what ways is the current theory of belonging before believing damaging to the true church?
2. How can we involve the unsaved in our fellowship and make them know with certainty that they are cherished and loved?
3. In what ways can Christians express their authentic relationship with God to this generation?

23 Dining with a royal host

Ezekiel Chapters 45–46

If Christians are to enjoy God forever, he must be central to our lives. To this end God has provided access into his most holy presence and invites us to dine with him. The God who is altogether beyond our understanding is at the same time knowable, personal, and approachable.

What would you say is central in your life? Family? Work or career? Other? Being aware of what your life revolves around brings real perspective on what is important. The thing that is central in your life may change and shift. Think about the television or computer games. In our home it is an on-going battle to be fair to our children in allowing them time to relax by watching TV or playing a favourite computer game. But every now and again it just feels as though these things are no longer a pastime but rather central to their enjoyment of life. It is at moments like these that as a family we initiate a digital detox! This means we re-orientate our focus and spend more quality time together as a family. I think if we are honest it can be like that in our walk with God. Every now and again things clutter our lives and our focus on God shifts to peripheral vision. It is good to be aware that the battle for our affections is lifelong and we need to deliberately cut out unnecessary distractions to get our focus back on God, restoring him to the central position in our lives. Central themes colour our experiences, so it is vital that God is the one who colours our experiences more than anything else. God does not leave us in the dark as to how this is possible.

In chapter 21 we took the view that the final temple is Christ and his believers. In all that is being said in these chapters of Ezekiel there will have been some application for orderly worship in the temple that was built following the decree of Cyrus (Ezra 1:1–2) and the return of the exiles to their own land. Of course not all that is outlined here was accomplished upon their return. So although not every detail will fit, much of what we read in Ezekiel's latest vision sets out principles of orderly worship for the church in the last days. This includes our duty towards God and our duty towards others.

The Lord's portion of the land 45:1–6

As the exiles are encouraged to lift their eyes from their current situation, directions are given for the distribution of the land when they return to it. Measurements are given for the allotment of land for the Lord's house and surrounding holy district (45:1–3). In an ever-widening arrangement, we find that immediately aligned with the temple area is an area designated for the Zadokite priests to build their homes; next to that is land for the Levitical priests; and next to that is land for the whole house of Israel (45:4–6). Two things emerge from this order of things. Firstly, it is interesting that the first portion of the land is assigned to the Lord for his house. Secondly, the Lord's portion is to be physically central to the whole life of Israel.

There is surely a simple principle here for the people of God in any generation. It is right and fitting that the Lord should be first in our thinking whether in the giving of our time or our tithe. All that we have belongs to the Lord; indeed all that exists belongs to the Lord. David wrote, 'The earth is the Lord's and the fullness thereof, the world and those who dwell therein' (Psalm 24:1). We are merely stewards of God's creation, so it is fitting that the first portion of anything belongs to the Lord. If we are to glorify the name of the Lord, as Ezekiel has been stressing throughout his prophecy, then it must surely begin by putting him first in all things. Upon their return from exile the Israelites are to assign the first of the land for the Lord's use, so that the land and all the tithes and offerings to the Lord should be first in their hearts and minds. The Lord must be centre of all. He must be the priority of all of his children if we are to avoid slipping again into the mistakes of the past where God was so grievously side-lined.

It is right and fitting that the Lord should be first in our thinking whether in the giving of our time or our tithe.

The prince's portion of the land 45:7–12

The portion of land to both sides of the temple area is to be given to the prince (45:7). The reason for this is so that he will have no need to extort land from others. There is to be no oppression under the new administration, no more taking land that belongs to others. Perhaps there is an allusion to the episode of Naboth's vineyard in these words (1 Kings 21:1–16), an example of the exploitation of the poor so that the wealthy could increase their already full coffers. At the very least God is demanding an end to all forms of exploitation and oppression and demanding justice and righteousness in all our dealings, including the use of fair weights and measures (45:9–12). In our times large international businesses are constantly being exposed for failing to pay their workers even the legal minimum wage. Christians should be at the forefront of exposing such exploitation, and work for justice for all.

The administrator prince 45:13–46:18

We are introduced to a series of offerings and gifts. Although the freewill offering is considered as recurring (46:14) and the exact occasion and purpose for all the offerings is uncertain, it may be that at least some of these had the primary role of dedicating the new temple.

Offerings for making atonement for the people 45:13–17

Ezekiel now lists the details of a series of offerings of grain, oil, and sheep that are to be given to the prince. These offerings are raised by means akin to a tax system (45:13–16).

The people are obliged to bring this offering (45:16) and the reason these gifts are given to the prince is that he is to ensure the correct administration of them on behalf of the people at the various feasts, new moons, and Sabbaths.[1] Most notably, the prince is to make atonement on behalf of the people and the whole house of Israel (45:15–17).

Offerings for making atonement for the temple 45:18–20

The temple is a special place dedicated to the service of God and as such it is to be purified. In a symbolic act, blood from the sin offering is to be put on the door posts, ledge of the altar, and on the gate posts to the inner court. Christians as the final temple need the application of the blood of Christ for the atonement of their sins. There is a once-for-all application of that blood when a person is born again. But there is also the need for repeated repentance for our sin. Perhaps this is what is alluded to in the next section.

Sin offerings for prince and people 45:21–25

> Our faith and practice should be seven days a week.

Furthermore the prince is to provide a sin offering on behalf of himself and all the people (45:22). These offerings are to continue for a period of seven days (45:23–25). I am drawn to John Gill's understanding of this. He suggests that it is typical of the fact that our relationship with Christ is not simply a Sunday thing but rather something that should affect us every day of the week. Our faith and practice should be seven days a week. Furthermore, the prince is clearly not a reference to Christ, the messianic prince, as some have suggested, since Christ would have no need to make a sin offering on his own behalf. As Chris Wright puts it, this seems to be '… a very human figure offering sacrifices for his own sins …'[2]

Offerings concerning the Sabbath and other special days 46:1–15

The east gate of the inner court is to be kept shut six days a week but is to be opened on the Sabbath and day of the new moon. It is through the vestibule of this gate that the prince is permitted to enter and leave the inner court (46:1–2, 8). Ezekiel now details the prince's role in administering all the varied offerings that the people are to bring to him in the temple. These offerings include burnt offerings, peace offerings, and grain offerings (46:2–7). It is the role of the priests to make the actual offerings before the Lord (46:2), but it seems that it is the role of the prince to see that provision is assured; and that they are done in an orderly fashion (46:4–7) even down to crowd control possibly for safety reasons (46:8–10). As Block comments,

> Ezekiel's vision of hundreds of thousands of people thronging the temple courts 'before Yahweh' on the prescribed festival days would have been a logistical nightmare, which this ordinance sought to manage … Every detail in the worship of Yahweh was ordered.[3]

There are further regulations regarding the use of the inner gate. The gate is to be opened only for the duration of the offerings (46:11–15).

Inheritance regulations in the land 46:16–18

In a brief section on some aspects of inheritance rights, the Lord sets out some simple rules to ensure equity and justice. That the inheritance relates to land specifically seems clear from verse 18. If the prince makes a gift of land to any of his sons it will remain the property of his sons as an inheritance. If however he makes a gift out of his inheritance to any of his servants, this gift is to be seen more as a short to mid-term lease. Any such gift is to be returned to the prince's own inheritance in the year of liberty (46:16–17). The other side of the matter is now set out. Just as the prince's inheritance belongs perpetually to him and his family, so too the inheritance of the people belongs perpetually to them and their families and is protected from any form of abuse. The prince may not take any land from the people to pass on as an inheritance to his sons. The reason is stated clearly: no one is to be left homeless. God remains the true landowner and he is to be central to all the affairs of his people'. Here he is setting out principles of fairness, justice, and equality so that no one should suffer deprivation. The principles of social concern in these words should be reflected in the way the church today works to protect the vulnerable in society.

The kitchens and boiling places 46:19–24

Ezekiel is taken out through the side rooms and passageways of the temple and his attention is drawn to the priest's kitchens (H on diagram of temple area). These are the kitchens where the Zadokite priests are to prepare the guilt and sin offerings and bake the grain offerings. This area and the food prepared there is to be kept within the inner court to avoid contamination of the holy offerings (46:19–20).[4] He is then led out to the outer court and shown other kitchens in the four corners of the courtyard (K on diagram of temple area). This is where the Levites are to prepare the offerings and sacred meals on behalf of the people.[5] Although God is altogether holy and to be feared, yet he provides the means whereby his people can dine in his presence. God is over and above all things and yet he is approachable, personal, and knowable. As Block points out,

God is over and above all things and yet he is approachable, personal, and knowable.

> Herein lies the relevance of this text for the modern believer. True worshippers fall down before the transcendent majesty of God, and with the Seraphim of Isaiah 6 proclaim his holiness, but with joyful hearts they accept his gracious invitation to eat the communion meal ... in his presence.[6]

I am reminded of those words of Christ to the church at Laodicea in Revelation 3:20, 'Behold I stand at the door and knock. If anyone hears my voice and opens the door, I will come in to him and eat with him, and he with me'. Commenting on this verse Hendriksen says,

> How wonderful! He, as it were, descends from the throne of His glory in order to dine with this individual who in himself is so poor and pitiable. Christ and the believer dine together, which in the East was an indication of special friendship and of covenant relationship. In other words, the believer has blessed fellowship with his Saviour and Lord (Jn. 14:23; 15:5; 1 Jn. 2:24). That fellowship begins even in this present life. It is perfected in the hereafter when the conqueror shall sit with Christ on His throne, just as Christ, the Conqueror, sat down with His Father on His throne.[7]

The covenantal relationship between God and his people found expression in their coming into his special presence to eat their sacrificial meals. The same can be observed today as God invites his people to remember the cost of their atonement and enjoy fellowship around the Lord's table. Many who have dined at the table of Her Majesty the Queen testify to it being a privilege, a humbling experience, and a steep learning curve in terms of protocol. All of this and more can be said of participation in the Lord's Supper. It is an immense privilege to be invited to dine with the Royal Host, and a healthy focus on this most gracious invitation alone will go a long way to keeping the Lord at the centre of our increasingly busy lives.

FOR FURTHER STUDY

1. Consider the following verses: Matthew 6:19–21, 6:33; Proverbs 16:3; John 3:30; Romans 8:5. What bearing do these verses have on the final temple in the light of Ezekiel's teaching about the centrality of God in the land?
2. Read 1 Kings 2:1–16. How does this shed light on the message of Ezekiel 45:7–12?

TO THINK ABOUT AND DISCUSS

1. In what ways can you ensure that God is truly central to worship in your church and in your life during the rest of the week?
2. Can you think of ways for you personally and for your church collectively to work for social justice?
3. In our family we periodically impose a digital detox to realign our focus. Can you think of any areas in your life where a similar detox might prove helpful in realigning your focus on God?

24 Christ makes all things new

Ezekiel Chapters 47–48

God makes a new covenant[1] with his people, each of whom is a new creation in Christ.[2] He has already promised through Ezekiel to give his people a new heart and a new spirit,[3] and a new temple where they can worship him.[4] There is the further promise of new heavens and a new earth, and new resurrected bodies[5] for his children to dwell there in a new relationship with him for all eternity. These are just some of the things intertwined with Ezekiel's final vision in these closing chapters.

We have reached the final vision in Ezekiel's marathon. The judgement of the early chapters is now well and truly history and these closing chapters are full of hope for the exiles by the Chebar canal. There are promises of greater equality and justice for the land they will return to. There are promises of an abundance of life and fruitfulness that they have never known before. And most significantly, they have the promise that God, who had abandoned them because of their sinful behaviour, will so commit to them that he will never again be compelled to leave them bereft of his life-giving presence. God will so order the new society that he will be able to dwell in the midst of his people without his holiness consuming them. God is going to make all things new.

New life for the land 47:1–12

The river's accelerated growth 47:1–5

We are introduced once again to Ezekiel's angelic surveyor as Ezekiel is taken on a riverside walk to inspect the river's development over its first two kilometres. This is a miraculous river, and not a literal one, as can be seen from its accelerated growth in volume and depth and in its supernatural life-giving properties. The water begins as a trickle from under the threshold of the entrance to the temple. Flowing in an easterly direction the river seemingly disappears underground almost immediately, reappearing as a trickle somewhere just off to the southern side of the outer east gate. The angelic surveyor takes Ezekiel a further 500 metres eastwards (1,000 cubits) to find that the water is now ankle deep. Five hundred metres further along it is knee deep, after another 500 metres it is up to the waist, and in his final measurement 500 metres further along we are told that the river is so deep that one could not cross it (47:1–5). In the space of two kilometres what started as a trickle is now a vast river flowing so deep and wide and perhaps so fast that no one can cross it. This is not the normal development of a river and certainly not normal in terrain where the only source is a trickle at the beginning. This is not a literal river, just as the temple is not a literal temple, but rather a way of expressing a truth that God wants to communicate to his people in a way that is easy for them to understand.

God wants to communicate to his people in a way that is easy for them to understand.

The river's life-giving properties 47:6–12

Ezekiel is now directed back to the river bank where his angelic surveyor draws his attention to the many trees growing there, introducing Ezekiel to the theme of abundance that this river represents (47:6–7). The man then proceeds to tell him that this river flows east into the sea and how its miraculous powers make even the sea waters fresh, bringing abundant life in its waters. It is a reference to the Dead Sea which is given its name because it is so salty that no creature could live in it. This is to change, and fishermen will reap the benefits of its bounteous supply of fish (47:8–10). But just in case the exiles begin to fret over the loss of any salt industry, they are consoled with the knowledge that not all the waters will become fresh (47:11). As Block notes, 'The preservation of some pocket of saltiness is intentional, recognizing the economic benefit of the minerals found in and around the Dead Sea'.[6] Our attention is drawn back to the trees on the river banks. We are told that the banks will grow all sorts of trees that miraculously bear fresh fruit every month, and leaves that will have healing properties (47:12). Whether directly through nutrient-rich waters, or indirectly through providing commerce and trade opportunities, the river will produce and preserve life. Perhaps there is even a hint here that in the new heavens and new earth we will return to a much closer relationship with the land, living off it more directly—just as Adam did in the original Eden.

Water as a symbol of fruitfulness and blessing is of course a common theme in the Bible. Most commentators recognise a connection between Ezekiel's latest vision and the river that flowed from the Garden of Eden, watering every kind of tree that was pleasing to the eye and good for food (Gen. 2:10–14). Other passages also draw on this theme of water as an expression of God providing for his people.[7] Zechariah 14:8 also talks of living water flowing from the Lord's house. It is easy to see the parallel with Ezekiel's river. As Stuart points out, these and other passages play on the fact that for the Hebrews many parts of their land had very little water, therefore talk of flowing water teeming with life would have been a great encouragement to them.

But perhaps the most significant parallel passage on this theme is Revelation 22:1–5. As in Ezekiel's vision of the river, John speaks of a river flowing from the presence of God. As the river flows with abundant life-giving water, so the love of God is ever flowing towards his children. Hendriksen writes, 'This river is the river of life for it symbolizes eternal life, salvation full and free, the gift of God's sovereign grace. And what is life but fellowship with God?'.[8] God is at the very heart of this source of life; the river flows from his house. Furthermore, just as the river in Ezekiel's vision teems with life and brings abundant life to the land through which it flows, so too there is a promise of renewal for the land itself in the age to come. As Chris Wright points out, 'Though portrayed in the symbolic language of prophetic vision, the environmental healing depicted in Ezekiel's vision should not be simply spiritualized. There is an ecological dimension to the full biblical understanding of God's saving purpose which should not be overlooked'.[9] Christ makes all things new and that includes the rejuvenating of an earth that has been so spoiled by poor stewardship on our part.

Christ gives the living water

The Lord Jesus Christ in talking with the Samaritan woman speaks of giving people living water (John 4:10–13). Reaching out beyond the Jewish people, Jesus offers this living water to a Gentile woman. Those who drink of the water that Christ offers will have life abundant. The living water is the Holy Spirit (John 7:37–39) which was poured out on the day of Pentecost on all who believed Peter's message, both Jew and Gentile. The parallel with Ezekiel is hard to avoid. In Ezekiel's vision the river starts as a trickle and soon becomes a fast-flowing life-giving river. Jesus talks of the water he will give starting as a spring of water welling up to eternal life. He is pointing to that part of God's promise of life-giving water that is already here, already available. The vision of the river we read about in Ezekiel is being fulfilled in the offer that Jesus made to the Samaritan woman by the well and the worshippers in the temple. This living water is applied to all who accept him in repentance and faith today. It is the promise of spiritual life, abundant life in him. This life-giving water is already available but will come to its ultimate fulfilment in the new heavens and new earth that the Apostle John talks of in Revelation chapters 21 and 22. This is part of what theologians call the tension between the already fulfilled and not yet fulfilled promises of Scripture. As Christians we enjoy God's presence as he dwells in our hearts by the Holy Spirit, but we still look forward to the ultimate fulfilment of that promise of living with God for all eternity (Eph. 1:13–14; Rev. 21:3).

As Christians we enjoy God's presence as he dwells in our hearts by the Holy Spirit, but we still look forward to the ultimate fulfilment of that promise of living with God for all eternity.

New division of the land 47:13–48:29; and 45:1–12

In words reminiscent of Numbers chapter 34 the Lord now addresses one of his covenant promises: that the land is to be divided up equally among the twelve tribes of Israel (47:13–14). New boundary lines are established for the twelve tribes of Israel, but not yet allocated (47:15–20). A new element to the dividing up of the land is that Gentiles are to be included (47:21–23). The portions with their boundaries are now allocated to the twelve tribes of Israel (48:1–7 and 48:23–29). The central portion is set aside for the Lord's sanctuary (48:8–22 and 45:1–6). This portion for the sanctuary includes sub-divisions for the temple (48:8–10); Zadokite priests (48:10–12); Levite priests (48:13–14); common land for dwellings andproduction of food (48:15–20); and the prince (48:21–22 and 45:7–12). There are some noticeable changes between the original division of the land of Canaan and the land as envisioned in Ezekiel. These differences are clearly apparent by briefly comparing maps based on both the Numbers passage and the new boundaries suggested here in Ezekiel. Chris Wright in his commentary talks of the land in Ezekiel's new divisions being '... a dramatic departure from the historical locations of some of the tribes',[10] and sliced up with mathematical perfection to symbolize equality and order among the people of God.[11] This vision of equality seems to be the heart of the division of the land in Ezekiel.

The land divisions as described here have never been realised historically for physical Israel, and were never intended to be. Once again we see Ezekiel encouraging the exiles by speaking in terms that would have resonated with them. It will be a great encouragement for them to realise that one day God would restore their land to them; but Ezekiel goes beyond the land to the Israelites and includes land for the Gentiles. Some of the differences to God's new division of the land in Ezekiel can be summed up as: Ezekiel's division has no land east of the Jordan; Ezekiel's division is more 'mathematical' (Wright) and more equally divided; and finally Ezekiel's division is to include the Gentiles.

So what does it all mean? It points to equality and justice and God-centeredness[12] in God's new covenant: seen in part now with the gospel that is going to all nations; and to be seen in full in the new heavens and new earth. This is not referring to historic Israel at any point, past or future, but rather to the true Israel of God, all who are children of Abraham by faith in Christ the Messiah. This inclusion of the Gentiles is taken up by the apostle Paul in his letter to the Romans. He says, 'Or is God the God of the Jews only? Is he not the God of Gentiles also? Yes, of the Gentiles also, since God is one—who will justify the circumcised by faith and the uncircumcised through faith' (Rom. 3:29–30). It was always God's intention that salvation would extend beyond ethnic Israel and include the Gentiles. Indeed, not all who are ethnic Israel shall be saved. The division that Paul describes in Romans chapters 9–11 shows that there has always been a division between ethnic Israel and the true Israel of God, between the physical seed of Abraham and the spiritual seed of Abraham, between the children of the flesh and the children of the promise (Rom. 9:8). Christ is the seed (singular) of Abraham through whom all the promises of God will be fulfilled (Gal. 3:16). The true Israel of God are all those, both Jew and Gentile, who are justified by faith in Christ (Rom. 5:1). Paul makes it clear that all the promises to the descendants of Abraham were ultimately to be fulfilled in Christ (2 Cor. 1:20). Within the fellowship of God's people there is to be equality. Beyond the fellowship of God's people we should be at the forefront of fighting for justice for all. In all that we do, both within and outside the church, Christ our Immanuel—God with us—is to be at the very heart of both what we do and why we do it. Our actions and our motives are to be

In all that we do, both within and outside the church, Christ our Immanuel—God with us—is to be at the very heart of both what we do and why we do it.

governed by the one who brings to fulfilment all that Ezekiel is here portraying.

New name for the city in the land 48:30–35

In the closing verses of Ezekiel's prophecy our attention is drawn once again to the city and to two things in particular. Firstly there are to be twelve gates equally spread around the walls with three entrances on each side of the city, and they are to be named after the twelve tribes of Israel (48:30–34). But secondly, and without doubt the most significant thing we are told about the city, is its name. No longer to be known as Jerusalem, but its name shall be 'The LORD Is There' (48:35). The many gates seem to emphasise access for true believers. But access to the city is only significant in that it is access into the very presence of God himself. Block notes, 'Like Ezekiel's restoration oracles, this name announces the undoing of a past evil situation'.[13] God will remedy the mistakes of the past. Because the Lord was sidelined previously, his people must now to keep their focus on the God who dwells in their midst. As noted above, this final paragraph of Ezekiel's message refers to the city of God. The city's name, The Lord Is There, is a stark contrast to what we saw earlier in Ezekiel when, as a result of Israel's sin God departed from the temple. In the new covenant the abiding characteristic is that God will always be present. This is the core message of Ezekiel to the poor wretched Israelites who

In the new covenant the abiding characteristic is that God will always be present.

are far from home, enslaved by a foreign power, and far from their beloved city and temple. In the new city God will always be by their side.

Christ makes all things new

As a child growing up in Northern Ireland we used to have a peculiar way of saying something was similar. We would say it was the same only different. In Revelation 21:1–5 the apostle John sees the new heavens and new earth and a new city of God descending from heaven. That city is the dwelling place of God. But more than that, the Lord himself says, 'Behold I am making all things new' (Rev. 21:5). The word 'new' in the original Greek conveys the idea, not of a totally different or other creation, but of a rejuvenated earth, city etc. It is the same only different. The effects of sin which began with Adam's disobedience in the Garden of Eden will be removed.

Society can try to usher in a new utopia of equality and fairness, but the nature of man is sinful and such projects will always fail. Better education for all; fairer distribution of wealth and economic justice; peace between nations; social reforms, and even ecological harmony, are all worthy ambitions in any society. But God alone can usher in true peace, true reforms, a fairer society, a replenished ecology system and a world where there will be no more tears or heartache or pain. Christ alone can make all things new. That begins now as he makes a new creation of each individual who confesses their sin and trusts in him. But one day we will experience the fullness of that new relationship with God in Christ as we are raised in new imperishable bodies (1 Cor. 15:53) and dwell with him in the new heavens and new earth. In an act of pure unadulterated grace, Christ makes all things new.

I am a new creation,
no more in condemnation,
here in the grace of God I stand.
(©1983 Kingsway's Thankyou Music)

FOR FURTHER STUDY

1. Compare Ezekiel 47:1–12 with Genesis 2:10–14. In what ways can Ezekiel's vision be understood as a restoration of Eden?
2. Read Revelation 22:1–5 and list the similarities and parallels with Ezekiel 47:1–12.
3. What light do the following passages shed on Ezekiel 47:1–12? Zechariah 14:8; Psalm 46:4, 65:9; Joel 3:18.
4. Consider Jesus' use of the water analogy in John 4:10–13 and 7:37–39. What light do these passages shed on the fulfilment of Ezekiel 47:1–12?
5. In Revelation 21:5 the Lord declares that he makes all things new. Using a concordance to help, consider the themes of (i) the new covenant; (ii) the new creation in Christ; (iii) the new heavens and new earth; (iv) our new resurrected bodies.

TO THINK ABOUT AND DISCUSS

1. How can you apply the principles of equality and justice raised by Ezekiel in: (i) your personal or family life; (ii) your church; (iii) your role in society? What other biblical principles can you think of that have relevance to the discussion?
2. There is both an already fulfilled and a not yet fulfilled nature to these final two chapters of Ezekiel. What does this mean? What impact should this have on us today in relation to (i) worship; (ii) ecology; (iii) social engagement?
3. As a child of God, how should the knowledge that you are a new creation in Christ affect how you live?

Endnotes

Preface

1 See article in the Daily Mail, 18 October 2007. Quote, 'In my business, asking people to risk their lives is part of the job, but doing so without giving them the chance to understand that there is a life after death is something of a betrayal … Qualities and core values are fine as an acceptable moral baseline for leadership, but the unique life, death, resurrection and promises of Christ provide that spiritual opportunity that I believe takes the privilege of leadership to another level.' http://www.isleofman.com/News/details/27009/general-sir-richard-dannatt-speaks-about-his-faith-during-flying-visit-to-the-island

Introduction

1 Rifkind, Hugo. 'Truth has gone the way of the toaster review.' *The Times*, Tuesday, January 24, 2017. The backdrop to his comment was the debate over numbers attending the inaugural speech of President Donald Trump. It all started with Trump's press secretary, Sean Spicer, accusing journalists of deliberate false reporting and was followed up later by a senior White House aide telling NBC's *Meet the Press* on Sunday that Spicer was simply offering 'alternative facts.' My use of this comment does not reflect any political opinion, but simply draws attention to where postmodernism has brought us at time of writing.

2 Of course, authenticity can mean something different for each generation, and even for individuals. Philosophers such as Camus, Sartre and Heidegger differed on what it meant but held in common the idea of a world without God where man was free to make his own choices and to create his own meaning for life. In

practice this meant you could be authentic to yourself, living for the moment, rather than living subject to God's watchful eye. Being an authentic Christian on the other hand is about being Christ-centred rather than me-centred. It is not about being perfect but rather imperfectly reflecting God at work in us, as we endeavour to make choices that glorify God and serve the good of our neighbour. Ezekiel certainly reflects such authenticity.

3 Schaeffer, Francis A. *The Church at the end of the Twentieth Century* in *The Complete Works of Francis A. Schaeffer, Vol. 4: A Christian View of the Church*, Paternoster Press, 1998, p. 33

Overview

1 Schaeffer, Francis A. *Genesis in Space and Time:* in *The Complete Works of Francis A. Schaeffer, Vol. 2: A Christian View of the Bible as Truth*, Paternoster Press, 1998

2 Wright, C. J. H. *The Message of Ezekiel*, The Bible Speaks Today Series, Inter-Varsity Press, Leicester, 2001, pp. 40–41

3 Jeffery, Peter *Opening Up Ezekiel's Visions,* Opening Up Series, Day One Publications, Leominster, 2004, p. 9

4 See Table 1

5 See Table 2 for one suggested breakdown

6 Reminiscent of the words in Isaiah 48:11 'For my own sake, for my own sake, I do it, for how should my name be profaned? My glory I will not give to another.'

7 Luc, Alex. A Theology of Ezekiel: God's name and Israel's history: *The Journal of the Evangelical Theological Society*. (1998). (electronic edition.). Garland, TX: Galaxie Software.

8 Wright, Christopher J. H. *The Mission of God: Unlocking the Bible's grand narrative*, Inter-

Varsity Press, Leicester, 2006, p. 122

9 Owen, John. *The Glory of Christ: in The Works of John Owen, Vol. 1*, Banner of Truth Trust, Edinburgh, 1987, p. 294

Background and summary

1 Block, Daniel I. *The Book of Ezekiel Chapters 1–24,* The New International Commentary on the Old Testament, Eerdmans Publishing Co, Grand Rapids Michigan, 1997, p. 1

2 Ezekiel— יְחֶזְקֵאל Made up of חָזַק meaning 'to be strong', and אֵל meaning 'God'

3 See John Piper's superb book *Let the Nations be glad: The Supremacy of God in Missions*, Inter-Varsity Press, Leicester, 2003, especially his summary of Jonathan Edwards on the unity of motives for world missions in chapter 6, p. 203.

Chapter 1

1 Calvin, John. *Calvin's Commentaries 22-Volume Set*, Volumes XI–XII, Baker Books, Grand Rapids Michigan, 1998, Vol. XI, p. 62

2 Gill, John. *Exposition of the Old and New Testaments, Vol. 6, Ezekiel to Malachi*, The Baptist Standard Bearer, Arkansas, 2006 Reprint, p. 3

3 Wright, C. J. H. *The Message of Ezekiel*, The Bible Speaks Today Series, Inter-Varsity Press, Leicester, 2001, p48

4 Stuart, Douglas. *Ezekiel*, The Communicator's Commentary Series, Old Testament, Volume 18, Word Books, Dallas, 1989, p. 32

5 On this see Wright, p. 50 fn18. Wright suggests that 'spirit of life' rather than 'spirit of the creatures' makes more sense of the singular in the original language.

6 In Josh. 3:11–13 the people of God were encouraged to cross into the Promised Land in the knowledge that the ark of the covenant of the Lord of all the earth was passing over before

them into the Jordan. See also Ps. 97:5

7 The word used is *Shaddai* meaning the Almighty, an ancient title for God. See for example Block, Daniel I. *The Book of Ezekiel Chapters 1–24,* The New International Commentary on the Old Testament, Eerdmans Publishing Co, Grand Rapids Michigan, 1997, p. 103

8 Block, ibid. p. 105

9 Block, ibid. p. 114

10 Henry, Matthew. *Commentary on the Whole Bible, Vol. 4, Isaiah to Malachi*, MacDonald Publishing Company, Virginia, p. 766

11 Calvin, ibid. p. 148

Chapter 2

1 Block, Daniel I. *The Book of Ezekiel Chapters 25–48*, The New International Commentary on the Old Testament, Eerdmans Publishing Co, Grand Rapids Michigan, 1997, p. 198

2 For further discussion on the possible interpretations of the 390 years plus the 40 years see Block, ibid. p. 170 ff. Wright, C. J. H. *The Message of Ezekiel*, The Bible Speaks Today Series, Inter-Varsity Press, Leicester, 2001, pp. 74–80; Calvin, John. *Calvin's Commentaries 22-Volume Set*, Volumes XI–XII, Baker Books, Grand Rapids Michigan, 1998, p. 174

3 Gill, John. *Exposition of the Old and New Testaments, Vol. 6, Ezekiel to Malachi*, The Baptist Standard Bearer, Arkansas, Reprint, p. 21

4 Isa. 52:10 'The Lord has bared his holy arm before the eyes of all the nations, and all the ends of the earth shall see the salvation of our God.'

5 Morris, Leon. *The Epistle of the Romans*, Eerdmans Publishing Co, Grand Rapids Michigan, 1988, p. 93

6 Lev. 21:5

7 Deut. 21:12; Isa. 15:2; Jer. 16:6; Amos 8:19; Mic. 1:16; Ezek. 7:18

8 2 Sam. 10:4–5

9 This chapter only touches on the immense subject of church discipline, so I encourage the reader to explore further what is possibly a much neglected area of church life.

10 Chapel, Bryan. *Holiness by Grace: Delighting in the Joy That Is Our Strength*, Crossway Books, Illinois, 2001, p. 174

Chapter 3

1 See Ezek. 6:7, 10, 13, 14; 7:4, 9, 27.

2 Calvin, John. *Calvin's Commentaries 22-Volume Set*, Volumes XI–XII, Baker Books, Grand Rapids Michigan, 1998, p. 218

3 Block, Daniel I. *The Book of Ezekiel Chapters 1–24*, The New International Commentary on the Old Testament, Eerdmans Publishing Co, Grand Rapids Michigan, 1997, p. 265

4 See Ralph Martin's essay: http://www.diovive.com/english/Filosofia/influence_humanism.htm

5 The term *Pluralism* refers to the growing diversity in western culture. It is often used to refer to 'the diversity of race, belief systems, heritage, language, culture, and religion in many Western and other nations.' See Don Carson, *The Gagging of God: Christianity Confronts Pluralism*, Apollos, Leicester, 1996, p. 13ff. See also Carson's analysis of how the nature of tolerance has changed with the advent of pluralism on p. 32.

6 Stuart Murray, *Post-Christendom*, Paternoster, Milton Keynes, 2004, p. 235

7 Carson, ibid. p. 32

8 See Galatians 5:11 and surrounding argument

9 Chapel, Bryan. *Holiness by Grace: Delighting in the Joy That Is Our Strength*, Crossway Books, Illinois, 2001, p. 138

10 See for example their appeal

for a King like the nations around them in 1 Samuel.

11 Stuart Murray, ibid. p. 237

12 'In evangelism we should neither try to force people to believe the gospel, nor remain silent as if we were indifferent to their response, nor rely exclusively on the dogmatic proclamation of biblical texts (vital as authoritative biblical exposition is), but rather, like the apostles, we should reason with people from both nature and Scripture, commending God's gospel to them by rational arguments.' John Stott, *Issues Facing Christians Today: New perspectives on social and moral dilemmas*, Marshall Pickering, London, 1990, p. 52

13 Morrisson, James L. *Standing Firm in the Faith: Finding God's Strength in Challenging Times*, 2010, p. 5 www.standingfirminthefaith.com/Download/StandingFirmInTheFaith.pdf

14 Thomas, Derek. *God Strengthens: Ezekiel Simply Explained*, Welwyn Commentary Series, Evangelical Press, Darlington, 1993, p. 61

15 Gill, John. *Exposition of the Old and New Testaments, Vol. 6, Ezekiel to Malachi*, The Baptist Standard Bearer, Arkansas, 2006 Reprint, p. 30

16 Ibid. p. 32

17 See for example Psalm 119:160; Isaiah 40:8; and 1 Peter 1:25

18 Block, Daniel I. *The Book of Ezekiel Chapters 1–24*, The New International Commentary on the Old Testament, Eerdmans Publishing Co, Grand Rapids Michigan, 1997, p. 271

19 Bridges, Jerry. *The Discipline of Grace: God's Role and Our Role in the Pursuit of Holiness*, Nav Press, Colorado, 1994, p. 77

20 See Philippians 2:10–11; Romans 14:10–12; and Isaiah 45:23

21 Grudem, Wayne. *Systematic*

Theology: An Introduction to Biblical Doctrine, IVP, Leicester, 1994, p. 715

22 Thomas, Derek. *God Strengthens: Ezekiel Simply Explained*, Welwyn Commentary Series, Evangelical Press, Darlington, 1993, p. 61

Chapter 4

1 Block, Daniel I. *The Book of Ezekiel Chapters 1–24*, The New International Commentary on the Old Testament, Eerdmans Publishing Co, Grand Rapids Michigan, 1997, p341. This is an important theme in Ezekiel and one that will be revisited in Ezek. 36:26

2 Thomas, Derek. *God Strengthens: Ezekiel Simply Explained*, Welwyn Commentary Series, Evangelical Press, Darlington, 1993, p. 71

3 Ezekiel 8:1–11:25 is a unit sandwiched between Ezekiel being taken by the Spirit to Jerusalem (Ezek. 8:1–3) and being brought back in the vision to his home (Ezek. 11:24–25).

4 Wright, C. J. H. *The Message of Ezekiel*, The Bible Speaks Today Series, Inter-Varsity Press, Leicester, 2001, p. 110

5 See for example Matthew Henry and John Gill.

6 See for example Douglas Stuart and Derek Thomas.

7 Wright, C. J. H. *The Message of Ezekiel*, The Bible Speaks Today Series, Inter-Varsity Press, Leicester, 2001, pp. 102–103

8 Jaazaniah son of Shaphan. Stood as leader in the midst of the 70 ancients (elders) of Israel with censers in their hands, worshipping idols portrayed upon the wall of the court of Jehovah's house; seen by Ezekiel (8:11). Shaphan was the scribe who read to Josiah the law. The son's spiritual privileges increased his guilt (2 Kings 22:10–14). His very name, meaning'

Jehovah hears,' gave the lie to the unbelief which virtually said 'Jehovah seeth not' (Ezek. 9:9; Ps. 10:11,14; 50:21; 94:7,9). The elders incurred further guilt in usurping the priests' office by offering incense. See Fausset's Bible Dictionary in Bible Works 6.

9 https://www.goodreads.com/quotes/7090336-religion-is-what-you-do-with-your-solitude

10 Note, this explanation is taken from the ISBE Bible dictionary, Electronic format in Bible Works 6.

11 Wright, C. J. H. *The Message of Ezekiel*, The Bible Speaks Today Series, Inter-Varsity Press, Leicester, 2001, p. 108

12 Gill, John. *Exposition of the Old and New Testaments, Vol. 9, Galatians to Revelation*, The Baptist Standard Bearer, Arkansas, 2006 Reprint, p. 573

13 Block, Daniel I. *The Book of Ezekiel Chapters 1–24*, The New International Commentary on the Old Testament, Eerdmans Publishing Co, Grand Rapids Michigan, 1997, p. 333

14 Ibid. p. 334

15 Ibid. p. 320

16 Ibid. p. 338

17 Calvin, John. *Calvin's Commentaries 22-Volume Set*, Volumes XI–XII, Baker Books, Grand Rapids Michigan, 1998, p. 360

18 See 2 Cor. 6:16; Rev. 21:3

19 Henry, Matthew. *Commentary on the Whole Bible, Vol. 4, Isaiah to Malachi*, MacDonald Publishing Company, Virginia, p. 810

20 Block, Daniel I. *The Book of Ezekiel Chapters 1–24*, The New International Commentary on the Old Testament, Eerdmans Publishing Co, Grand Rapids Michigan, 1997, p. 359.

Chapter 5

1 Interestingly God does not call Zedekiah 'King' perhaps an indication of his disdain for

him and playing on the fact that he is merely the puppet of Nebuchadnezzar. See Block, Daniel I. *The Book of Ezekiel Chapters 1–24*, The New International Commentary on the Old Testament, Eerdmans Publishing Co, Grand Rapids Michigan, 1997, p. 373
2 Jamieson, Fausset, and Brown Commentary; Electronic Edition in e-Sword® Bible Software. Comment on Ezekiel 12:10
3 Block, Daniel I. *The Book of Ezekiel Chapters 1–24*, The New International Commentary on the Old Testament, Eerdmans Publishing Co, Grand Rapids Michigan, 1997, p. 374
4 Kostenberger, Andreas J. *The Missions of Jesus and the Disciples according to the Fourth Gospel, with Implications for the Fourth Gospel's Purpose and the Mission of the Contemporary Church*, Wm. B. Eerdmans Publishing Company, 1998 p. 217
5 See for example Romans 2:4; 2 Corinthians 7:10; 2 Timothy 2:25.
6 Morris, Leon. *The Apostolic Preaching of the Cross*, third edition, The Tyndale Press, London, 1965, p. 210
7 Manila Manifesto www.lausanne.org/content/manifesto/the-manila-manifesto

Chapter 6

1 Jeffery, Peter. *Opening Up Ezekiel's Visions*, Opening Up Series, Day One Publications, Leominster, 2004, p. 41
2 'Proof texting' has been defined in a number of ways but the essential meaning is using passages of Scripture to support whatever position the preacher wants to hold. It often involves using a text of the Bible as a spring-board into a subject that is then developed more according to the imagination of the

preacher than according to the context within which it is set in Scripture.

3 'My Heart is Filled with Thankfulness' by Keith Getty and Stuart Townend. Copyright© 2003 Thankyou Music

4 Block, Daniel I. *The Book of Ezekiel Chapters 1–24*, The New International Commentary on the Old Testament, Eerdmans Publishing Co, Grand Rapids Michigan, 1997, p. 413.

5 Block goes as far as to suggest they were 'instruments of black magic.' ibid. p. 414.

Chapter 7

1 Wodehouse, P. G. *The Inimitable Jeeves*, Arrow Books, London, 2008, p. 140

2 Calvin, John. *Calvin's Commentaries 22-Volume Set*, Volume XII, Baker Books, Grand Rapids Michigan, 1998, p. 46

3 Ecclesiastes 5:1

4 Comfort P. W., 'Idolatry' in Hawthorne, Martin, Reed, Eds. *Dictionary of Paul and his Letters*, IVP, Leicester, 1993, p. 426

5 Lowman, Pete. *A Long Way East of Eden*, Paternoster Press, Milton Keynes, 2002, p. 257

6 See for example God's response to the churches at Pergamum and Thyatira in Revelation chapter 2.

7 Compare Matthew 11:20 ff.

Chapter 8

1 Lewis C. S. *The Screwtape Letters: C. S. Lewis Signature Classics Edition*, Harper Collins Publishers, London, 2002, p. 58. First published in 1942 by Geoffrey Bles.

2 Octavius Winslow. *Personal Declension and Revival of Religion in the Soul*, Robert Carter, 1847, p. 9

3 Psalm 80:8, 14; Isaiah 3:14; 5:1–7; Jeremiah 2:21; 6:9; 8:13; Hosea 10:1; 14:7

4 Whitacre R. A. Vine, Fruit of the Vine, in *Dictionary of Jesus*

and the Gospels, Eds. Joel B. Green, Scot McKnight, I. Howard Marshall, Intervarsity Press, Leicester, 1992, p. 867

5 http://www.jewishencyclopedia.com/articles/14304-temple-of-herod ; also: http://www.bible-history.com/court-of-women/jewish_encyclopedia.html

6 Jeremiah 2:21

7 LXX ἄμπελον καρποφόρον πᾶσαν ἀληθινήν
Note:Jeremiah uses ἀληθινήν John 15:1 uses ἀληθινη The idea as Lenski points out is an emphasis on *real as opposed to true or truthful* i.e. Christ is the *real* vine ... Israel as the vine *in all things real* was a picture of Christ. Hebrew used is אֱמֶת refering to firmness, faithfulness, truth.

8 Spurgeon, C. H. *Miracles and Parables of our Lord*, Baker Book House, Grand Rapids Michigan, 1989, Vol. 3, p. 151

9 Spurgeon, ibid. p.151

10 Piper, John. *Glorifying God by Bearing Fruit in Union with Christ*, www.desiringgod.org/messages February 3, 2014.

11 See also Hendriksen, William. *The Gospel of John: New Testament Commentary*, Baker Book House, Grand Rapids Michigan, 1953, p. 294 for a clear and thorough understanding of the central message of John 15.

12 The reference to being burned at both ends is a reference to the two deportations that had already taken place:

1. 722 BC the Northern Kingdom taken into exile by the Assyrians (1st deportation)
2. 598 BC most of the Southern Kingdom including many from Jerusalem taken into exile by the Babylonians (including Daniel and Ezekiel) (2nd deportation)
3. 586 BC 2nd Babylonian invasion (3rd deportation) yet to come in

approximately two years' time

13 Deuteronomy 7:6 'For you are a people holy to the LORD your God. The LORD your God has chosen you to be a people for his treasured possession, out of all the peoples who are on the face of the earth.' Deuteronomy 14:2 'For you are a people holy to the LORD your God, and the LORD has chosen you to be a people for his treasured possession, out of all the peoples who are on the face of the earth.'

14 Block, Daniel I. *The Book of Ezekiel Chapters 1–24*, The New International Commentary on the Old Testament, Eerdmans Publishing Co, Grand Rapids Michigan, 1997, p. 459

15 Block points out that given the covenantal relationship that has been broken here, the Hebrew word used is even stronger than simply adultery. See his comments on p. 459 of his commentary.

16 It further reminds us of the magnitude of what happened on the cross. Sproul writes, 'His figure on the cross was the most grotesque, obscene mass of concentrated sin in the history of the world.' Truth of the Cross; Kindle ed. Loc. 832

17 Block, Daniel I. *The Book of Ezekiel Chapters 1–24*, The New International Commentary on the Old Testament, Eerdmans Publishing Co, Grand Rapids Michigan, 1997, p. 521

18 www.truthinhistory.org/the-welsh-revival-of-1904-1905-2.html

19 Martin, Kenneth. *Power: A devotional commentary on The Acts of the Apostles*, Published by Kenneth Martin, Craigavon, United Kingdom, 2014, p. 6

20 'This passage offers helpful insight into the biblical perspective on guilt and shame. Against the grain of popular thinking today, this oracle is unrestrained in its

shaming of unfaithful Israel.' See Block, ibid. p. 522

21 Compare Ezek 17:15 with 2 Chron 36:9–13

22 Stuart, Douglas. *Ezekiel*, The Communicator's Commentary Series, Old Testament, Volume 18, Word Books, Dallas, 1989, p. 149

Chapter 9

1 The exact meaning depends on whether the Hebrew conjunction Vav is translated as and or but. See Wright's analysis of this in his commentary pp. 181–189.

2 The actual making of carved or even cast images was never a sin but rather making such with a view to worshipping them. Under God's direction Moses was even commanded to make figures of Cherubim for the Ark of the Covenant, and this crafting of images was perfectly acceptable as the articles made were not objects of worship.

3 Dr. Rabbi Zev Farber http://thetorah.com/punishing-children-for-the-sins-of-their-parents/

4 Dr. Rabbi Zev Farber, ibid.

5 Calvin, John. *Calvin's Commentaries 22-Volume Set*, Volumes XI–XII, Baker Books, Grand Rapids Michigan, 1998, pp. 250–251

6 Calvin, John. *Calvin's Commentaries 22-Volume Set*, Volumes XI–XII, Baker Books, Grand Rapids Michigan, 1998, p. 259

7 Grudem, Wayne. *Systematic Theology: An Introduction to Biblical Doctrine*, IVP, Leicester, 1994, p. 713

8 Wright, C. J. H. *The Message of Ezekiel*, The Bible Speaks Today Series, Inter-Varsity Press, Leicester, 2001, p. 189

9 Calvin, ibid. p. 260

Chapter 10

1 'Ezekiel refuses to dignify them with the title *melek*, 'king.' Block, Daniel I. *The Book of Ezekiel Chapters 1–24*, The New International

Commentary on the Old Testament, Eerdmans Publishing Co, Grand Rapids Michigan, 1997, p. 598

2 Calvin, John. *Calvin's Commentaries 22-Volume Set*, Volumes XI–XII, Baker Books, Grand Rapids Michigan, 1998, p. 267

3 Henry, Matthew. *Commentary on the Whole Bible, Vol. 4, Isaiah to Malachi*, MacDonald Publishing Company, Virginia, p. 860

4 Calvin, ibid. p. 268

5 Wells, David F. *Above all Earthly Pow'rs: Christ in a Postmodern World*, Eerdmans, Grand Rapids, 2006, p. 314

6 Wells, ibid. p. 315

7 Block, ibid. p. 611

8 Stuart, Douglas. *Ezekiel*, The Communicator's Commentary Series, Old Testament, Volume 18, Word Books, Dallas, 1989 p. 168

9 Thomas, Derek. *God Strengthens: Ezekiel Simply Explained*, Welwyn Commentary Series, Evangelical Press, Darlington, 1993 p. 133.

10 D. J. Wiseman, JEHOIACHIN, in *The New Bible Dictionary*, Intervarsity Press, London, 1962, p. 602

11 Thomas, ibid. p. 133

12 Hendriksen, William. *More than Conquerors*, Baker Book House, Michigan, 1940, (Commemorative Edition 1982) p. 91

13 See 1 Samuel 13:14 and Acts 13:22

14 Block, ibid. p. 611

Chapter 11

1 See also Roland De Vaux, *Ancient Israel: Its Life and Institutions*, The Biblical Resource Series, Eerdmans, Grand Rapids Michigan, 1958, (1997 Edition), pp. 48–50

2 Wright, Christopher J. H. *Old Testament Ethics for the People of God*, Intervarsity Press, Leicester, 2004, p. 85

3 Wright, ibid. p. 92

4 Williamson, Paul R. *Sealed with an Oath: Covenant in*

God's unfolding purpose, Intervarsity Press, Illinois, 2007, p. 96

5 *Bamah* means high place and is often used in the Bible to refer to Canaanite sanctuaries. See De Vaux, ibid. p. 284

6 See Wright's summary in *Old Testament Ethics,* ibid. p. 296

7 For further study on the Sabbath read *Call the Sabbath a Delight*, by Walter Chantry (Banner of Truth); and *From Sabbath to Lord's Day: A Biblical, Historical and Theological Investigation*, edited by D. A. Carson (Wipf & Stock Pub).

8 Morris, Leon. *The Epistle to the Romans*, Eerdmans, Grand Rapids, Michigan, 1998, p. 94

9 Hendriksen, William. *Romans: New Testament Commentary*, Baker, Grand Rapids, Michigan, 1980, p. 85

10 Wright, C. J. H. *The Message of Ezekiel*, The Bible Speaks Today Series, Inter-Varsity Press, Leicester, 2001, p. 165

11 'Those with an overly optimistic view of the human condition tend to dismiss this text … as damaging to one's mental well-being. While all human beings do indeed have intrinsic dignity by virtue of their status as images of God, notions of self-worth must be distinguished from ideas of worthiness. Our status as God's image provides the basis for his unique interest in us, but our fallen condition disqualifies us from claiming this statue as a natural right. God did not express his love in Jesus Christ in response to our worthiness, but to redeem us from our unworthiness. The fundamental problem with most of us is not deficient self-esteem but an inadequate divine-esteem.' Block, Daniel I. *The Book of Ezekiel Chapters 1–24*, The New International Commentary on the Old Testament, Eerdmans Publishing Co, Grand Rapids Michigan, 1997, p. 659

12 Adams, Jay, E. *The Biblical View*

of Self-esteem, http://www.chapellibrary.org/files/6513/7643/2891/bvos.pdf

13 Calvin, John. *Calvin's Commentaries 22-Volume Set*, Volumes XI–XII, Baker Books, Grand Rapids Michigan, 1998, p. 342

14 Calvin, ibid. p. 345

Chapter 12

1 Stuart, Douglas. *Ezekiel*, The Communicator's Commentary Series, Old Testament, Volume 18, Word Books, Dallas, 1989, p. 204

2 Counting Religion in Britain, January 2018; Posted on February 2, 2018 by Clive D. Field. http://www.brin.ac.uk/2018/counting-religion-in-britain-january-2018/

3 Block, Daniel I. *The Book of Ezekiel Chapters 1–24*, The New International Commentary on the Old Testament, Eerdmans Publishing Co, Grand Rapids Michigan, 1997, p. 764

4 Calvin, John. *Institutes of the Christian Religion*, The Westminster Press, Philadelphia, Vol. 1, 1960, p. 405 or 2.8.41–44

5 Gill, John. *A Body of Doctrinal and Practical Divinity*, The Baptist Standard Bearer, Arkansas, 1989 reprint, p. 860

6 Gill, John. *Exposition of the Old and New Testaments, Vol. 6, Ezekiel to Malachi*, The Baptist Standard Bearer, Arkansas, 2006 Reprint, p. 115

7 Owen, John. *Eshcol, A Cluster of the Fruit of Canaan:* in The Works of John Owen, Vol. 13, *Ministry anxd Fellowship*, Banner of Truth Trust, Edinburgh, 1987, p. 56

8 See http://www.christianitytoday.com/edstetzer/2014/february/marriage-divorce-and-body-of-christ-what-do-stats-say-and-c.html

Chapter 13

1 Bunyan, John. *The Pilgrim's Progress*, Banner of Truth

Trust, Edinburgh, 1997, pp. 36–37 Reprint of 1895 edition by John C Nimmo Ltd.

2 Bunyan, John. ibid. pp. 250–251

3 Possibly late December 592 or January 591 BC. We read in Ezek. 1:2 that he is first called on the 5th day of the 5th year of exile. Here in Ezek. 24:1 it is now the 10th day of the 10th month of the 9th year, i.e. a period of approximately 4 years and 5 months.

4 Block, Daniel I. *The Book of Ezekiel Chapters 1–24*, The New International Commentary on the Old Testament, Eerdmans Publishing Co, Grand Rapids Michigan, 1997, p. 797

5 This paragraph owes much to Christopher Wright's comments on the passage.

6 Block, ibid. p. 796

7 Wilberforce, William. *Real Christianity*, Pickering & Inglis, Basingstoke, 1982, (original 1829), p. 125

8 Owen, John. *An Exposition of Psalm CXXX: in* The Works of John Owen, Vol. 6, *Temptation and Sin*, Banner of Truth Trust, Edinburgh, 1987, p. 505

9 Psalm 130:7–8

10 Murphy, Thomas. *Pastoral Theology: The Pastor in the Various Duties of His Office*, Old Path Publications, New Jersey, 1996 (First published in 1877), p. 57

11 See Hooker's comments to this effect in Murphy's *Pastoral Theology*, ibid. p. 59

Chapter 14

1 http://www.livescience.com/17398-schadenfreude-affirmation.html

2 Ibid.

3 Block, Daniel I. *The Book of Ezekiel Chapters 25–48*, The New International Commentary on the Old Testament, Eerdmans Publishing Co, Grand Rapids Michigan, 1997, p. 3

4 In the original language the

escaped one or *fugitive* is the same word in 24:26 and 33:21

5 Barnes, Albert. Notes on the Old Testament, Ezekiel. http://biblehub.com/commentaries/barnes/ezekiel/25.htm

6 Block, ibid. p. 20

7 'Vengeance is mine says the LORD.' Deut 32:35—cited in Rom 12:19 & Heb 10:30

8 www.theworldcounts.com/stories/Child-Labor-Facts-and-Statistics

9 Tyre had been for many years subordinate to Sidon. From the 12th century BC we can date Tyre's great commercial and colonial activity. Its mariners pushed out to the West and founded colonies in Spain and North Africa, some of which, like Gades, Abdera and Carthage, became famous. They extended their commerce more widely than Sidon had ever done and ventured into the Atlantic and reached the coasts of Britain and West Africa. They reached out to the East also, and had their ships in the Red Sea and the Indian Ocean, and their land routes threaded all Western Asia. (International Standard Bible Encyclopaedia, Electronic Copy, in e-Sword Bible Study Programme)

10 The Message Bible

11 https://www.ancient.eu/article/107/

12 See footnote on Tyre above. For many years Tyre lived in the shadow of Sidon but in time became more dominant.

13 Wright, C. J. H. *The Message of Ezekiel*, The Bible Speaks Today Series, Inter-Varsity Press, Leicester, 2001, p. 238

14 Block, ibid. p. 18

15 Lane, Eric. *Proverbs*, Christian Focus Publications, Fearn, Ross-shire, 2000, p. 185

16 Wright, ibid. p. 246

17 Wright, ibid. p. 248

18 Thomas, Derek. *God Strengthens: Ezekiel Simply Explained*, Welwyn Commentary Series, Evangelical Press, Darlington, 1993, p. 206

19 Wright, ibid. p. 230

20 Stuart Townend & Mark Edwards Copyright © 2007 Thankyou Music (Adm. by CapitolCMGPublishing.com excl. UK & Europe, adm. by Integrity Music, part of the David C. Cook family, songs@integritymusic.com)

Chapter 15

1 Wright, C. J. H. *The Message of Ezekiel*, The Bible Speaks Today Series, Inter-Varsity Press, Leicester, 2001, p. 72

2 Block, Daniel I. *The Book of Ezekiel Chapters 25–48*, The New International Commentary on the Old Testament, Eerdmans Publishing Co, Grand Rapids Michigan, 1997, p. 246

3 Jeffery, Peter. *Opening Up Ezekiel's Visions*, Opening Up Series, Day One Publications, Leominster, 2004, p. 92

4 Block, ibid. p. 248

5 Pink, Arthur W. *The Seven Sayings of the Saviour on the Cross*, Baker Book House, Grand Rapids, 1990, (first printed in 1958), p. 28

6 Stuart, Douglas. *Ezekiel*, The Communicator's Commentary Series, Old Testament, Volume 18, Word Books, Dallas, 1989, p. 313

7 See for example the short history of the Ulster Revival of 1857 http://www.revival-library.org/index.php/catalogues-menu/1857/the-ulster-revival-of-1859

8 Reymond, Robert. *Paul, Missionary Theologian: A Survey of his Missionary Labours and Theology*, Mentor, Christian Focus Publications, Ross-shire, 2000, p. 563

Chapter 16

1 So Block and Wright. 'Ezekiel chooses a metaphor for kingship that was well known throughout the ancient Near East, from Babylon to Egypt—the shepherd of the flock. He then launches into an attack on *the shepherds of Israel*—

meaning the historical kings of the period up to the exile.' Wright, C. J. H. *The Message of Ezekiel*, The Bible Speaks Today Series, Inter-Varsity Press, Leicester, 2001, pp. 274–275.

2 Block, Daniel I. *The Book of Ezekiel Chapters 25–48*, The New International Commentary on the Old Testament, Eerdmans Publishing Co, Grand Rapids Michigan, 1997, p. 283.

3 Gill, John. *Exposition of the Old and New Testaments, Vol. 6, Ezekiel to Malachi*, The Baptist Standard Bearer, Arkansas, 2006 reprint, p. 176.

4 Jeffery, Peter. *Opening Up Ezekiel's Visions*, Opening Up Series, Day One Publications, Leominster, 2004, p. 108.

5 Wright, ibid. p. 280

6 Wright, ibid. Luke 1:27, 32–33, 69; 2:1

7 Jeffery, ibid. p104–105

8 See for example http://www.opendoorsuk.org/

9 Hendriksen, William. *The Gospel of John: New Testament Commentary*, Baker Book House, Grand Rapids Michigan, 1953, p. 110.

Chapter 17

1 We read in Genesis 32:3 that the land of Seir is an alternative name for Edom. This is the mountainous tract bordering south-east Israel and was occupied by the descendants of Esau.

2 Edom, Edomites, in *The Illustrated Bible Dictionary*, IVP, 1980, p. 411.

3 Maynard, Dennis, R. *When Sheep Attack!*; Booksurge Publishers, USA, 2010, Introduction.

4 Schaeffer, Francis A. *Joshua and the Flow of Biblical History:* in *The Complete Works of Francis A. Schaeffer, Vol. 2: A Christian View of the Bible as Truth*, Paternoster Press, 1998, p. 288.

5 See also 1 John 3:15

6 Compare Matthew 5:21–22 with Matthew 18:15–20.

7 Romans 12:17–21

8 The phrase is coined by Barack Obama in his book, *The Audacity of Hope*.

9 See *Stop the Traffik: People Should Not Be Bought & Sold*, by Steve Chalke, Marston Book Service, 2009. The book contains many helpful insights into human rights abuses and some steps that have been taken by at least some multinational companies to make right mistakes of the past. Unfortunately it seems that for every one who is prepared to take positive steps to correct such exploitation, another is found wanting.

10 John Stott, *Issues Facing Christians Today: New Perspectives on Social and Moral Dilemmas*, Marshall Pickering, London, 1990, p. 157.

11 Block, Daniel I. *The Book of Ezekiel Chapters 25–48*, The New International Commentary on the Old Testament, Eerdmans Publishing Co, Grand Rapids Michigan, 1997, pp. 320–321.

12 Paradox Blessing, second verse, in *Celtic Daily Prayer*, Book Two, p. 1088.

13 Block,ibid. p. 333

14 Block,ibid.

15 Gen. 22:14 So Abraham called the name of that place, 'The Lord will provide'; as it is said to this day …'

16 Leupold H.C. *Exposition of the Psalms*, Evangelical Press, London, 1959, p. 989.

Chapter 18

1 It should be noted that most of the types of discharge that rendered a person impure occurred in the course of everyday life. It isn't clear why they were considered defiling although some think it is not so much that they were sinful but rather unclean in that they were in some way connected to death. See for example—Mooney, D. J. (2012, 2013,

2014, 2015). 'Leviticus, Book of', in J. D. Barry, D. Bomar, D. R. Brown, R. Klippenstein, D. Mangum, C. Sinclair Wolcott, W. Widder (Eds.), *The Lexham Bible Dictionary*, Bellingham, WA: Lexham Press. Logos Bible Software.

2 Wright, C. J. H. *The Message of Ezekiel*, The Bible Speaks Today Series, Inter-Varsity Press, Leicester, 2001; pp. 287–288.

3 Commenting on Luke 7:47, in his Notes on the New Testament, Albert Barnes writes: 'A man's love to God will be in proportion to the obligation he 'feels' to him for forgiveness. God is to be 'loved' for his perfections, apart from what he has 'done' for us. But still it is proper that our love should be increased by a consideration of his goodness; and they who feel—as Christians do—that they are the 'chief of sinners,' will feel under infinite obligation to love God and their Redeemer, and that no 'expression' of attachment to him can be 'beyond' what is due.'

4 Block, Daniel I. *The Book of Ezekiel Chapters 25–48*, The New International Commentary on the Old Testament, Eerdmans Publishing Co, Grand Rapids Michigan, 1997, p. 353. See also Chris Wright, *op cit*, p. 293.

5 Grudem, Wayne. *Systematic Theology: An Introduction to Biblical Doctrine*, Intervarsity Press, Leicester, 1994, p. 861

6 See also 2 Cor 7:11 for a ref where NT believers cleanse themselves.

7 Owen, John. *On Communion with God: in The Works of John Owen, Vol. 2*, Banner of Truth Trust, Edinburgh, 1987, p. 314

8 Bridges, Jerry. *The Discipline of Grace: God's role and our role in the pursuit of holiness*, NAV PRESS, Colorado Springs, 1994, p. 165

9 Wright, ibid. p. 300.

10 Bridges, Jerry. *Transforming Grace: Living Confidently in God's Unfailing Love*, NAV PRESS, Scripture Press Foundation, (UK) Ltd, Amersham-on-the-Hill, 1991, p. 46.

11 Owen, John. *The Work of the Holy Spirit: in The Works of John Owen, Vol. 4*, Banner of Truth Trust, Edinburgh, 1987, p. 277.

12 Luter A. B. Jr., 'Name' in Hawthorne, Martin, Reed, Eds. *Dictionary of Paul and his Letters*, IVP, Leicester, 1993, p. 628.

Chapter 19

1 Ephesians 2:1

2 This is not to deny that God can and does heal people. Indeed we are positively encouraged to pray for those who are sick (James 5:14). However, the burden of Ezekiel's writing, and passages such as Isaiah 53:5 and 1 Peter 2:24, is that people need to be saved from death, not sickness. In the original biblical languages the word for healed can mean either physical or spiritual healing. In both Isaiah and Peter the word is used in the context of sin and righteousness, not sickness and physical healing. It is another way of saying that sinners are pardoned from their sin and born again. They are now dead to sin and are to live godly lives.

3 De Vaux, Roland. *Ancient Israel—Its Life and Institutions*, p. 56 '…to be left unburied, a prey to the birds and the wild beasts, was the worst of all curses (1 Kings 14:11; Jer. 16:4; 22:19; Ezra 29:5)'. See also, Wright, C. J. H. *The Message of Ezekiel*, The Bible Speaks Today Series, Inter-Varsity Press, 2001, p. 304.

4 Jeffery, Peter. *Opening Up Ezekiel's Visions*, Day One Publications, Leominster, 2004, p. 111.

5 Gill, John. *Exposition of the Old and New Testaments, Vol.*

6, Ezekiel to Malachi, The Baptist Standard Bearer, Arkansas, 2006 Reprint, p. 192.

6 Block, Daniel I. *The Book of Ezekiel Chapters 25–48*, The New International Commentary on the Old Testament, Eerdmans Publishing Co, Grand Rapids Michigan, 1997, p. 375.

7 The three words, 'breath,' 'wind,' and 'spirit,' are represented in the Hebrew by the same word, and the context must determine which sense is intended. 'Both the Hebrew and Greek words rendered *spirit* in our Bibles (*ruach* and *pneuma*) carry this basic thought, and both have the same range of association. They are used of (1) the divine Spirit, personal and purposeful, invisible and irresistible; (2) the individual human consciousness (in which sense *spirit* becomes synonymous with *soul*, as for instance in Luke 1:46, 47); and (3) the wind that when aroused whirls leaves, uproots trees, and blows buildings over. (For examples of this latter use, see (a) Ezekiel 37:1–14, the dry-bones vision, where *ruach* is breath, wind, and Spirit of God in quick succession, and (b) the use of *pneuma* for the wind as well as for God's Spirit in John 3:8).' Packer, J. I. *Keep in Step with the Spirit*, IVP, Leicester, 1984, p. 57.

8 Block, ibid. p. 392.

9 Stott, John. *Basic Christian Leadership: Biblical Models of Church, Gospel and Ministry*, IVP Books, Illinois, 2002, p. 73.

10 Jeffery, ibid. p. 115.

11 Isaiah 55:10–11

12 Gill, John. *Exposition of the Old and New Testaments, Vol. 6, Ezekiel to Malachi*, The Baptist Standard Bearer, Arkansas, 2006 reprint, p. 194.

13 Wright, ibid. p. 313.

14 'The kingdom manifests itself through the church, and

thereby the future reign of God breaks into the present (it is 'already' here: Matt. 12:28; Rom. 14:17; and 'not yet' here fully: Matt. 25:34; 1 Cor. 6:9–10). Therefore those who believe in Christ will begin to experience something of what God's final kingdom reign will be like… Eventually Jesus will return and his kingdom reign will extend over all creation (1 Cor. 15:24–28)' Grudem, Wayne. *Systematic Theology: An Introduction to Biblical Doctrine*, IVP, Leicester, 1994, p. 864.

15 Prince of Peace—Isa 9:6 (cf. Ezek 34:24; 37:25–26); Immanuel, God in our midst—Isa 7:14 Mat 1:23 (cf. Ezek 34:24; 37:24–25); the Son of David—Matt 1:1; 12:23; Lk 1:32; Rom 1:3 (cf. Ezek 34:23–24; 37:24–25); and the good shepherd—John 10:1–21 (cf. Ezek 34:23; 37:24).

Chapter 20

1 See for example The Christian Institute briefings at www.christian.org.uk for up to date news on these and similar issues.

2 1 Timothy 6:12

3 There have been many attempts at identifying Gog. For example: Ambrose and Augustine saw Gog and Magog as a reference to the Goths who ravaged the Roman Empire in the 5th and 6th centuries '… which seemed to signal the end of Christian civilization as then known' (Wright, p. 325). Luther, Fairbairn, and Gill saw Gog as a reference to the Turks who were encroaching on 'Christian Europe' at that time. Johannes Cocceius, the Dutch theologian of the 17th century saw it as referring to a 'Romish Antichrist'. Dispensationalism sees it as a reference to Russia or the Soviet Union. See T.C. Mitchell's historical insight as noted below; and Stuart's insight in the text above.

4 T.C. Mitchell, 'Meshech', in

The New Bible Dictionary, Intervarsity Press, London, 1962, p. 811.

5 Stuart, Douglas. *Ezekiel*, The Communicator's Commentary Series, Old Testament, Volume 18, Word Books, Dallas, 1989, p. 355.

6 Block, Daniel I. *The Book of Ezekiel Chapters 25–48*, The New International Commentary on the Old Testament, Eerdmans Publishing Co, Grand Rapids Michigan, 1997, p. 450.

7 Block, ibid. p. 456.

8 Wright, ibid. p. 319.

9 Grier, W.J. *The Momentous Event: A Discussion of Scripture Teaching on the Second Advent*, The Banner of Truth Trust, Edinburgh, 1986, p. 36. First published in 1945.

10 Grier, ibid. p. 36.

11 Wright, ibid. p. 321.

12 Gill, John. *Exposition of the Old and New Testaments, Vol. 6, Ezekiel to Malachi*, The Baptist Standard Bearer, Arkansas, 2006 reprint, p. 205.

13 R. Fowler White, Re-examining the Evidence for Recapitulation in Rev 20:1–10 in *The Westminster Theological Journal* 51:2 (Fall 1989) p. 327.

14 Ibid.

15 Hendriksen, William, *More than Conquerors*, Baker Book House, Grand Rapids Michigan, 1940, p. 194.

16 http://www.christianitytoday.com/news/2017/january/top-50-countries-christian-persecution-world-watch-list.html

Chapter 21

1 'This belief in Yahweh's presence in his Temple was the whole reason for the worship celebrated there and for the pious customs of the faithful', Roland De Vaux, *Ancient Israel: Its Life and Institutions*, The Biblical Resource Series, Eerdmans, Grand Rapids

Michigan, 1958, (1997 Edition), p. 326.

2 Owen, John. *A Christian, God's Temple: in* The Works of John Owen, Vol. 9, *Sermons to the Churches*, Banner of Truth Trust, Edinburgh, 1987, pp. 285–295.

3 See comments on Francis Schaeffer's use of this term in the overview at the beginning of this book.

4 This is based on a cubit being about 45 centimetres. Ezekiel tells us in 42:15–20 that the temple area was 500 cubits long by 500 cubits wide.

5 Stuart, Douglas. *Ezekiel*, The Communicator's Commentary Series, Old Testament, Volume 18, Word Books, Dallas, 1989 p. 376.

6 Gill, John. *Exposition of the Old and New Testaments, Vol. 6, Ezekiel to Malachi*, The Baptist Standard Bearer, Arkansas, Reprint, p. 231.

7 'Elevated above the realm of the common and surrounded by massive walls, the absolute holiness of this area, established by the residence of the deity himself, was to be strictly guarded. Only the priests, specially consecrated, could enter here, and only the sacred gifts could be brought inside. While Yahweh may have condescended to dwell among his people, extreme measures will be prescribed to prevent the contagion of impurity inside and the contagion of holiness outside' Block, ibid. p. 592.

8 For a detailed figure of the altar see Block, ibid. p. 598.

9 Block, ibid. p. 601.

10 Block, ibid. pp. 612–613.

11 This section owes a great deal to the masterful mind of Edmund P. Clowney in his article *The Final Temple*, Westminster Theological Journal, Philadelphia, vol. 35, #2, 1973. What follows is a scant summary of his teaching. A copy of his paper can also be found at this website: http://

beginningwithmoses.org/oldsite/articles/finaltemple.htm

12 Clowney, ibid. p. 159. See also Schaeffer's superb treatise on this subject in Schaeffer, Francis A. *The God Who Is There: in The Complete Works of Francis A. Schaeffer, Vol. 1: A Christian View of Philosophy and Culture*, Paternoster Press, 1998.

13 Clowney, ibid. p. 161

14 Clowney, ibid. p. 162

15 Clowney, ibid. p. 164.

16 Clowney, ibid. p. 164 (emphasis mine).

17 C. H. Spurgeon in his sermon titled *One Greater Than the Temple* preached on January 23, 1876.

18 'The type and the Antitype cannot be separated. Israel's physical temple (or tabernacle) was the place in which God dwelt. Hence, it was the type of Christ's body, which also, and in a far more superior sense, was the dwelling-place of God' William Hendriksen, *The Gospel of John*, New Testament Commentary, Baker, 1988, p. 125.

19 Hendriksen, William. *The Gospel of John*, New Testament Commentary, Baker, 1988, p. 125.

20 Roland De Vaux, *Ancient Israel: Its Life and Institutions*, The Biblical Resource Series, Eerdmans, Grand Rapids Michigan, 1958, (1997 Edition), p. 330.

21 Clowney, ibid. p. 190

Chapter 22

1 'Yahweh hereby announces concretely that he would reside among the descendants of Israel forever. The tragedy of 11:23 will never be repeated.' Block, Daniel I. *The Book of Ezekiel Chapters 25–48*, The New International Commentary on the Old Testament, Eerdmans Publishing Co, Grand Rapids Michigan, 1997, p. 614.

2 See for example, David Robertson's article *Belonging Before Believing—A Recipe for*

a Dying Church, at www.christiantoday.com/article/belonging-before-believing-a-recipe-for-a-dying-church/39171.htm.

3 See for example census on church attendance at http://www.eauk.org/church/research-and-statistics/english-church-census.cfm.

4 Grudem, Wayne. *Systematic Theology: An Introduction to Biblical Doctrine*, IVP, Leicester, 1994, p. 853.

5 This was the understanding of these words when the temple was rebuilt under Herod between 19 and 9 bc. Gentiles or foreigners were permitted to enter the outer court but they were excluded from entering into any of the inner courts. And warning signs in Greek and Latin were placed giving strict warning that the penalty for such trespass was death. Our knowledge of these signs up to 1871 was from the writings of the Jewish historian Josephus. However, in 1871 archaeologists discovered one of these signs on which was written in the Greek language. It read: 'No foreigner is to go beyond the balustrade and the plaza of the temple zone. Whoever is caught doing so will have himself to blame for his death which will follow.' It was the responsibility of the Levites to guard against this happening.

6 Aaron and Levi were brothers. Zadok was a descendent of Aaron (1 Chron. 6:1–8).

7 Block, ibid. p. 636

8 Block, ibid.p. 640

9 Schaeffer, Francis A. *The Great Evangelical Disaster: in The Complete Works of Francis A. Schaeffer, Vol. 4: A Christian View of the Church*, Paternoster Press, 1998, p. 402.

10 Wright, C. J. H. *The Message of Ezekiel*, The Bible Speaks Today Series, Inter-Varsity Press, Leicester, 2001, p. 352.

Chapter 23

1 Block, Daniel I. *The Book of Ezekiel Chapters 25–48*, The New International Commentary on the Old Testament, Eerdmans Publishing Co, Grand Rapids Michigan, 1997, p. 659.

2 Wright, C. J. H. *The Message of Ezekiel*, The Bible Speaks Today Series, Inter-Varsity Press, Leicester, 2001, p. 354.

3 Block, ibid. p. 674.

4 On the matter of contagion see Block, ibid. p. 684.

5 Block, ibid. p. 685

6 Block, ibid. p. 686

7 Hendriksen, William. *More than Conquerers*, Baker Book House, Michigan, 1940, (Commemorative Edition 1982) p. 79.

Chapter 24

1 Jeremiah 31:31

2 2 Corinthians 5:17

3 See Chapter 18 above.

4 See Chapter 21 above.

5 1 Corinthians 15:35–49

6 Block, Daniel I. *The Book of Ezekiel Chapters 25–48*, The New International Commentary on the Old Testament, Eerdmans Publishing Co, Grand Rapids Michigan, 1997.

7 See also Ps46:4; 65:9; Joel 3:18.

8 Hendriksen, William. *More than Conquerors*, Baker Book House, Michigan, 1940, (Commemorative Edition 1982) p. 205.

9 Wright, C. J. H. *The Message of Ezekiel*, The Bible Speaks Today Series, Inter-Varsity Press, Leicester, 2001, p. 357.

10 Wright, ibid. p. 362

11 Wright, ibid. p. 363

12 See my comments on this theme in chapter 23.

13 Block, ibid. p. 739

Select bibliography

Block, Daniel I. *The Book of Ezekiel Chapters 1–24*, The New International Commentary on the Old Testament, Erdmans Publishing Co, Grand Rapids Michigan, 1997

Block, Daniel I. *The Book of Ezekiel Chapters 25–48*, The New International Commentary on the Old Testament, Erdmans Publishing Co, Grand Rapids Michigan, 1997

Calvin, John. *Calvin's Commentaries 22-Volume Set*, Volumes XI-XII, Baker Books, Grand Rapids Michigan, 1998

Chapel, Bryan. *Holiness by Grace: Delighting in the Joy That Is Our Strength*, Crossway Books, Illinois, 2001

Gill, John. *Exposition of the Old and New Testaments, Vol. 6, Ezekiel to Malachi*, The Baptist Standard Bearer, Arkansas, 2006 Reprint.

Henry, Matthew. *Commentary on the Whole Bible, Vol. 4, Isaiah to Malachi*, Macdonald Publishing Company, Virginia,

Jeffery, Peter. *Opening Up Ezekiel's Visions*, Day One Publications, Leominster, 2004

Stuart, Douglas. *Ezekiel*, The Communicator's Commentary Series, Old Testament, Volume 18, Word Books, Dallas, 1989

Thomas, Derek. *God Strengthens: Ezekiel Simply Explained*, Welwyn Commentary Series, Evangelical Press, Darlington, 1993

Wright, C. J. H. *The Message of Ezekiel*, The Bible Speaks Today Series, Inter-Varsity Press, Leicester, 2001